THE PERSISTENCE OF ↑

Modernism is commonly perceived as a response to the cataclysmic events of the early twentieth century. To what extent then can we explain its continued persistence? Madelyn Detloff argues for modernism's relevance to our own age, a time of escalating loss, retribution, and desire. Some of the social formations that inspired modernist cultural production – xenophobic nationalism and imperial hubris – are still with us. Writers such as Virginia Woolf and Gertrude Stein, who saw themselves as outsiders with a precarious sense of belonging to their dominant culture, are, Detloff claims, still able to give us insight into our contemporary narratives of loss, recovery, memory, and nation. Detloff extends her conceptualization to include current writers like Pat Barker and Hanif Kureishi, who have taken up the modernist thread in their own work; the result is an ambitious study that will appeal to all students and scholars of modernism.

MADELYN DETLOFF is Associate Professor of English and Women's Studies at Miami University, Ohio.

THE PERSISTENCE OF MODERNISM

Loss and Mourning in the Twentieth Century

MADELYN DETLOFF
Miami University, Oxford, OH

CAMBRIDGE UNIVERSITY PRESS
Cambridge, New York, Melbourne, Madrid, Cape Town, Singapore,
São Paulo, Delhi, Dubai, Tokyo, Mexico City

Cambridge University Press
The Edinburgh Building, Cambridge CB2 8RU, UK

Published in the United States of America by Cambridge University Press, New York

www.cambridge.org
Information on this title: www.cambridge.org/9780521182461

© Madelyn Detloff 2009

This publication is in copyright. Subject to statutory exception
and to the provisions of relevant collective licensing agreements,
no reproduction of any part may take place without the written
permission of Cambridge University Press.

First published 2009
First paperback edition 2010

A catalogue record for this publication is available from the British Library

Library of Congress Cataloguing in Publication data
Detloff, Madelyn, 1965–
The persistence of modernism : loss and mourning in the twentieth century / Madelyn Detloff.
p. cm.
Includes bibliographical references and index.
ISBN 978-0-521-89642-9
1. Modernism (Literature) 2. Loss (Psychology) in literature.
3. Woolf, Virginia, 1882–1941–Criticism and interpretation.
4. Stein, Gertrude, 1874–1946–Criticism and interpretation.
5. H.D. (Hilda Doolittle), 1886–1961–Criticism and interpretation. I. Title.
PN56.M54D48 2009
820.9´353–dc22
2008038893

ISBN 978-0-521-89642-9 Hardback
ISBN 978-0-521-18246-1 Paperback

Cambridge University Press has no responsibility for the persistence or
accuracy of URLs for external or third-party internet websites referred to in
this publication, and does not guarantee that any content on such websites is,
or will remain, accurate or appropriate.

For Mary, Pete, Kerianne, and Elizabeth

Contents

Illustration information	*page* viii
Acknowledgments	ix
List of abbreviations	xi
Introduction: "The captivating spell of the past"	1
Part One War, time, trauma	**21**
1 Woolf's resilience	23
2 Stein's shame	53
3 H.D.'s wars	80
Part Two The modernist patch	**117**
4 Pictures, arguments, and empathy	119
5 The promise and peril of *metic* intimacy	136
6 Orpheus, AIDS, and *The Hours*	154
Epilogue: Toward a survivable public mourning	166
Notes	177
Index	210

Illustration

Fred Spear, "Enlist," 1915. Boston Public Safety Committee.
Photo courtesy of the Princeton University Poster
Collection, Archives Center, National Museum of
American History, Smithsonian Institution.   171

Acknowledgments

While the entire manuscript has been heavily revised since they were originally published, sections of chapters 1, 3, and the epilogue have appeared in print.

Portions of chapter 1 appeared in "'Thinking Peace into Existence': The Spectacle of History in *Between the Acts*," *Women's Studies: An Interdisciplinary Journal* 28 (1999), 403–33. Portions of chapter 3 appeared in "'Father, don't you see I'm burning?' Identification and Remembering in H.D.'s World War II Writing," *Incest and the Literary Imagination* (Gainesville, FL: University Press of Florida, 2002), pp. 249–80, reprinted with permission of the University Press of Florida. Portions of chapter 3 and the epilogue appeared in "''Tis Not My Nature to Join in Hating, but in Loving': Toward Survivable Public Mourning," *Modernism and Mourning*, ed. Patricia Rae (Lewisburg, PA: Bucknell University Press, 2007), reprinted with the permission of Associated University Presses.

This manuscript has evolved over many years through many phases of my life. To list all of the people to whom I am indebted is a daunting task. Thank you to all of my peers, students, and mentors at the University of California, Santa Barbara; the University of California Humanities Research Institute; California State University, Los Angeles; and Miami University for their support and camaraderie. I am grateful to my editor at Cambridge University Press, Ray Ryan, for his patience and direction, to the anonymous readers of the manuscript, who made several helpful comments that have strengthened the final version of this book, my production editor, Tom O'Reilly, and to my fabulous copy editor, Kay McKechnie.

I am especially grateful to my friends and advisors at the University of California, Santa Barbara: H. Porter Abbott, Maurizia Boscagli, Julie Carlson, Aranye Louise Fradenburg, Victoria Harrison, Miranda Maupin, Judith Raiskin, and Joe Rollins. For material support, I wish to thank the University of California Interdisciplinary Humanities Center, the

American Association of University Women, and the University of California Humanities Research Institute.

To my former colleagues and students at Cal State LA – I admire you all for your dedication and grace under pressure. Special thanks to our fabulous "paintball" team and writing group, Hema Chari, Michelle Hawley, and Maria Karafilis. The English Department at Miami University has been intellectually and materially supportive of my research. I have benefitted tremendously from the feedback and advice of many friends and colleagues across the university. Among them special thanks to Yu-Fang Cho, Jim Creech, Sheila Croucher, Stefanie Dunning, Claire Goldstein, Eric Goodman, Carolyn Haynes, Elisabeth Hodges, Katie Johnson, Cheryl Johnson, Anna Kosofska, Sally Lloyd, Laura Mandell, Denise McCoskey, Mary McDonald, Tim Melley, Susan Morgan, Susan Pelle, Kate Ronald, Sven-Erik Rose, Martha Schoolman, Sherrie Shumavon, Jonathan Strauss, Keith Tuma, Liz Wilson, and Emily Zakin. Karen Mitchell and Susan Pelle are among the many wonderful graduate students who have inspired my work and teaching. Lynn Hall and Erin Douglas, graduate assistants extraordinaire, provided timely and as always impeccable assistance preparing the manuscript.

Over the years, I've been fortunate to meet many amazing feminist and queer scholars who have inspired my work. I'm grateful to the members of the H.D. International Society and International Virginia Woolf Society for their groundbreaking work and camaraderie. Thank you especially to Brenda Silver for her mentorship in my graduate school days; Carla Freccero for her intellectual companionship at the UCHRI; Patricia Rae for her generosity and leadership in putting together *Modernism and Mourning*. Patty Ingham, Siobhan Somerville, Amelia Montes, Mark Kerr, and Jeanne Scheper have sustained me with their friendship and support over the course of many years. Thank you to Gaile Pohlhaus, Jr. for being here in the nick of time. To my family, Theresa Raniere, the late Paul S. Raniere, James Detloff, Jo Ann Detloff, Mary Gammel, Pete Detloff, Kerianne Hearns, and Liz Raniere-Zimmerman – thank you for your love and encouragement.

I could not have completed this book without the friendship, encouragement, advice, and support of Chloé Hogg. Mary Jean Corbett, in addition to being a dear friend, has been a professional godsend who guided me through some of the roughest patches of the writing process. Finally, thank you does not seem adequate to express my deep appreciation to Robyn Wiegman for years of friendship, advice, and intellectual generosity. Her tireless and often unacknowledged mentorship makes it possible for so many of us to imagine better futures, and to work for their materialization.

Abbreviations

AROO	Virginia Woolf, *A Room of One's Own*, Foreword by Mary Gordon (New York: Harcourt [Harvest], 1989).
BA	Virginia Woolf, *Between the Acts* (New York: Harcourt, 1969).
"BN"	T. S. Eliot, "Burnt Norton," *Four Quartets. Collected Poems, 1909–1962* (New York: Harcourt Brace Jovanovich, 1971), pp. 173–210.
BP	Virginia Woolf, "The Memoirs of Sarah Bernhardt," 1908, *Books and Portraits*, ed. Mary Lyon (New York: Harcourt [Harvest], 1977), pp. 201–7.
BS	Hanif Kureishi, *The Buddha of Suburbia* (New York: Penguin, 1990).
D-V	Virginia Woolf, *The Diary of Virginia Woolf*, ed. Anne Olivier Bell and Andrew McNeillie, vol. 5 (New York: Harcourt Brace Jovanovich, 1984).
DM	Virginia Woolf, "Thoughts on Peace in an Air Raid," *The Death of the Moth and Other Essays*, ed. Leonard Woolf (New York: Harcourt [Harvest], 1970), pp. 243–48.
"FR"	H.D., "The Flowering of the Rod," *Trilogy*, Introduction and Reader's Notes by Aliki Barnstone (New York: New Directions, 1998).
Gift	H.D., *The Gift*, ed. Jane Augustine (Gainesville, FL: University Press of Florida, 1998).
"LG"	T. S. Eliot, "Little Gidding," *Four Quartets. Collected Poems, 1909–1962* (New York: Harcourt Brace Jovanovich, 1971), pp. 173–210.
L-III	Virginia Woolf, *The Letters of Virginia Woolf*, ed. Nigel Nicholson and Joanne Trautmann, vol. 3 (New York: Harcourt Brace Jovanovich, 1977).

M	Virginia Woolf, "On Being Ill," *The Moment and Other Essays* (New York: Harcourt Brace Jovanovich, 1948), pp. 9–23.
Mrs. D	Virginia Woolf, *Mrs. Dalloway*, Foreword by Maureen Howard (New York: Harcourt [Harvest], 1990).
"OB"-*MB*	Virginia Woolf, "Old Bloomsbury," *Moments of Being*, ed. Jeanne Schulkind (New York: Harcourt, 1985), pp. 181–201.
PL	Judith Butler, *Precarious Life: The Powers of Mourning and Violence* (New York: Verso, 2004).
PW	H.D., *Pilate's Wife*, ed. Joan A. Burke (New York: New Directions, 2000).
"R"-*MB*	Virginia Woolf, "Reminiscences," *Moments of Being*, ed. Jeanne Schulkind (New York: Harcourt, 1985), pp. 28–59.
"SP"-*MB*	Virginia Woolf, "A Sketch of the Past," *Moments of Being*, ed. Jeanne Schulkind (New York: Harcourt, 1985), pp. 64–159.
"TA"	H.D., "Tribute to the Angels," *Trilogy*, Introduction and Reader's Notes by Aliki Barnstone (New York: New Directions, 1998).
TBA	Hanif Kureishi, *The Black Album* (New York: Scribner, 2006).
TL	Virginia Woolf, *To the Lighthouse* (New York: Harcourt Brace, and Company, 1981).
TG	Virginia Woolf, *Three Guineas* (New York: Harcourt Brace Jovanovich, 1966).
TY	Virginia Woolf, *The Years* (Reprint, New York: Harcourt, 1965).
"WDNF"	H.D., "The Walls Do Not Fall," *Trilogy*, Introduction and Reader's Notes by Aliki Barnstone (New York: New Directions, 1998).

Introduction:
"The captivating spell of the past"

> The past will have been worked through only when the causes of what happened then have been eliminated. Only because the causes continue to exist does the captivating spell of the past remain to this day unbroken.[1]
>
> – Theodor Adorno

> [S]hock and loss have been common responses. But we must then go beyond them to some crucial distinctions. Take the hardest first: the discovery in ourselves, and in our relations with others, that we have been more effectively incorporated into the deepest structures of this now dying order than it was ever, while it was strong, our habit to think or even suspect.[2]
>
> – Raymond Williams

MODERNIST PATCHING

It is uncanny (in all of the unease-producing senses of the word) to think that the catastrophes and atrocities that are current news as I write this introduction are likely to have been superseded by new disasters and fresh outrages by the time the book goes to press. To cite, for example, the tsunami that hit Sri Lanka in December 2004, or hurricane Katrina which flooded New Orleans in August 2005, or the earthquake that struck Kashmir and Pakistan two months later, is to risk obsolescence. For the majority of people who were not directly affected, those events are now remembered (if at all) as anniversaries. Similarly, the epicenters of human-made violence – war, terrorism, military repression – have shifted from New York to Afghanistan, Bali, Iraq, Chechnya, Madrid, London, Lebanon, Myanmar, and Turkey in the space of six years. This is not to say that the anguish of those devastated by natural disaster, traumatized by terror attacks, or brutalized by war has abated because our front pages are filled with stories of violence and suffering from the next new calamity. Rather, I am describing what might be called a surrogation effect in the consciousness of onlookers, as one disaster supplants the previous one as a sign of humanitarian crisis requiring immediate redress. As Joseph Roach suggests, however, surrogation is never complete, and traces of the old supplanted object remain in the performances of the new.[3] The surrogation effect ensures that consciousness of a new disaster does not overwrite the old like a new computer file being written onto the finite memory of a hard drive. Quite the contrary – the new file in human or collective memory exists alongside, or is imbricated with, the memory of the old. The old file, to continue the computer metaphor, is not overwritten by material from the new, but is nevertheless changed – patched – because of its relation to the new. The "Great War," for example, became World War I only after the war in Europe from 1939 to 1945 gave a sense of seriality to the two very different conflicts. The "Gulf War" of 1991, similarly, became the "First Gulf War" after the US-led invasion of Iraq in 2003. The new event restructures our understanding of the old, even as the old informs our perception of the new.

The concept of "patching" is an intriguing metaphor for the workings of (old-fashioned) human memory because the patch – a bit of new code that inserts itself into an already existing program in order to shore up security vulnerabilities or to smooth out conflicts that prevent certain operations from running properly – does more than cover over an existing gap; it changes the very functioning of the program. The patch and the virus, then, work by the same mechanism. Their difference is in their effects. One enhances the system's functioning in the present, and the other causes the system to operate in excess of its capacities, so that its memory becomes so overloaded that it ceases to function effectively. This is one way that theorists describe the workings of ordinary memory and traumatic memory, which overwhelms the psyche. For now, I would like to resist the lure of that analogy and focus on what the concept of patching might tell us about the relationality of past and present in more general terms: what it means to live on in a present that is shaped by past events. To understand the past in a relational sense is thus not simply to know what came before, but to know something about how one comes to function in the present. As Edward Said notes, "there is no just way in which the past can be quarantined from the present."[4]

Said's epidemiological analogy – the language of "quarantine" implying the threat of the present becoming infected by the past – is not unique. Adorno takes up the metaphor of contagion in "Working through the Past," suggesting that post-World War II efforts to make anti-Semites "aware of the mechanisms that cause racial prejudice within them" would include isolating the "propaganda tricks" that foster race hatred so that they could be known and used as "a kind of vaccine."[5] (H.D., writing at roughly the same time [1958] as Adorno, uses a similar language of "inoculation" to describe her own efforts to work through her past connections to Ezra Pound.) In Said's formulation, the past (the imperial past) is like the patch or viral code that continues to function in the present; it is part of the operating system of a present that is geopolitically different from the past, but nevertheless saturated with its effects. As Said explains, "although that era [of "high nineteenth-century imperialism"] clearly had an identity all of its own, the meaning of the imperial past is not totally contained within it, but has entered the reality of hundreds of millions of people, where its existence as shared memory and as a highly conflictual texture of culture, ideology, and policy still exercises tremendous force."[6] In the same vein, Paul Gilroy argues that "the political conflicts which characterize [contemporary] multicultural societies can take on a very different aspect if they are understood to exist firmly in a context supplied by imperial and colonial history . . . the imperial and colonial past continues to shape political life in the overdeveloped – but-no-longer-imperial countries."[7]

In a different, but contiguous, context I analyze the persistence of modernism in contemporary responses to war, terror, and trauma. A set of discourses that crystallized during a time of escalating loss, retribution, and violence from 1914 to 1946, modernism did not end neatly with the end of World War II. Read as a whole century, rather than as two halves separated by the war, the arc of the twentieth century might be imagined as parabola-shaped, with World War II at the vertex of a curve that begins and ends with uncannily symmetrical constellations of troubling social formations, from xenophobic nationalism to state-sponsored homophobia, to interethnic violence. Because modernism has been with us for over a century and does not promise to become obsolete in the near future, understanding its persistence is instructive for twenty-first-century readers facing the ethical and political complications of widespread suffering and loss.

If the wounds of the early twentieth century promise to remain with us – not metaphorically, but actually — examining modernist strategies of resilience may help us to understand these wounds from the perspective of the *longue durée*. Early twentieth-century writers such as Stein, Woolf, and H.D. thus provide conceptual resources for living in the midst of loss and violence. Similarly, twenty-first-century postimperial British writers such as Hanif Kureishi and Pat Barker offer frameworks for understanding the current resurgence of violence and loss haunting the United States, Britain's successor to imperial power.

The impetus of this book is therefore to learn something from the way modernist writers and thinkers grappled with the world-shaping and world-shattering events that marked the first half of the twentieth century. Understanding modernism as a constellation of discourses about widespread loss and violence has the benefit of circumventing definitional debates about modernist orthodoxies – high or low, early or late, radical or reactionary, populist or elitist, luddite or technophilic. Sidestepping such debates, I analyze the function of (and the felt need for) apocalyptic rhetoric during times of terrible loss and devastation, such as the air raids of World War II. In the wake of such events, it is especially important to recognize the rhetorical patterns available for speaking about large-scale collective trauma, and to help elucidate the "collateral" effects of those forms. These rhetorical patterns occur in a variety of modernist works, from H.D.'s and Stein's experimental prose to the long poems *Four Quartets* and *Trilogy*, to Woolf's memoirs and novels, to contemporary cultural productions that recirculate "patched" forms of modernism.

In general (although *Trilogy* presents a notable exception), Woolf, H.D., and Stein are wary of triumphant or transcendent redescriptions of trauma. Their writing questions the construction of believing, heroic, sacrificial, even fascist, subjects willing to fight and die in order to belong to a larger collective entity. To take these three writers as exemplars of modernism is thus to characterize modernism as a resistant, even resilient cultural formation, rather than a cynical and ironic one. This stance may seem a bit heretical, given that the usual suspects in a study of modernism generally include Eliot, Pound, Conrad, Joyce, and *maybe* Woolf, Stein, and/or H.D. I center my analysis on the latter three rather than the former four precisely because Woolf, Stein, and H.D. – "queer" women whose citizen status (as Woolf reminds us in *Three Guineas*) could be trumped by marriage or nullified by heterosexism – occupy the position of "*metics*," subjects who belong, but not quite fully, to a culture. As I argue below, *metic* sensibility offers an alternative to forms of cosmopolitanism that are complicit with imperial and/or elite privilege. Eliot and Pound, less marginalized than H.D., Stein, or Woolf, enjoyed full membership in Anglo-American culture of the early twentieth century, and thus are less central to a modernism infused with *metic* sensibility. Conrad and Joyce, both postcolonial expatriates, were, on the other hand, closer to *metic* status. A longer study would have included chapters on both. My focus here, however, is primarily on reading H.D., Stein, and Woolf as *metics* by virtue of their gender and sexuality who wrote in a geopolitical context permeated by trauma, bloodshed, and imperial unraveling.

In addition to contending with the shattering events (war, revolution, genocide) that marked the new century, modernist thinkers were faced with a more gradual shift (not unconnected to percussive eruptions of war, revolution, and racism) in the status of Europe as the imperial "center" of the world. "By 1914," as Said notes, "Europe held a grand total of roughly 85 percent of the earth as colonies, protectorates, dependencies, dominions, and commonwealths."[8] As Jed Esty notes in his study of late modernism, the erosion of the British empire coincided with "the putative death of English modernism."[9] For Esty, this relationship is complex, rather than a simple chain of causation. Nevertheless, Esty argues that the later modernism of Woolf, Eliot, and Forster abandoned the "metropolitan perception" of high modernism for an "anthropological turn" toward "little" England. This "anthropological turn" was, for Esty, a precursor to the inward focus of British cultural studies, which urged the examination of Englishness as a particular object of ethnographic attention, rather than as the deracinated ideal of universal "civilized" subjectivity. Therefore, according to Esty, cultural studies and late modernism are both genealogically connected to British imperialism and imperial decline.

Esty's attempt to link modernism to the development of cultural studies is a continuation of a long-standing critical conversation about the political investments of modernist literature and culture. We can trace the debate about modernist politics at least as far back as "The Leaning Tower," Woolf's 1940 response to younger writers' critiques of Bloomsbury's alleged quietism. The Leavises and the *Scrutiny* group, as Brenda Silver demonstrates, further contributed to this characterization of modernism as alienating and excessively highbrow.[10] And Raymond Williams, although an admirer of Bloomsbury, furthered this association of modernism with formal, rather than political, concerns by attributing the creation of a "modern absolute" – a high modernist aesthetic style that outlived its conditions of cultivation – to the historical development of the imperial metropolis.[11] Between Williams, who argues for the persistence of a reified "modern absolute" in the late twentieth century, and Esty, who argues for a turn from metropolitan modernism to "little Englandism" and cultural studies, there is a third position which I endeavor to trace throughout this book – the historical development and redeployment (in patched form) of a modernism that is not "absolute," but rather dynamic and co-evolving with (neo)imperialism and its violent effects.

The either/or view of modernism as reified and absolute or frustrated into provincial retrenchment depends upon imagining modernism from the vantage of Eliot or Joyce, rather than Woolf or H.D., or (to use the categories formulated by Bonnie Kime Scott), from that of the "men of 1914," rather than the "women of 1928."[12] Williams, for example, associates the metropolitan orientation of modernism with alienation or with "an individual lonely and isolated within the crowd" of "strangers."[13] Esty links this apparent isolation to "a cosmopolitan humanist language supported by English cultural hegemony ... a European artistic elite increasingly bound to itself and split from its constituent societies."[14] In the case of Woolf, arguably the most prominent of English modernists and certainly the most prominent of the "women of 1928," these characterizations don't ring true. Woolf was both a cosmopolitan and a *metic*. As both Christine Froula and Jessica Berman argue, Woolf's cosmopolitanism was not entirely aligned with "English cultural hegemony," but was rather infused with her anti-establishment political thought. Berman, for example, suggests that:

Woolf's writings engage themselves directly with the political crisis in Great Britain in the period from 1929 to 1931, and with the entwined discourses of community and action so often in question in this period. In *Orlando* and *The Waves* in particular we can see the way in which narrative action becomes praxis, the expansion of the subject substitutes for the consolidation of personal political power, and the construction of alternative models of community pushes a cosmopolitan ideal.[15]

Froula, moreover, challenges the characterization of Bloomsbury as remote, disengaged, and elite, instead reading its "enlightenment project" as deeply political: "Integrating aesthetics with internationalist perspectives on economic, political, and social institutions at a moment when the *sensus communis* was under urgent debate, Bloomsbury challenges myths of modernism as an antirealism 'remote from the sphere of everyday practices.'"[16]

Bloomsbury's political values notwithstanding, cosmopolitanism cannot entirely escape the charge of elitism. Only the privileged classes can afford to move from metropolis to metropolis, to speak with the urbane knowingness of frequent travelers, to cross borders without worrying that a rifle barrel, detention facility, or vulnerable refugee camp awaits them on the other side. One person's mobility might be another person's migrancy; one person's *belonging to the world* might be another person's *exile*. The term "cosmopolitan," derived as Martha C. Nussbaum tells us from the Greek "*kosmou politês*" or "world citizen," does not quite describe the differential vulnerability of border crossers, world travelers, and stateless persons, precisely because the term *politês* implies a form of citizenship, a sense of full belonging in the imaginary community of the global *polis*.[17]

The *metic*, on the other hand, is not quite a citizen of the world, and not quite a citizen of a nation. In ancient Greece, the *metic* was officially designated an outsider dependent upon the goodwill of a citizen sponsor in order to remain within the *polis*. Thus he or she operated within the *polis* without being fully enfranchised by it. Significantly, Antigone, an important figure of resistance for Woolf, calls herself a *metic* after being sentenced by Creon, thus calling attention to both her statelessness and expulsion from the familial.[18] As an expression of this *metic* sensibility, Woolf's often cited declaration that "as a woman I want no country. As a woman my country is the whole world" takes on a resonance that is not quite a claim to world citizenship (*TG*, p. 109).[19] Far from advocating uncomplicated cosmopolitanism, Woolf resignifies a negative condition – a gendered sense of un-belonging (because marriage trumps nationality) – into inspiration for affiliation across borders and accountability to the world beyond the provincialism of one's geographic location.

As I mention above, Williams characterizes the modernist as "an individual lonely and isolated within the crowd."[20] Esty extrapolates from this characterization an image of the modernist as an alienated artist trapped on one side of a "schism between art and society."[21] Woolf belies this characterization as well, as she certainly was not a writer who found art at odds with social relevance. In *Three Guineas*, for example (a text that grapples with the pressing question, "how are we to prevent war?"), Woolf considers the "intellectual liberty" of the writer to be crucial to combating militarism (*TG*, pp. 3, 97). In that text, Woolf exhorts her readers to "Go to the pubic galleries and look at pictures; turn on the wireless and rake down music from the air; enter any of the public libraries which are now free to all" in order to find (for example, the poetry of Sophocles) "a most profound analysis by a poet, who is a psychologist in action, of the effect of power and wealth upon the soul" (*TG*, p. 81). Whether or not we agree with Woolf's analysis of *Antigone*, we can hardly say that her sentiment is that of an artist who finds a great "schism between art and society."[22] Indeed, as Anna Snaith, Froula, and Alex Zwerdling (among many others) have noted, Woolf was very engaged with the political concerns of the day, had a wide and varied social network of friends ranging well beyond the artistic elite, taught at a working-class college (one of the activities Williams credits for the formation of cultural studies), and corresponded with a great number of people from positions high and low.[23]

Finally, Esty's suggestion that Woolf's "late modernist" works are part of a larger cultural turn toward pastoral Englishness, as an antidote to the unease caused by imperial unraveling, bears some scrutiny. For Esty, Woolf's last novel, *Between the Acts*, "uses the pageant to recast history as heritage – as the rehearsal of familiar gestures, songs and scenes. Woolf (like Forster) struggles to break narrative momentum by posing insular culture against the rapid transformations of capitalist modernity, enduring pastoral folkways against perpetual Hegelian struggle."[24] This seems to me a Streatfield-ish reading of *Between the Acts*, which depicts insularity as an impossible fantasy. Esty reads Lucy Swithin's contemplation of a prehistoric European continent undivided by the English Channel as "the starting point for a comforting narrative about the birth of culture as an island story."[25] The "aeroplanes" that cast their shadow over Reverend Streatfield's attempt to sum up Miss LaTrobe's pageant, however, suggest a less nostalgic reading of Lucy's fantasy, reminding us of the proximity of England to the continent (*BA*, p. 200). England may yet be an island, but in the age of aeronautics, it is no longer insular.

ARTICULATING LOSS

While Britain's shift from empire to "little England" is important to chart, it is equally important to register the effects of imperial migration (from Europe to the USA), mutation (from an empire of colonies and dominions to an empire of bases), and translation (from nation-based imperialism to globalization).[26] In a similar vein, modernism, as a literary-historical period, might, like the "age of empire," be over, and yet the meaning of the modernist past, to paraphrase Said, "is not totally contained within" its periodization. To write after World War II is to write in the wake of a conflict that killed an estimated 50 million people – half of them civilians – and with the knowledge of genocide perpetrated in the center of "civilized," modern, industrialized, philosophically "enlightened" Europe.

Theodor Adorno refers to the magnitude of this brutal knowledge in his frequently misquoted lines, "To write poetry after Auschwitz is barbaric. And this corrodes even the knowledge of why it has become impossible to write poetry today."[27] Taken in the context of his full argument in "Cultural Criticism and Society," Adorno's comment is not a moratorium on poetry, but rather an indictment of criticism that reifies a "high" or "pure" culture purportedly unsullied by contact with ideology, politics, or the masses. Earlier in the same essay, Adorno argues that "cultural criticism" misrecognizes material suffering in the name of aesthetic universalisms: "Where there is despair and measureless misery, he [the cultural critic] sees only spiritual phenomena, the state of man's consciousness, the decline of norms. By insisting on this, criticism is tempted to forget the unutterable, instead of striving, however impotently, so that man may be spared."[28] This transvaluation reifies "culture" as static and elite, at the very moment that western Europe's "presupposed intellectual progress" was fundamentally called into question by the barbarism of National Socialism. If so-called pure culture is civilizing, then how can one explain the depravity of Nazism and its death camps? One cannot, and that impossibility unmasks the civilizing pretensions of high culture and the cultural criticism that placed it above ideology, politics, and everyday struggles for material existence.

It is tempting to say, then, that modernism faltered at this moment in history precisely because its "civilizing" projects (imperial and domestic) were shown up by the colossal brutality of the death camps and the bystanders who turned a blind eye to their existence. On the left, Bloomsbury's faith in the equality and justice-forging potential of "intellectual liberty" seems to have been misplaced, or premature (*TG*, p. 97). On the right, Yeats' and Eliot's belief in the salvific potential of traditional culture seems too tainted by complicity with fascism for one to be at ease with their civilizing impulses. And Pound is perhaps the quintessential example of the arrogant "cultural critic" Adorno critiques. His post-World War II position at the center of his self-proclaimed "Ezuversity" in St. Elizabeth's hospital presents a nightmare version of modernism's transatlantic migration, mutation, and translation from the cosmopolitan urbanity of the imperial metropolis to the formalist isolationism of the New Critical syllabus. If "to write poetry after Auschwitz is barbaric," then to award Pound the first Bollingen Prize for poetry in 1948 for his *Pisan Cantos* is in this context the epitome of barbarism, the apotheosis of cultural criticism's descent into sterile formalisms that "forget the unutterable."

The persistence of modernism is important to track precisely because there *is* poetry *and* barbarism after Auschwitz. To chart the migration of the meanings of modernism is to depart from the rarified and reifying "cultural criticism" so fervently condemned by Adorno, and to move in the direction of cultural studies – albeit a cultural studies that is imagined differently from the "island story" that Esty tells. Describing a methodology for cultural studies of modernism, Rita Felski (following Stuart Hall, Larry Grossberg, and Ernesto Laclau) describes "articulation" as:

> a theory of social correspondences, non-correspondences, and contradictions or alternatively as a theory of how contexts are made, unmade, and remade . . . Articulation thus seeks to explain how segments of the social field may join together to form temporary unities without resorting to a view of the social whole as an expressive totality whose essential features are mirrored in every one of its parts.[29]

Tracing modernist articulations of loss, violence, and their attendants – trauma, consolation, and retribution – illuminates the contours of our own encounters with imperial "blowback" in this already bloody first decade of the twenty-first century.[30] To attempt this genealogy is somewhat different from suggesting that we learn from the past as exemplum (the notion that history provides a "case study" for the present), for it is clear that modernist articulations (from attempts to liken the "war on terror" to the war against the Nazis, to neofascism, to renewed calls for cosmopolitanism) are still with us, even if their correspondences and contexts have shifted. The modernist past is thus not an inert object to be studied in its alterity, but rather a "structure of feeling" (to use Williams' phrase) functioning in a "patched" present still troubled by modernist constellations of personal trauma, militarized violence, and "imperial loss."[31]

The third term, "imperial loss" requires some explanation. It fits in the category of what Freud calls "loss of a more ideal kind."[32] For the melancholic, this loss might be unarticulated, unavowed, or not understood fully. As Freud explains, "the object has not perhaps actually died, but has become lost as an object of love," or "a loss of the kind has been experienced, but one cannot see clearly what has been lost," or the "patient" "knows whom he has lost but not *what* it is he has lost in them."[33] Imperial loss might then be the loss of the idea of British rule (or American world dominance) as an object of love, or admiration, or pride. Williams himself indicates this loss of ideal in his "Afterword to *Modern Tragedy*," noting that, "when a social order is dying, it grieves for itself."[34]

Gilroy continues this thread, arguing that "since [1945] the life of the [British] nation has been dominated by an inability even to face, never mind actually mourn, the profound change in circumstances and moods that followed the end of the empire and consequent loss of imperial prestige."[35] Imperial loss thus becomes melancholic when the unavowed privileges of empire erode without the privileged ever having acknowledged "what it is [they have] lost in them."[36] When the first two kinds of loss (personal trauma and militarized violence) are complicated by "loss of a more ideal kind" (loss of faith in civilization, in decency, democracy, fairness, progress), one might expect mass melancholia to be the resulting "structure of feeling." Modernism, in its patched form, reminds us that there are other, less destructive ways to deal with the ambivalence of ideal loss.

While it would be impractical to catalogue exhaustively the "correspondences, non-correspondences, and contradictions" among loss, trauma, politics, belonging, subject-making, abject-making, violence, recuperation, and memorialization that have carried over from the first half of the twentieth century to the present, I wish to enumerate three key clusters of questions that remain salient in our patched present. First, what are the sociocultural effects of public commemorations of shattering loss? How might particular acts of remembrance shape the meanings we give to the past, and how does that construction of the past shape our possible futures? This is an especially pressing question in times of war, when, as Elaine Scarry reminds us, the wounded or killed body serves to substantiate unanchored concepts, lending its "incontestable reality" to the winning side's interpretation of contested issues.[37] How does one commemorate the *particularity* of loss when catastrophe and atrocity seem to renew themselves with alarming frequency? This question opens up a dizzying hall of mirrors for even the least cynical of those exhorted to remember, as imperatives to commemorate compete both synchronically and diachronically with other calls to mourn, to remember, to redress.

Second, how can we fashion non-lethal (non-suicidal) responses to death-bearing forms of power? The answer to this question is not simple, and it is one that troubled the pacifist and League of Nations movements that were formed in response to World War I. By the mid 1930s the rise of fascism and the growing militarization of Germany would demand more complex responses from those opposed to militarism, but equally opposed to Hitlerism. It is not a simple thing to oppose imperialism and yet advocate military intervention in response to atrocities in (for example) Bosnia, Rwanda, the Sudan, as empire is often justified using the same altruistic arguments that are used to support "peacekeeping" missions. There is the additional problem of identifying when an ethical intervention becomes an imperial one.

Finally, how do we describe and represent atrocity without resorting to apocalyptic narratives? As Michael André Bernstein argues in his work on tragic emplotments of the *Shoah*, "We try to make sense of a historical disaster by interpreting it, according to the strictest teleological model, as the climax of a bitter trajectory whose inevitable outcome it must be."[38] Such a closed narrative gives way to resignation in the face of the religious sublime. The counter-coin side of this concern is the fear of moral relativism – and the related charge that a nuanced approach to catastrophe or atrocity is akin to "siding with the enemy" or dishonoring the dead.

We can approach these questions by examining the memorializing impulses of disparate modernist works, from H.D.'s and Eliot's long poems to Stein's World War II writings, to Woolf's memoirs and novels. Woolf seems especially aware of the consequences of triumphant or redemptive descriptions of public violence, overtly questioning the construction of believing, heroic, sacrificial, subjects willing to fight and die in order to belong to a larger collective. H.D. and T. S. Eliot, on the other hand, both produce austere, moving, redemptive, responses to World War II in their long poems of the 1940s. Reading *Four Quartets* and *Trilogy* together elucidates the function of (and the felt need for) apocalyptic rhetoric during times of terrible loss and devastation. Such times compel us to recognize the rhetorical patterns available for speaking about large-scale collective trauma, and to understand the "collateral" effects of those forms when they are mobilized to justify further retributive violence.

Moreover, the revenants of modernist responses to loss resurface in late twentieth- and early twenty-first-century work by contemporary writers such as Hanif Kureishi, Pat Barker, and Susan Sontag. For example, in her essays on illness, the arts, literature, representation, and violence, Sontag continues Woolf's intellectual, ethical, aesthetic aims. Her last works, *Regarding the Pain of Others* and "Regarding the Torture of Others," bring to mind modernist concerns about the slippery relationship between the collective and the individual, and the permeable boundary between spectatorship and participation. It is this slippage, between spectatorship and identification, between witnessing and participating, that Barker – well known for her depiction of shell shock in her World War I *Regeneration* trilogy – examines in her newer novels, *Border Crossing* and *Double Vision*. Like Sontag, Barker extends Woolf's aesthetic and antiwar vision into the twenty-first century, and testifies to Woolf's continued relevance as a political/ethical thinker. *Double Vision* specifically engages with Sontag's *Regarding the Pain of Others*, mediating, in

Woolfian fashion, Sontag's ethical concerns about representation, atrocity, and responsibility through the creative dilemmas a female artist must work through in order to achieve her vision.[39]

Woolf's purported reliance on the unmediated truth-value of photographic evidence of war's "horror and disgust" is problematic for Sontag because, "photographs of the victims of war are themselves a species of rhetoric."[40] For Barker, the artist or photojournalist is not let off the hook in the face of the rhetoricity of images, but rather must be attentive to the cultural work done by representations of atrocity. The ethical import of that cultural work is dependent on the onlooker's willingness to ask Sontag-like questions of her or his own reaction to depictions of suffering: When does witnessing become voyeurism? When do recording and reporting violent events become complicity, feeding the spectators' desire for more killing, revenge, atrocity? When do photographs, ostensibly the "guarantor[s] of reality," mislead?[41]

The slippage between spectatorship and identification, between witnessing and participating, troubles psychoanalytic attempts to grapple with trauma and representation, memory and our responsibility to the present. As Ruth Leys suggests in her genealogy of trauma, current debates within and in response to recovery movements (represented in the work of Judith Herman, for instance) retrace some of the contested theoretical terrain covered by Freud, Janet, Ferenczi, and Prince.[42] One of the aims of *The Persistence of Modernism* is therefore to forge connections between two clusters in trauma studies that often are theorized separately: the first focused predominantly on historical atrocities, such as genocide, war, and imperial violence, and the second on personal, intimate or familial traumas such as the death of loved ones or sexual abuse. The interconnections between subjectivity, sociality, and loss, on the one hand, and national identity, public mourning, and trauma-producing practices on the other, are complicated and rife with the potential for insensitivity or oversimplification. This is in part because of the theoretical slippage between what might be called the traumatic foundations of subjectivity – the sense that *assujetissement* (subject-making) is a compensation for the originary bereavement caused by individuation from our primary love objects – and traumatic identifications that are the result of particular experiences that may be shared, but are not universal. Even so, one can make distinctions between the universalizing gesture that makes loss constitutive to subjectivity, and an examination of losses that may be felt to be personal (rather than public), and radically isolating (rather than communal). It is important to articulate the connections between the personal and the communal, especially since one of the effects of a large-scale "public" trauma (such as war) is to depersonalize those who are most affected by its sweeping violence.

Modernism gives us many models for writing about enormous devastation and loss. Because there is not a one-to-one connection between high modernism and ideologically problematic responses to loss, it is helpful to examine how and when modernist cultural productions reify (even glorify) violence and loss, and how and when they resist the lure of traumatic reification. Nevertheless, some of the more beautiful aesthetic products of modernism are among the most problematic – transforming suffering into "terrible beauty" so successfully that beauty comes to be seen as the sublime effect of loss and violence. For example, Yeats' "Easter 1916," which is at first a very ambivalent elegy, transforms the capital punishment of unsuccessful revolutionaries into a symbol of Irish nationalism. The poem thus partakes of what Herbert Marcuse calls "the ideology of death" – "the idea of death as the *telos* of life."[43] According to this worldview, life is "redeemed" through a fitting death, which "gives 'meaning' to life, or is the precondition for the 'true' life of man."[44] This view of death, for Marcuse, leads to a culture that glorifies the sacrifice of self and others.

At the heart of "the ideology of death" is the myth of transcendence, of an outside to time from which God plays the ultimate salvager, arranging the accidents and catastrophes of our lives into coherent, triumphant narratives. Such is the case in Eliot's *Four Quartets*, which "redeem[s] the time" of the Blitz. If redemptive narratives, such as those that foster "the ideology of death," are suspect for their potential to turn loss into political gain, so too are narratives that refuse categorically the possibility of consolation, of living on in the wake of trauma. This is the drawback of theories that tout the "unspeakability" of trauma and the incommunicability of pain. Rather than focusing on the speaker's inability, it might be more fruitful to focus on the potential listener's ability to hear, to see, and to recognize trauma when its effects are articulated by others.

There is some ground between a position that insists upon the absolute incommunicability of suffering and a position that triumphantly resignifies trauma for its own ideological purposes. Woolf, more fully than others, explores this terrain between resignation and redemption, and therefore her work functions as a persistent refrain throughout this book. Her efforts led her to develop what I will call resilient writing, after studies on the resilience of survivors of trauma. Resilient writing differs from redemptive writing in its refusal to make loss into a metaphor for something else. It diverges from the "unspeakable" hypothesis by recognizing the attempts of survivors to invent, if necessary, new methods for recognizing and communicating suffering, without suggesting that those methods are always and only symptoms of trauma's inescapable hold. Another way to describe resilient writing would be to suggest that it respects the dynamic relationships between the particularity of suffering and the temporality of living, of continuing on after, or even in the midst of, suffering. Resilience, then, might be seen as a complex adaptation to traumatic circumstances – but an adaptation that does not "get over" or transcend the past as redemptive narratives imply. Rather, the past, like the "patch," becomes part of the continuously emerging present.

I begin Part I of this book, a reading of war, time, and trauma, with a defense of Woolf's resilience. Despite Scarry's contention that pain is incommunicable, Woolf developed rhetorical strategies such as *apophasis* and a "radial" prose that allowed her to communicate suffering through its effects. I connect Woolf's personally resilient style to her arguments for resilient pacifism in her antifascist triptych, *Three Guineas*, and her World War II novel, *Between the Acts*, and investigate the performative function of Woolf's staging of history as a spectacle in the pageant that ends that novel. In her critique of the consolidation of national identity at the expense of the despised "queer" figures in the village, Woolf foregrounds the production of "abjects" who make the formation of nationalist subjects possible. Until this production of subjects at the expense of abjects can be resisted, Woolf suggests, we are only fighting the fascism beyond our borders, while turning a blind eye to the fascism within.

In Chapter 2, I analyze the fear of "ethical contagion" that contemporary critics (such as Janet Malcolm) confront when dealing with the biographical complexities of Stein's life. A Jewish lesbian who flirted with fascism, worked for the French resistance, and managed to survive World War II in Vichy France, Stein does not provide a cohesive politicized identity that can be taken up neatly by later critics. Rather, Stein's fabulously unexemplary life mobilizes what Eve Sedgwick calls the "double movement shame makes: toward painful individuation, toward uncontrollable relationality," and evokes in contemporary critics a phenomenon I describe as vicarious compunction.[45] Stein herself explores the tension between individuation and relationality in *The Making of Americans*, where she develops an ethics of antimetaphor that can alleviate some of the disease that accompanies ionic identifications. Stein's refusal to trope, combined with her "forensic" historiographic methods, enables her to resist redemptive figurations of history. While her flat renderings of the past may seem empathically stunted, given the tumultuous events she lived through, Stein's "detective" stories and histories, such as *Blood on the Dining-Room Floor*, *Everybody's Autobiography*, *The Geographical History of America*, and *Reflection on the Atomic Bomb*, nevertheless offer an alternative to triumphal or apocalyptic versions of history, a topic I address at length in the following chapter.

In Chapter 3, a reading of H.D.'s World War II writings, I examine the ethical consequences of redemptive narratives of catastrophe, arguing that they participate in "the ideology of death." Aligned with the apocalyptic visions of Yeats and Eliot, H.D.'s *Trilogy* represents the destruction of the war as cleansing, an opportunity for cultural rebirth. I read the poem against H.D.'s interwar prose (her "Madrigal" trilogy and *Pilate's Wife*), as well as *The Gift*, a childhood memoir that is haunted by the fear of sexual violence and the uncanny death of girls. Through its repetition of the image of burned girls, *The Gift* presents the story of a daughter who has a knack for noticing the everyday perils of girlhood, and for making connections between private traumas and the publicly acknowledged traumas of war. While *Trilogy* symbolically "redeems" the lives of the burned girls who haunt *The Gift*, H.D.'s interwar prose offers a more pointed critique of the "ideology of death" implicit in wartime stories of heroic sacrifice and rebirth. Her interwar prose therefore offers us a model for thinking through the consequences of sacrificial logic, and, especially in her posthumously published *Pilate's Wife*, provides an alternative vision of collective organizing and resistance.

Part II, "The modernist patch," examines the reanimation of modernist responses to loss and violence in contemporary film and fiction, opening with an analysis of Sontag's frequent remarks on the ethics of representations of pain and atrocity. I address Sontag's critique of Woolf's *Three Guineas*, arguing that she misreads the ethical nature of Woolf's demand that onlookers recognize their own self-positioning in social systems that cause suffering. Sontag's work on Sarajevo is especially helpful for introducing the "patched present," as the ghost of World War II and the Nazi death camps seems to haunt our understanding of late twentieth-century eruptions of violence and "ethnic cleansing" in the former Yugoslavia. Sontag's skepticism about the empathetic pull of photos of suffering helps to elucidate the limits of "sentimental nationalism." This is an important cautionary note to sound during a time when national sentiment has been mobilized to justify actions and policies that run counter to international standards for human rights. I ultimately take issue with Sontag's reading of Woolf's rhetorical use of photos of suffering in *Three Guineas* and conclude with a discussion of Barker's recent novel about art and atrocity, *Double Vision*. Barker presents a less pessimistic and more helpful vision of the artist's, the photographer's, and the reporter's attempts to respond ethically to "the pain of others."

In Chapter 5, I propose an alternative to cosmopolitan thinking by reappropriating, as I discussed earlier, the ancient Greek term "*metic*" – a resident alien who lives in the city as an officially designated non-citizen. The Ancient *metic* is more privileged than the subaltern or the dispossessed, but can be dispossessed, exiled, or made a slave if the citizens of the city withdraw their patronage. Modern *metics*, too, are situated precariously between belonging and unbelonging. Woolf and Kureishi explore the potential of translocal, queer, *metic* intimacies to forge affiliations across differences that are so often mobilized in the service of extreme nationalism or fanatical racism. Kureishi's protagonists (often biracial, bisexual, or otherwise marked as non-heteronormative) negotiate the polarities of the two violently enforced isms of fundamentalism and racism, attempting to forge space for erotic and affectional freedom while challenging both racism and extremist forms of cultural nationalism. I contend that Kureishi's work extends Woolf's own exploration of the promise of queer *metic* intimacies, and elucidates the stakes of cultural production in postimperial Britain – especially during a time when the ideologies of both racism and fundamentalism have made complex cross-class, cross-race, cross-cultural affiliations seem either dangerous or impossible.

Chapter 6 begins with a reading of Woolf's suicide, which, especially in the 2002 film *The Hours*, has been narrated from a gendered perspective that reiterates what Klaus Theweleit calls "the politics of Orpheus." I argue that *The Hours* unwittingly conspires with the lethal public fantasy of a post-AIDS world without gay men. The film therefore directly contradicts the message of *Mrs. Dalloway*, which situates particular deaths in their sociopolitical contexts. This effect is due to the film's omission of Woolf's overt critique of various death-producing sites of cultural power – the medical and psychiatric institutions, the parliament, the peerage, and the military. *The Hours*, as a film that urges us to put the AIDS pandemic behind us, colludes with the unequal dynamics of biopower, which works by regulating life – making some live, and "letting" others die.

The Persistence of Modernism concludes with an examination of the uncanny returns of imperial loss, or what Chalmers Johnson calls the "Sorrows of Empire."[46] This "sorrow" is entwined with the melancholy of those who have lost, in the wake of torture scandals and pre-emptive invasions, a sense of American idealism, as well as those who grieve over losses that are far less symbolic – the deaths of thousands in the terrorist attacks of September 11, the wars in Afghanistan and Iraq, and the other natural and unnatural disasters that have marked the first decade of the twenty-first century. Writing on the eve of World War II, with keen awareness of the growing menace of fascism in Europe, Woolf invoked the figure of Antigone in *Three Guineas*. As a bereaved sister who bravely questions Creon's autocratic attempts to legitimate his power by managing public grief, Antigone performs an act of commemoration that is socially engaged and stubbornly resistant to hegemonic cooptation. Her actions also call to mind contemporary Antigone figures who mourn and yet dissent, questioning the state's attempts to control the meaning of the deaths of their fallen loved ones. Reading Woolf's "versioning" of the Antigone story alongside Butler's more recent musings on Antigone's "predicament," I advocate forms of public mourning that intervene in, rather than repeat, vicious cycles of violence.[47]

One of the interventions that Woolf makes in her 1940 essay "Thoughts on Peace in an Air Raid" is insisting on the necessity of "making happiness." While at first glance this claim seems hopelessly naïve, it is embedded in the context of the nuanced political analysis of fascism, nationalism, and unequal gender and class relations, an analysis that Woolf articulated throughout her works of the 1930s. If our intimate, particular, and ordinary lives are connected to large-scale political matters such as war and peace, this is not simply because the "tyrannies and servilities of the private house" are related to the "tyrannies and servilities" of the public world as the micro is related to the macro, but because this is how biopower works (*TG*, p. 142). Biopower is two pronged – focusing on the life and health of the individual on the one hand, and the life and health of the species on the other hand. This does not necessarily mean that biopower is life-affirming, but rather that power based on the right of the sovereign to take the lives of the subject (literally, the power of the sword) has (largely) been superseded by systems of power that justify their operations by functioning as the purported stewards of the life of the individual and the "race." Despite its function as "a power organized around the management of life rather than the menace of death" biopower is every bit as lethal as the sovereign power of previous epistemes, perhaps more so.[48] "Wars," Foucault argues, "were never as bloody as they have been since the nineteenth century, and all things being equal, never before did regimes visit such holocausts on their own populations."[49] If, for Foucault, resistance to biopower involves a turn to "bodies and pleasures," Woolf and Kureishi expand our understanding of the creativity of pleasure – sensual and artistic. In his response to a friend who argued that after September 11 there is no more use for the type of creative work that he does, Kureishi contends that, "If both racism and fundamentalism are diminishers of life – reducing others to abstractions – the effort of culture must be to keep others alive by describing and celebrating their intricacy, by seeing that this is not only of value but a necessity."[50] *The Persistence of Modernism* is dedicated to understanding, articulating, and responding to that necessity.

PART I

War, time, trauma

CHAPTER I

Woolf's resilience

> So if one dies, it'll be a common sense, dull end – not comparable to a days walk, & then an evening reading over the fire. Hospital trains go by. A hot day to be wounded. Anyhow, it cant last, this intensity – so we think – more than 10 days. A fateful book this. Still some blank pages – & what shall I write on the next 10? This idea struck me: the army is the body: I am the brain. Thinking is my fighting.
> (*D-V*, 15 May 1940)

In *Ghostly Matters: Haunting and the Sociological Imagination,* Avery Gordon urges us to be aware (and beware) of seemingly invisible effects of power that function as "a seething presence, acting on and often meddling with taken-for-granted realities."[1] Illuminating the sociological dimensions of "haunting," Gordon explains, "requires attention to what is not seen, but is nonetheless powerfully real; requires attention to what appears dead, but is nonetheless powerfully alive; requires attention to what appears to be in the past, but is nonetheless powerfully present."[2] Understanding the persistence of modernism requires similar habits of perception. For this reason Virginia Woolf, who was minutely attentive to both discernable and "invisible" complexities of power, is a fitting figure with which to begin a discussion of modernist articulations of loss, trauma, and resilience.[3]

Although it would be foolhardy to suggest that a single author could adequately attend to the concerns outlined in my introduction, Woolf did address many of the issues that still haunt us in a patched but persistent modernism today: the implications of commemorating shattering losses; the connections between acts of remembrance and our imagined futures; the difficulty of commemorating the particularity of loss when catastrophe and atrocity occur so frequently; and the necessity for forging non-lethal responses to the deadly forms of power. Woolf attends to these issues on two levels: on the level of craft, through her associative use of metonym to figure the "negative space" of absence precipitated by loss; and on the level of philosophy, through her refusal to reify rage- or threat-produced national identities. These levels are not mutually exclusive, of course, as they both implicitly critique the logic of substitution that permeates metaphorical understandings of mourning and identification.[4] When loss is figured metaphorically, the particularity of the referent is lost, becoming something else – insight, the consolation of philosophy, the occasion for building character, the impetus for a beautiful elegy – anything but loss *as* loss. Identity formation follows a similar metaphorical structure, since, in Freudian terms, the formation of the ego involves the compensatory incorporation of a lost cathexis.[5] Wendy Brown, although she does not use the language of mourning and melancholia, analyzes a similar consolatory move in the formation of "politicized identity" that "enunciates itself, makes claims for itself, only by entrenching, restating, dramatizing, and inscribing its pain in politics."[6] In this dynamic, identity becomes the consolation for a history of suffering, but in the process, that history of suffering comes to be regarded as if it were an ontological fact of being, rather than a historical condition subject to change.

Acknowledging the particularity of loss was important to Woolf's worldview, especially during a time when, as Herbert Marcuse argues, "the ideology of death" was sweeping across the continent, sanctifying death as the means to obtain the "true," or transcendent, life. Resistance to "the ideology of death" functions as a conceptual sinew in much of Woolf's work, connecting her minute examinations of quotidian personal life with her bold analyses of public events and policies. In what follows, I trace this sinew, first focusing on reifying readings (in contrast to her own resilient responses) to Woolf's much discussed mental illness. In the second half of this chapter, I analyze Woolf's resistance to the ideology of death in her later works, *Three Guineas* and *Between the Acts*, which can be read as primers for refusing troubling forms of militant nationalism.

"WHAT VARIETY OF FIGURES WILL DO JUSTICE"? – PAIN AS NEGATIVE SPACE

Woolf's attempts to find words for seemingly "unspeakable" experiences such as abuse, mental illness, trauma, and grief, are well known and widely discussed by scholars such as Louise DeSalvo, David Eberly, Suzette Henke, Roger Poole, Mark Spilka, and Diana Swanson.[7] Elaine Scarry, whose 1985 book, *The Body in Pain*, is still the authoritative text on the rhetoric of torture and war, even begins her discussion of the "unsharability" of pain with a quotation from Woolf's "On Being Ill": "English, which can express the thoughts of Hamlet and the tragedy of Lear, has no words for the shiver and the headache."[8] The "difficulty of expressing physical pain" is, for Scarry, at the center of concentric circles of pain, the politics of (mis)communicating pain, and human creativity.[9] Given Scarry's concentric schema, it is perhaps not coincidental that Woolf – who was able to invent prose capable of expressing "unspeakable" trauma – chose to write in a "radial" style, conjuring associations by charting submerged transfers of energy.[10] Pain may be, as Scarry argues, ultimately incommunicable, but Woolf is, in the very essay that Scarry cites, able to communicate the experience of pain by tracing its effects. Her perception is seismographic – able to register the subterranean tremors that emanate from traumatic ruptures. She does this by indicating the negative space at the inarticulate center of loss through associative, metonymic language. Hence she expresses her affinity for the French painter Jacques Raverat's suggestion that uttering a word is like "throwing a pebble in a pond," "there are splashes in the outer air in every direction, and under the surface waves that follow one another into dark and forgotten corners" (*L-III*, p. 106).

Noting the connections between Woolf's associative style and her avowed experiences of illness may allow us to think our way out of a troubling either/or that seems to permeate Woolf studies: that Woolf was either primarily a trauma survivor (with her subsequent breakdowns stemming from abuse) or primarily mentally ill, and only incidentally, or coincidentally, a survivor of abuse. This either/or is indicative of larger cultural attitudes about mental illness – that it is something of which to be ashamed, that it is a weakness of will or moral lapse that needs to be defended against or explained. Even Thomas Caramagno, whose *The Flight of the Mind: Virginia Woolf's Art and Manic Depressive Illness* is one of the least judgmental discussions of Woolf's mental illness, begins his discussion as if Woolf needs to be defended for being ill: "Biology lifts from Woolf's shoulders the derogatory weight of responsibility for her illness. It allows us to see that her fiction was not necessarily produced by hypothetical unconscious conflicts, her supposed flight from sex, or her morbid preoccupation with death."[11] But why is the "derogatory weight of responsibility" connected to her illness in the first place? Why does mental illness open one to being discredited, stigmatized, accused of violations against reason and self-control? In part because "madness" is so often a metaphor for something else. As Sontag argues:

Nothing is more punitive than to give a disease a meaning – that meaning being invariably a moralistic one. Any important disease whose causality is murky, and for which treatment is ineffectual, tends to be awash in significance. First, the subjects of deepest dread (corruption, decay, pollution, anomie, weakness) are identified with the disease. The disease itself becomes a metaphor. Then in the name of the disease (that is, using it as a metaphor), that horror is imposed on other things.[12]

In earlier feminist scholarship, notably in Sandra Gilbert and Susan Gubar's influential *The Madwoman in the Attic*, published a year after Sontag's *Illness as Metaphor*, "madness" becomes a metaphor for female anger and resistance to the restraints placed on women through sexist cultural practices. This metaphorical trajectory is honed even more precisely in some biographical treatments of Woolf's status as a survivor of sexual abuse. In the most extensive discussion of this subject, DeSalvo's *Virginia Woolf: The Impact of Childhood Sexual Abuse on Her Life and Work*, childhood sexual trauma becomes the privileged hermeneutical key to understanding Woolf's intricate, philosophical, often fragmented narratives, which come to stand metaphorically for her damaged psyche. Through an overdetermined privileging of trauma, the survivor's life is constricted to a radical embodiedness. In a dynamic similar to the formation of "politicized identity" that Brown describes, Woolf's woundedness becomes an identity, and her utterances mere symptoms of her abuser's power.[13] Such a reading has the consequence of overshadowing Woolf's innovative experiments with narrative and her "capacity for self-extension," a capacity that Scarry links to the politically productive function of the imagination.[14] Woolf exercises her "capacity for self-extension," by representing the "unspeakable" through the writerly equivalent of "negative space" – illustrating the shape of a void by filling in the details around the empty space on the canvas.

Although it has been tempting to read Woolf's innovative prose as a symptom of her traumatic "dissociation," it may be more productive to think of her illness as a resource *as well as* a disability that she managed, more or less successfully, for much of her life.[15] What if Woolf's experiences of hypomania enabled her to perceive the reverberations, the concentric circles of sorrow, more acutely, and thus made it possible for her to communicate her experiences of trauma more adroitly?[16] At the conclusion of "On Being Ill," for example, Woolf uses metonym – a crushed fold in a Victorian curtain – to communicate the "agony" of Lady Waterford (*M*, p. 23). This phrase echoes a section of "Reminiscences" (1907–8), where the young Woolf attempts to describe the death of her mother to her nephew, Julian:

Written words of a person who is dead or still alive tend most unfortunately to drape themselves in smooth folds annulling all evidence of life. You will not find in what I say, or again in those sincere but conventional phrases in the life of your grandfather, or in the noble lamentations with which he fills the pages of his autobiography, any semblance of a woman whom you can love. ("R"-*MB*, p. 36)

This concession is a good example of Woolf's distinctive use of *apophasis* – a means of assertion through negation. Woolf uses this technique of negation and then performative affirmation to great rhetorical effect in her writing – suggesting that something is impossible, then proceeding to perform the very thing that can't be done. In *A Room of One's Own*, for example, she begins by stating that she "should never be able to fulfill what is, I understand, the first duty of a lecturer – to hand you after an hour's discourse a nugget of pure truth to wrap up between the pages of your notebooks," and then immediately embarks on an extraordinary lecture that leaves the audience with her succinctly stated and generously supported sentiment that in order to write "a woman must have money and a room of her own" (*AROO*, p. 4). Later in *A Room of One's Own*, Woolf notoriously asserts, "it is fatal for any one who writes to think of their sex" – an assertion which might give feminists pause, until we realize that this death sentence comes at the end of a beautifully crafted, very much alive book (if the scores of reprints since 1928 mean anything) that is all about thinking of one's sex in relation to the history of literary production (*AROO*, p. 104).

Similarly, in "Reminiscences," after her disclaimer to Julian – "you will not find . . . any semblance of a woman you can love" – Woolf paints an intimate portrait of her mother, from her quirky sayings to her daily acts of charity, letter-writing, matchmaking, etc. Again resorting to *apophasis*, Woolf regrets that, "no one ever wrote down her sayings and vivid ways of speech since she had the gift of turning words in a manner peculiar to her," and then proceeds to catalogue at least six of her mother's peculiar sayings in the next paragraph ("R"-*MB*, p. 36). This intimate portrait notwithstanding, it is probably fair to say that Woolf most accurately represents Julia Stephen by registering the impact of her loss:

If what I have said of her has any meaning you will believe that her death was the greatest disaster that could happen; it was as though on some brilliant day of spring the racing clouds of a sudden stood still, grew dark, and massed themselves; the wind flagged, and all creatures on the earth moaned or wandered seeking aimlessly. But what variety of figures will do justice to the shapes which since then she has taken in countless lives? The dead, so people say, are forgotten, or they should rather say, that life has for the most part little significance to any of us. ("R"-*MB*, p. 40)

Here, to return to painterly language, Woolf communicates the psychic pain of loss *as loss* by depicting negative space – filling in the background around an unpigmented space until the absence at the center of a rather bleak canvas ("where life has for the most part little significance to any of us") takes on an almost palpable form.[17] Focusing on Woolf's representation of loss as negative space might give us a way to distinguish the "unspeakable" from the "incommunicable." While it may be the case that words are not available to describe one's suffering to another, it may yet be possible to communicate the fact that *one is suffering* to another who cannot share, but at least can witness, one's pain. This effort is represented by the second of Scarry's concentric circles, "the political and perceptual complications that arise as a result of [the] difficulty" of expressing pain.[18]

The ethical stakes of expressing pain are especially profound, and yet it is something of a mystery that it is so difficult, since, as mood disorder specialist Peter Whybrow explains, the ability to communicate and perceive emotional information is apparently at the primordial core of what makes us social beings: "Emotion – so obviously unleashed in acute grief – is an ancient signaling system that we share in common with many other mammalian species living in social groups. Emotion and emotional expression evolved as a preverbal system of communication millions of years ago."[19] The preverbal may be all we have to express acute pain, which, as Scarry argues, "does not simply resist language but actively destroys it, bringing about an immediate reversion to a state anterior to language, to the sounds and cries a human being makes before language is learned."[20] But even at the preverbal level, emotional communication is not as automatic as it may seem. Consider Whybrow's own description of breaking down in tears at his father's funeral: "For the people assembled that day I did not need the language of words; my feelings were communicated in my tears and facial expression, in the preverbal language of emotion."[21] But how much did this successful communication depend on a receptive audience, aware of the context of Whybrow's non-verbal communication? If he were to break out in tears in the middle of a party, would he be able to forgo "the language of words" to communicate his feelings, or would his outburst isolate him from a group that does not share or understand his feelings? (This, incidentally, is the situation faced by someone with a mood disorder such as depression or bipolar illness, whose emotional state may seem unexplainable or out of sync with the observable context of the person's life.) With this in mind, we might say that the "complications that arise as a result of the difficulty of expressing pain" are not so much the result of the radical or inherent inexpressibility of pain *in language*, but rather a breakdown in our perceiving apparatus

Woolf's resilience

due to an insufficient context for understanding a sufferer's pain. In fact, most of the atrocities that we call "unspeakable" – incest, torture, and genocide – are more aptly called "unhearable." That is, they're not comprehensible on the part of the listener, because a context (social, political, ethical) for understanding (and alleviating) the sufferers' pain is missing, misleading, or underdeveloped.[22]

In order to build a context that would make even a preverbal communication of pain understandable, we are in need of language, or at least what Scarry would call the world-making capacity of the imagination. This would bring us to the third concentric circle in Scarry's scheme. For Scarry, creativity is something like the inverse of pain, because it is an expansion of self beyond its isolated limits, rather than a reduction of the self to the facts of the body.[23] While the "total reinvention of the world" through the imagination is unrealistic, impossible, one can, through the creation of artifacts ("a sentence, a cup, a piece of lace"), "alter" the world on a much more modest scale.[24] "Imagining a city, the human being 'makes' a house," explains Scarry.[25] "Imagining a political utopia, he or she instead helps to build a country; imagining the elimination of suffering from the world, the person instead nurses a friend back to health."[26] Although the imagined thing is impossible or unreal, the creative effort nevertheless brings about material change.

This leads us back to Woolf's "On Being Ill" and the "impossibility" of fully communicating pain in language. English "has no words for the shiver and the headache," Woolf proclaims. But this assertion can be read as yet another example of *apophasis*, for Woolf suggests not that language will always be insufficient, but that sufficient words must be invented through artifice:

> The merest schoolgirl, when she falls in love, has Shakespeare or Keats to speak her mind for her; but let a sufferer try to describe a pain in his head to a doctor and language at once runs dry. There is nothing ready made for him. He is forced to coin words himself, and taking his pain in one hand, and a lump of pure sound in the other (as perhaps the people of Babel did in the beginning), so to crush them together that a brand new word in the end drops out. (*M*, p. 11)

Woolf's statement, therefore, is not merely an indictment of the limitations of language, but also an indication of its future possibilities. Moreover, she is aware of the creative potential of associative thinking in her description of being ill:

> In health, meaning has encroached upon sound. Our intelligence domineers over our senses. But in illness, with the police off duty, we creep beneath some obscure

poem by Mallarmé or Donne, some phrase in Latin or Greek, and the words give out their scent and distil their flavour, and then, if at last we grasp the meaning, it is all the richer for having come to us sensually first, by way of the palate and the nostrils, like some queer odour. (*M*, p. 19)

Despite the many traumas she experienced and the debilitating aspects of her mental illness, Woolf herself emphasizes the strength and elasticity of creative work, the "capacity for self-extension." From this perspective it is possible to revalue Woolf's difference – as a prolific, admirable, industrious, and ethical artist who most likely happened to have what we now call bipolar illness. Moreover, Woolf's resilience might be worth emulating, especially as she provides strategies for registering loss without reifying identities as ontologically constituted by loss or trauma that must be reconstituted through aggressive identification. In this sense, Woolf takes issue with forms of national identification that are constituted by threat (the circle-the-wagons form of national identification implicit in the phrase "you are with us or against us"). Her insights might also complicate our understanding of contemporary theories of subjectivity, notably Butler's characterization of subject formation as the effect of reappropriated and displaced melancholic rage.[27] As Butler explains, "Survival, not precisely the opposite of melancholia, but what melancholia puts in suspension – requires redirecting rage against the lost other, defiling the sanctity of the dead for the purpose of life, raging against the dead in order not to join them."[28] Butler's reading of "melancholic rage," however, depends on a Freudian understanding of melancholia and mania as dual poles of the same process conditioned by the "mental economics" of the psyche.[29] For Freud, that is, "mania" is the release of psychic energy that has been "bound" and directed inward in the condition of melancholia.

If we uncouple mania from melancholia, we might see it instead as Kay Redfield Jamison does – a condition that is very debilitating when it leads to psychotic episodes, but also as a difference that can be advantageous to creative persons when their illness is kept in check. Citing recent studies, Jamison concludes that mania may enhance "fluency, rapidity, and flexibility of thought on the one hand, and the ability to combine ideas or categories of thought in order to form new and original connections on the other."[30] Woolf's "fluency, rapidity, and flexibility of thought," channeled in the service of her political and ethical values, led her to propose that we "think peace into existence," even as she lived through the disheartening early years of World War II (*DM*, p. 243). In the remainder of this chapter, I trace her efforts to imagine a future where air raid shelters are no longer necessary.

"Consider the gun slayers, bomb droppers, here or there"[31]

"... let's talk in words of one syllable, without larding, stuffing or cant. Let's break the rhythm and forget the rhyme. And calmly consider ourselves" (*BA*, p. 187) (Woolf's emphasis). Thus the anonymous "megaphonic" voice exhorts the audience of a fictional village pageant in Woolf's final novel, *Between the Acts*. Given that the novel is set in June, 1939, when the Nazis already occupied Austria and Czechoslovakia and were threatening Poland, Woolf's call to avoid "larding, stuffing, or cant" was perhaps more difficult to heed than one might imagine during a time of peace. As she notes in her diary in 1940, propaganda and bathetic patriotism had reached a fevered pitched on that other "megaphonic," disembodied voice, the BBC:

We have now been hard at hero-making. The laughing, heroic, Tommy – how can we be worthy of such men? – every paper, every BBC rises to that dreary false cheery hero-making strain. Will they be grinding organs in the street in 6 months? Its the emotional falsity; not all false; yet inspired with some eye to the main chance. So the politicians mate guns & tanks. No. Its the myth making stage of the war we're in. (*D-V*, 3 June 1940)

Despite the sentimental pull of the "false cheery hero-making strain," Woolf urges dispassionate self-reflection during the crisis of the Battle of Britain, a move as counterintuitive as her efforts to think about peace during an air raid. This anti-sentimental stance is a continuation of Woolf's Bloomsbury-influenced project of cultivating honest self-criticism, something, as Froula notes, that she deemed necessary to "enlightened" politics. "In a half-century blighted by two European 'civil-wars,'" Froula explains, "Bloomsbury carried forward and made new the Enlightenment project's self-critical and emancipatory force and meaning . . . Bloomsbury carries the Enlightenment struggle for civilization dialectically into the twentieth century in its pacifism and internationalism, its sense of history not as inevitable progress but as an unending fight for a future that is always open and free."[32]

Given the enormous scope of brutality and destruction that accompanied World War II, it may seem trivial to think of writing as a contribution to culture in a time of crisis. An objection, too, might be leveled at Woolf's attempts to "think peace" during the particular crisis of World War II. If one is against war, is one in effect, if not intention, pro-German at this historical juncture? Or can one be committed to peace and the destruction of the Nazis at the same time? Woolf seems to think this is possible, at least in her 1940 essay "Thoughts on Peace in an Air Raid," where her thoughts are also with the RAF pilots defending England during the Battle of Britain:

> Arms are not given to Englishwomen either to fight the enemy or to defend herself. She must lie weaponless to-night. Yet if she believes that the fight going on up in the sky is a fight by the English to protect freedom, by the Germans to destroy freedom, she must fight, so far as she can, on the side of the English. How far can she fight for freedom without firearms? By making arms, or clothes or food. But there is another way of fighting for freedom without arms; we can fight with the mind. We can make ideas that will help the young Englishman who is fighting up in the sky to defeat the enemy. (*DM*, pp. 243–44)

There is a temporal logic to Woolf's address in this essay: first, defeat "Hitlerism" abroad and in the sky, and "subconscious Hitlerism" – "the desire for aggression; the desire to dominate and enslave" – wherever it is, even in England (*DM*, p. 245). The RAF men in the planes must defeat Hitler's forces in the sky, and, in support of the RAF pilots, the women in the air raid shelters must use their intellectual abilities to defeat the ideology of Hitlerism. Then, after Hitlerism is defeated, the work of building a lasting basis for peace must be done. For Woolf, this involves a shift in ideology and the interpellation of new subjects for whom "honour" requires exercising creative instincts, rather than martial ones: "We must help the young Englishmen to root out from themselves the love of medals and decorations. We must create more honourable activities for those who try to conquer in themselves their fighting instinct, their subconscious Hitlerism. We must compensate the man for the loss of his gun" (*DM*, p. 247).

Because Woolf advocated a wholesale change in the way we think about ingrained traditions, beliefs, and norms, her World War II writing might best be considered a project addressed to the future, rather than to her difficult present. That is, her twenty-first-century readers might be in a better position to appreciate her critique of militarism and nationalism than her contemporaries were. As an address to the future, her contribution to culture is the one she felt herself best equipped to make. In April 1939, she articulated this belief clearly. Rather than "learning to do something that will be useful if war comes," she notes in her memoir, "I feel that by writing I am doing what is far more necessary than anything else" ("SP"-*MB*, p. 73).[33] In May 1940, in the middle of writing *Between the Acts*, she holds firm to her convictions, writing in her diary, "The idea struck me: the army is the body. I am the brain. Thinking is my fighting" (*D-V*, 15 May 1940). Even later, in August of that year, Woolf more fully articulates her commitment to "thinking" as a means of fighting fascism:

Unless we can think peace into existence we – not this one body in this one bed but millions of bodies yet to be born – will lie in the same darkness and hear the same death rattle overhead. Let us think what we can do to create the only efficient air raid shelter while the guns on the hill go pop pop pop and the searchlights finger the clouds and now and then, sometimes close at hand, sometimes far away, a bomb drops. (*DM*, p. 243)

If thinking was Woolf's fighting, then *Between the Acts* is a testament to how tenaciously she could fight the logic of war and patriotic sacrifice. Militarism, for Woolf, was not defense, and the death of the "laughing, heroic, Tommy" was something not to be glorified or mythologized, but rather to be lamented as a horrible waste of human life (*D-V*, 3 June 1940). The only true "defense," "the only efficient air raid shelter," would be the prevention of war, and the only way to prevent war would be to counter and dispel ideologies that consider war justifiable, even inevitable. The novel is therefore Woolf's attempt to understand, on a minute and daily level, how it is that human beings come to accept the extreme forms of nationalism and supremacist ideology that are overtly expressed in fascism. If we could intervene at the level of belief, of "memory and tradition," Woolf suggests, perhaps the sentiments that lead to war might be prevented, if not now, at least for the "millions of bodies yet to be born."

Nevertheless, the allure of "myth-making," not to mention "larding, stuffing, and cant," can be difficult to resist when the violence of war is so close to home. And when we know, with the benefit of hindsight, that the history Woolf was living would turn out to be so calamitous, the temptation to "backshadow" is similarly strong. Michael André Bernstein, who coined the term, describes "backshadowing" as the practice of retrospectively interpreting events as omens – preparatory signs that lead to the ill-fated end as if that end were preordained.[34] The danger of backshadowing is that it encourages fatalism by characterizing efforts to imagine a different outcome as hopelessly naïve. Fatalism, when it masquerades as realism, may compel a seemingly stoical acceptance of pain and calamity. In this situation, heroism is characterized as the ability to endure pain and injustice, rather than to resist it.

Although Woolf resisted both "hero-making" and teleological narrative closure in her work, it is tempting to backshadow when interpreting *Between the Acts* – to read it as the last act in the drama of her life, a prelude to her suicide, her final testament against the patriarchal forces that led Europe into World War II. Many critics read *Between the Acts* as a sign of Woolf's despair over the fate of civilization should the Nazis succeed in their threatened invasion of England. Zwerdling, for example, argues that "Woolf had come to the end of her idealism and was forced to recognize the barrenness of the [pacifist] faith she could not bring herself to give up."[35] Poole suggests that the novel exhibits "a state of mind in which suicide, far from being 'insane,' becomes a natural, and even understandable, desire."[36] So too, Nancy Topping Bazin and Jane Hamovit Lauter argue that the novel's concluding scene "verifies Woolf's vision of the likely death of civilized life – of a return to cave dwelling where nothing but survival matters."[37]

Writing *Between the Acts* in the midst of the devastation of World War II, Woolf was certainly realistic about the brutality of supposedly "civilized" human beings.[38] However, the very act of writing *Between the Acts* suggests her political engagement, rather than despair. Far from admitting the futility of pacifism, the novel is an attempt to intervene in the production of discourses that Woolf found most responsible for the promotion of war, although necessarily – given the circumstances of the text's writing – her intervention is nuanced with tensions, allegiances, and ambivalences. I am certainly not alone in suggesting that *Between the Acts* participates in pacifist, feminist, antifascist, or antihomophobic discourse. James English, for example, examines the "pressure" *Between the Acts* "brings to bear on the 'we' of a certain village-community version of English nationalism."[39] Penny Farfan traces important connections between performance and Woolf's "feminist-pacifist" sentiments,[40] and Stephen Barber analyzes Woolf's subversive production of queer subjectivities in the novel.[41] I wish to take their analyses a step further to show how Woolf implicated dominant pedagogy, historiography, nationalism, heteronormativity, and sexism in the ideology of war. Woolf does not merely reveal the interconnectedness of these discourses, but rather demonstrates their performative function: exposing how the reiterated citation of historical precedent (the "memory and tradition" of *Three Guineas*) consolidates proper nationalist subjects at the expense of scapegoated outsiders-within. She then disrupts nationalist historical narrative though the ironic performance of the pageant of British history that is depicted at the end of *Between the Acts*. Her self-consciously performative historiography encourages its dual audiences (the 1939 audience of the novel's historical pageant and the present-day audience of the novel) to react to national history in ways that promote political accountability rather than patriotic identification.

Between the Acts itself scrupulously refuses to backshadow. Rather than presenting a tragic narrative that scripts the onset of World War II as inevitable, Woolf sets her novel in the summer of 1939, when the outbreak of world war was definitely a strong possibility, but not an absolute inevitability. Because it is set just before the declaration of war, the text is thus able to make use of what Bernstein calls "sideshadowing," "a gesturing to the side, to a present dense with multiple, and mutually exclusive, possibilities for what is to come."[42] For Bernstein, "sideshadowing's attention to the unfulfilled or unrealized possibilities of the past is a way of disrupting the affirmations of a triumphalist, unidirectional view of history in which whatever has perished is condemned because it has been found wanting by some irresistible historico-logical dynamic."[43] Woolf, by investing the historical moment of June 1939 with many possibilities seen from multiple viewpoints, was able to circumvent the "irresistible" closed circuitry of tragically emplotting the historical events she was living through.[44] For Bernstein, focusing on the possibilities open to ordinary people at any particular moment in time does not invalidate the importance of events as they actually occurred in the past, but rather encourages our own accountability for the decisions we make and actions we take in the present time. By showing what might have been, sideshadowing reminds us that human beings, not impersonal fates or forces, have made the decisions, participated or refrained from the actions, condoned or resisted the policies that precipitated historical events. Woolf gives us a brief glimpse of those human beings in *Between the Acts*.

Woolf is able to construct a demystifying counterdiscourse through her rhetorical and stylistic choices (moving from linear "argument" to pictorial and then dramatic forms). Her efforts unmask the reifying effects of "memory and tradition" that performatively construct subjects willing to fight and die for national ideals. The formation of such voluntarily sacrificial subjects might be interrupted, Woolf suggests, by acknowledging the centrality of homophobic repudiation (the violent disavowal of queer "abjects") to the formation of national subjects and thus showing how it is that national belonging is predicated on violent exclusion, rather than the putatively innate bonds of Englishness.[45] Ultimately, Woolf's formal and substantive concerns coincide in her depiction of a "mirror-staging" scene dramatized by the outcast lesbian playwright Miss La Trobe (*BA*, pp. 186–89). Rather than a unifying vision of British subjecthood, La Trobe's mirroring provides a vision of subjects who are in history – consolidated and reconsolidated by the temporal flux of events and ideas – and not simply the inheritors of history. This vision of a contingent and disparate national populace with tenuous claims to cultural inheritance undermines the uncritical use of precedent to foster the exclusionary and violent national identifications that are used to justify war.

MEMORY, TRADITION, AND "REALITY... UP FOR GRABS"

To understand Woolf's construction of counterdiscourse, it is necessary to return to *Three Guineas*, her attempt to analyze the psychological causes of war, rather than its violent symptoms. When she does make reference to the violent symptoms of war, she does so in a mere two paragraphs. Comparing photographs of war's violent consequences (dead bodies, bombed houses) to the "pictures of other people's lives and minds" offered by biography and history, Woolf suggests that the pictorial evidence leaves less room for ideological redescription than does historical narrative:

> Those photographs are not an argument; they are simply a crude statement of fact addressed to the eye. But the eye is connected with the brain; the brain with the nervous system ... When we look at those photographs some fusion takes place within us; however different the education, the traditions behind us, our sensations are the same; and they are violent. (*TG*, p. 11)

Without verbal content, such graphic images, Woolf suggests, are less likely to be coopted into a rationalizing narrative. "Argument," in this context, is an unreliable communicator of the meaning of violence, since the rhetorical persuasiveness of an argument depends on shared cultural assumptions about what is rational. Although, as Sontag notes, Woolf was perhaps too optimistic in her assumption of any imaginary consensus produced by the pictures, the fictional letter-writer of *Three Guineas* can count at least on her interlocutor's agreement about the necessity to end war, for in its rhetorical framing the text is generated by his question, "How in your opinion are we to prevent war?" (*TG*, p. 3).[46] Consensus notwithstanding, Woolf posits a gulf between those who have been educated differently. Those who have been brought up to believe that "honour" is a concept worth defending with one's life, for example, will be more likely to consider a duel an acceptable way to respond to an insult to one's integrity. Cultural assumptions similarly influence one's judgment about the "reasonableness" of war. Moreover, those who are in power have more reason to celebrate the rationalizing narratives of "civilization" and hence will be more inclined to redescribe war in terms that justify its violence (*TG*, pp. 7–8). Thus it is possible for the ruling class to consider war "a profession; a source of happiness and excitement; and . . . an outlet for manly qualities" (*TG*, p. 8). "Outsiders" who are "differently influenced by memory and tradition" will be less likely to consider the alleged benefits of violence with the same enthusiasm (*TG*, p. 18). For Woolf, pictorial images, because they are not narratives, can help circumvent the disproportionate ideological effects of "memory and tradition." The graphic images, she suggests, will provide a common ground for an ethical stance against the violence of war:

You, Sir, call them "horror and disgust." We also call them horror and disgust. And the same words rise to our lips. War, you say, is an abomination; a barbarity; war must be stopped at whatever cost. And we echo your words. War is an abomination; a barbarity; war must be stopped. For now at last we are looking at the same picture; we are seeing with you the same dead bodies, the same ruined houses. (*TG*, p. 11)

Woolf's suggestion that visual evidence might persuade people to reject war and its horrors is similar to the position taken by John Berger more than forty years later in his arguments against nuclear war. Describing a book of pictures painted by survivors of the nuclear bomb dropped on Hiroshima, Berger argues, "the face of horror, the reaction which has now been mostly suppressed, forces us to comprehend the reality of what happened."[47] Arguments about the "strategic" use of nuclear weapons inevitably set up hypothetical scenarios in which their deployment is justified. When one believes that one can prepare for nuclear war, one begins to create the conditions that make such a war thinkable and frighteningly possible. The use of such terrible agents of destruction should be unthinkable, says Berger; this fundamental immorality should not be disguised by the desensitizing term "military strategy." For Berger, such redescriptions deflect our attention from the evidence of atrocity. "One of evil's principal modes of being," argues Berger, "is *looking beyond* (with indifference) that which is before the eyes . . . Only by looking beyond or away can one come to believe that such evil is relative, and therefore under certain conditions justifiable. In reality – the reality to which the survivors and the dead bear witness – it can never be justified."[48]

"Looking beyond," a facility developed through desensitizing cultural conditioning, is more than an individual lapse in ethical responsibility. It is, as Scarry contends, an integral element of the structure of war. Injured bodies come to represent abstract ideals. In both torture and war, Scarry argues, the pain of the body is used to confer meaning on an issue of importance to those in power: "the incontestable reality of the body – the body in pain, the body maimed, the body dead and hard to dispose of – is separated from its source and conferred on an ideology or issue or instance of political authority impatient of, or deserted by, benign sources of substantiation."[49] The resignifying function of war transforms death, war's product, into a meaning-making practice. Wounding, too, is a practice that serves to substantiate abstract concepts. Scarry notes that the pain combatants feel as a result of injury has an immediacy and palpability that is transferred to the ideology of the ultimate victor. Woolf points out the ethical implications of this transfer in her critique of the "myth-making" stage of war. Will the injured soldiers who are used by the British media to rouse patriotic sentiment "be grinding organs in the street in 6 months?"(*D-V*, 3 June 1940) Once they are used to confer legitimacy to British ideals, will the soldiers be effectively "used up"?

This concern for those who have been used up by the war continues a theme Woolf develops in *Mrs. Dalloway* through her depiction of Septimus Smith, who refuses to make the cognitive transfer required of war. That is, he refuses to accept that British civilization (with its ambulances, industries, and social niceties) is worth the death of his killed friend. If death is the price of war, the way of life purchased with that death seems hardly worth the sacrifice (*Mrs. D*, p. 88). Woolf echoes this sentiment again in 1940, writing in her diary, "It's all bombast, this war. One old lady pinning on her cap has more reality" (*D-V*, 15 May 1940). The reference to the "old lady's" reality may be read as a sign of existential quiescence, a withdrawal of focus from the harsh realities of war to a more benign domestic scene. However, when read in the context of Woolf's lifelong response to war, and her address to the future in "Thoughts on Peace," the "old lady's" reality is not the least bit trivial. The diary passage is more accurately read as a resistance to the violent symbolic exchange required of war. Woolf is suspicious of any political reality that must be substantiated by the wounded body. The "old lady's" reality, suffused with custom and habit, needs no such substantiation. As Scarry notes, one's cultural affiliation is deeply inscribed on the body through such habitual actions as pinning one's cap. National or cultural customs of the body are far more indelible than allegiances to verbal or ideological cultural constructs; therefore war must alter bodies in order to secure the meaning of those abstract constructs. "Whether the body's loyalty to these political realms is more accurately identified as residing in one fragile gesture or in a thousand," Scarry explains, "it is likely to be deeply and permanently there, less easily shed, than those disembodied forms of patriotism that exist in verbal habits or in thoughts about one's national identity."[50] Woolf's diary entry suggests that the old lady's act of pinning on her cap is one of those "fragile gestures" that signify her cultural allegiance more indelibly than abstract patriotic "bombast."

A poetic and free-associative use of words in *Between the Acts* has been read as a sign of Woolf's retreat from reality. Sally Sears argues that words "inauthenticate reality" in the novel: the "puppetlike" characters are paralyzed by their purposelessness in a world on the brink of war: "It is above all in the medium of language that the characters take flight from the realities of their experience."[51] The novel's poetic fragments, however, may be read as an attempt to represent reality accurately, rather than to evade it. As Quentin Bell notes, Woolf discusses her attempts to achieve "radial" rather than "linear" prose in her correspondence with Raverat.[52] "The difficulty about writing," Bell explains, "was that it has to be – as [Raverat] put it – 'essentially linear' – one can only write (or read) one thing at a time. Writing a word ... was like casting a pebble into a pond: 'There are waves that follow one another into dark and forgotten corners.'"[53] In reply to Raverat's distinction between the pictorial and the written, Woolf suggests that modern writers "are trying to catch and consolidate and consummate ... those splashes of yours; for the falsity of the past ... is precisely I think that they adhere to a formal railway line of sentence, for its convenience, never reflecting that people don't and never did feel or think or dream for a second in that way."[54] Rather than a bankruptcy of meaning, Woolf's scattered bits of language might instead signify simultaneity of thought and focus. If war, as Scarry notes, is an elaborate attempt to "fix" the meaning of "unanchored" cultural constructs, Woolf's poetic fragments attempt the obverse, leaving important cultural constructs (British history, traditional social relations, the cultural meaning of the landscape) remarkably unfixed.

Melba Cuddy-Keane argues that Woolf's attempt to represent "the multiplicity of reality" inspired her to experiment with genre, developing a new form of political comedy.[55] Although the text does display moments of social cohesion, Woolf consistently undermines these moments with instances of dispersion and disjunction. The pageant ends, in fact, with the gramophone oscillating between "Unity – Dispersity" while the wheels of the departing cars "scurred on the gravel" (*BA*, p. 201). Given the tension between "unity" and "dispersion" in the novel, it seems more appropriate to consider the novel a form of satire as English does, reading the comic moments as facilitators of a satiric critique of British culture.[56] Ultimately less skeptical about the possibilities for social unity and communal "inclusiveness" than Woolf herself, Cuddy-Keane nevertheless makes a significant link between genre and "the necessarily fragmentary nature of any attempt to articulate 'truth.'"[57] Woolf's desire to represent simultaneous realities explains her shift from the narrative mode of representation (employed in *The Years*) to the dramatic.[58]

From its conception, Woolf considered *Between the Acts* a dramatic work. "Pointz Hall [the original title of *Between the Acts*] is to become in the end a play," she notes in her diary (*D-V*, 9 May 1938). Dramatization allows her to circumvent the falsifying "formal railway line of sentence" and instead present a multiplicity of voices that interrupt, contradict, nuance the representation of the historical moment depicted in the text. Although Woolf's representations are still verbal, her move toward dramatization distances her from "argument," which in *Three Guineas* she considers so unreliably linked to "memory and tradition." The dramatic form best suited to Woolf's project of unfixing reified meanings is satire, which makes use of irony to destabilize taken-for-granted customs and cultural beliefs. As I note above, Woolf undertook the project of *Between the Acts* with a clear sense of her ethical stance – to "create the only efficient air raid shelter" by dispelling the logic of militarism. Her decision to script English history as a satire, rather than a tragedy, despite setting its performance in the summer of 1939, allows her to sideshadow, to challenge versions of history that script the onset of war as inevitable. The fatalism intimated by the unstoppable downward momentum of tragedy, together with the focus of tragedy on errors of judgment made by great men, makes that genre unsuitable for a political vision that insists that change is possible (however improbable) if enough "insignificant" people work for it. When we foreclose attempts to imagine different alternatives to war, Woolf seems to say, we foreclose our ability to "think peace into existence."

Significantly, the only character in *Between the Acts* who believes that the outbreak of war is inevitable is Giles Oliver, also the only main character likely to go to war. Giles has inherited the "memory and tradition" Woolf notes in *Three Guineas*. Impatient with his family and neighbors' enjoyment of the countryside, he characterizes their lives as trivial and contemptible. This perspective coincides with what Scarry calls the structure of war, which makes everything but itself appear unreal and insignificant. "War," Scarry argues,

is in the massive fact of itself a huge structure for the derealization of cultural constructs and, simultaneously, for their eventual reconstitution . . . The declaration of war is the declaration that "reality" is now officially "up for grabs," is now officially not only to be suspended but systematically deconstructed ... The lies, fictions, falsification, within war ... themselves together collectively objectify and extend the formal fact of what war is, the suspension of the reality of constructs, the systematic retraction of all benign forms of substance from the artifacts of civilization, *and simultaneously*, the mining of the ultimate substance, the ultimate source of substantiation, the extraction of the physical basis of reality from its dark hiding place in the body.[59]

Giles' reaction to his relatives and neighbors is an indication that the deconstructive process of war has already begun, even though war has not been officially declared. To Giles, Mrs. Swithin's reality (the "old lady's" reality) is trivolous:

Giles nicked his chair into position with a jerk. Thus only could he show his irritation, his rage with old fogies who sat and looked at views over coffee and cream when the whole of Europe – over there – was bristling like ... He had no command of metaphor. Only the ineffective word "hedgehog" illustrated his vision of Europe, bristling with guns, poised with planes. At any moment guns would rake that land into furrows; planes splinter Bolney Minster into smithereens and blast the Folly. He, too, loved the view. And blamed Aunt Lucy, looking at views, instead of – doing what? (*BA*, p. 53) (Woolf's ellipses)

In Giles' mind, the villagers' reality is made unreal, or at least unrealistic, by the daily reports of escalating aggression on the continent. Although the landscape and the structures upon it have not, at this moment in history, been destroyed by the war, Giles' impatient discounting suggests that such "artifacts of civilization" and pleasure, along with the "old fogies" that appreciate them, have already been rendered insignificant by the very threat of war. Although Woolf's depiction of Giles as surly and in need of outlets by which to assert his aggressive masculinity suggests that she is critical of his participation in the deconstruction of everyday reality, she is careful to present war as a very real threat. The current events that are noted in the newspaper and the line of fighter planes that interrupt the Reverend Streatfield are constant reminders of this threat. So too, Lucy Swithin's fantasy of a world before human civilization, although clearly not a viable option for the future, does provide a reminder of what war destroys – the people who populate the land and the material artifacts of civilization.

Mrs. Swithin's focus on "pre-history" has been read negatively as a sign of Woolf's fear that European society will regress to a savage state of pre-civilization or positively as "a longing for a world that is not defined by patriarchy."[60] Both readings[61] assume that Mrs. Swithin's viewpoint mirrors that of Woolf, although the novel suggests that her fantasies are influenced by reading "An Outline of History" (*BA*, p. 8), a text presumably much like the traditional "lop-sided" history Woolf found wanting in *A Room of One's Own* (*AROO*, p. 45). Nevertheless, Mrs. Swithin's fantasies can be read as a commentary on the material effects of war. As Scarry has argued, war, rhetorically as well as materially, undoes the enabling work of human creation.[62] That is, human beings create material artifacts – shelters, beds, clothes – to relieve the burdens of the sentient body. Relieving the body of its burdens allows energy for the artistic, intellectual, interpersonal pursuits that make pleasure and culture possible. Mrs. Swithin's fantasy of a world before humanity reminds us, through their absence, of such enabling "artifacts of civilization." War, as Scarry makes clear, achieves its purpose by reminding us of our embodiedness primarily through wounding the body of the soldier, but also by damaging and destroying the shelters that house and protect civilians.

Between the Acts' focus on the manor house "Pointz Hall" is significant in this respect, for as a shelter it enables its residents to "escape from nature" and it facilitates a great deal of social interaction (*BA*, p. 8). The staging of Miss La Trobe's pageant of English history outside, where players and audience alike are subject to the weather, reinforces the importance of such shelters (*BA*, pp. 179–80). Giles' vision of Bolney Minster blown to "smithereens" further emphasizes the possibility that war will destroy this (admittedly minor, but nevertheless cherished) seat of civilization. Woolf must certainly have been aware of this possibility, for her former house at Tavistock Square was destroyed by a bomb in October of 1940, while she was writing *Between the Acts*.[63] In her diary she notes the plight of Londoners lining up for shelter in subway stations during air raids (*D-V*, 20 October 1940). With this in mind, the pageant's tableau depicting "Civilization" being rebuilt brick by brick – certainly a metaphor for cooperation and collaboration – takes on literal as well as figurative significance (*BA*, p. 181).

THE ABJECT ANSWERS: PERFORMATIVE HISTORIOGRAPHY

The playwright Miss La Trobe's vision for the future, communicated through her parodic staging of British history, provides a counterpoint to Giles' logic of inevitability. We know the outcome of Giles' vision for the future, for history did ultimately follow this pattern. The ordinary antics of village folk were rendered insignificant in comparison to the feats of the military. That Woolf set her novel in the months preceding England's declaration of war suggests that she wanted us to take La Trobe's vision seriously. What if, the novel asks, La Trobe's worldview were prevalent in 1939, and not the exclusionary vision of Whitehall, of the gentry, of the fascists on the continent? As I shall argue later, La Trobe offers an alternative to Giles' fatalistic vision precisely because she offers alternatives within her rendering of history. In her history, England's development – from child to glutted empire to truncheon-waving policeman – is not an inevitable unfolding of destiny, but rather a series of "citations" that are made more apparent by the actors' mis-citations and unconvincing performances.

"Citation," in Butlerian theories of subject formation, refers to the process of reiterating regulatory norms in order to naturalize the identity of a subject. This reiteration of socially prescribed parameters for constituting oneself as a subject masks itself as the expression of the essence of a purportedly "natural" subject.[64] Whereas Butler is concerned primarily with the central role the assignation of "sex" plays in subject formation, Woolf's depiction of the process of citation demonstrates its importance to the formation of national subjects whose sexuality enables them access to the claim of subjecthood. (This process, by extension, also creates categories of people who are not granted access to full subjecthood.) Demonstrating this process, *Between the Acts* shows how the performativity of sex and what Homi K. Bhabha has identified as the performativity of nation are intertwined.

According to Bhabha, a nation must continually "narrate" itself through the dual movements of "pedagogical" recitation and display of "historical origins or events" (similar to the recitation of Woolf's "memory and tradition") and the performative creation of the subjects through the continuous reiteration and transformation of "the scraps, patches, and rags of daily life" into signs of national culture that interpellate "a growing circle of national subjects."[65] In Bhabha's formulation, the nation's performative interpellation of national subjects is continually destabilized by the specter of internalized liminality, the "outsiders" from "extrinsic Other nations" who must, uneasily, be incorporated as "insiders."[66] The destabilizing threat of the abjected outsider who inhabits the inside of national/cultural boundaries is conceptually similar to Butler's formulation of the disavowed, yet haunting threat of identification with the internalized queer abject who defines the peripheries of the subject. As Butler notes, "the subject is constituted through the force of exclusion and abjection, one which produces a constitutive outside to the subject, an abjected outside, which is, after all, 'inside' the subject as its own founding repudiation."[67] In other words, the abject is named or brought into discursive being first, in order to prop up the fantasy of a coherent, bounded, natural subject. The subject is dependent on the abject for its very definition. Although, as Bhabha's postcolonial arguments attest, the logic of repudiation (the emphatic rejection of the internalized outsider within) is not exclusive to homo/heterosexual identifications, the visceral and irrational abjection of homosexuality in Euro/American culture makes this particular kind of repudiation exemplary. Hence Butler surmises that "much of the straight world has always needed the queers it has sought to repudiate through the performative force of the term."[68]

Though she did not have Butler's or Bhabha's theoretical language available to her, Woolf's rendering of history as performative makes use of this conceptual linkage to expose the logic of repudiation that facilitates national identity. Particularly in her critique of the consolidation of national identity at the expense of La Trobe and Dodge, the despised queer figures in the village, Woolf anticipates the philosophical link Butler makes between (disavowed) homoerotic desire and notions of "proper" subjecthood. *Between the Acts* therefore extends her analysis (articulated in *Three Guineas* and continued in "Thoughts on Peace in an Air Raid") of the gendered dimensions of class and national identity. Furthermore, Woolf links gender performance to the exclusionary formation of a collective English or German or Italian "we," and to the will to dominate she calls "Hitlerism." "Let us try to drag up into consciousness the subconscious Hitlerism that holds us down," she argues:

It is the desire for aggression; the desire to dominate and enslave. Even in the darkness we can see that made visible. We can see shop windows blazing; and women gazing; painted women; dressed-up women; women with crimson lips and crimson fingernails. They are slaves who are trying to enslave. If we could free ourselves from slavery we should free men from tyranny. Hitlers are bred by slaves. (*DM*, p. 245)

To trace the dimensions of national identity that might lead to fascism (or "Hitlerism"), Woolf implicitly examines two aspects of subject formation that Butler makes explicit: the citational and the repudiative. The citational process, as I mentioned above, masks its own operation and produces the illusion of authenticity, individuality, uniqueness. Although the reiteration of regulatory norms is, for Butler, inescapable in any performance of identity, Woolf provides a particularly telling example of how cultural authority is garnered through citation in her depiction of the Oliver/Swithin family's promotion of itself as the inheritor of English tradition. This example, admittedly taking place on the manifest level and not the deeply interior levels Butler examines, elucidates the process of citation through its very literalness: through repeated allusions to literary masterpieces, reference sources, and blood ties to other landed gentry. Mrs. Swithin and Bart Oliver, for example, are constantly quizzing themselves about the origins of phrases, details about the English countryside, classical history. This banter may seem trivial, but the reiteration of this information demonstrates the family's access to cultural capital and therefore augments their class identity. This demonstration is contrasted to the language of the nursemaids and other servants. Bond, for example, is limited to monosyllabic utterances: "'Hi-Huh!' he cried suddenly. It was cow language presumably, for the particoloured cow" (*BA*, p. 28). Woolf contrasts Bond's scarcely verbal utterance with the Oliver/Swithin family's demonstration of cultural literacy. This rapid chain of associations begins with Bart Oliver looking up the origin of "touch wood" in the encyclopedia, Mrs. Swithin wondering who "rode out to the sea," Bart confidently demonstrating his knowledge of English geography, and the family discussing the Pharaohs' dental prosthetics. It culminates with Bart asserting, "The Swithins were there before the Conquest" (*BA*, pp. 28–31). In addition to buttressing the authority of those who already have been vested with authority, citation naturalizes the logic of repudiation that operates behind the scenes of subject development. The gentry are the gentry because they are not country bumpkins who speak in monosyllables, nor village idiots, nor servants who believe that the ghost of Lady Ermyntrude haunts the lily pond. Their authority is maintained through the citation of ancestry (represented, for example, by the portrait of the ancestor and his horse), but this authority is backed in the last instance by the last link in their chain of citations – proverb, myth, science, history, lineage . . . conquest.[69]

Woolf examines this dialectical construction of subjects and abjects in her thoughts on Professor von X in *A Room of One's Own*: "Women have served all these centuries as looking-glasses possessing the magic and delicious power of reflecting the figure of man at twice its natural size" (*AROO*, p. 35). Conquest and colonialism are made possible by the self-confidence produced by such mirroring. "Without that power probably the earth would still be swamp and jungle . . . The Czar and the Kaiser would never have worn their crowns or lost them. Whatever may be their use in civilised societies, mirrors are essential to all violent and heroic action" (*AROO*, pp. 35–36). Twelve years later, Woolf still makes use of the mirror metaphor in the last act of La Trobe's historical pageant, but her use of mobile fragments shatters the power of the self-consolidating mirroring described in *A Room of One's Own*. In the final scene of the pageant, called, suggestively, "Present Time. Ourselves," Woolf unsettles the complacent audience members by forcing them to contemplate unflattering and fragmented images of themselves:

> Out they leapt, jerked and skipped. Flashing, dazzling, dancing, jumping. Now old Bart... he was caught. Now Manresa. Here a nose... There a skirt... Then trousers only... Now perhaps a face... Ourselves? But that's cruel. To snap us as we are, before we've had time to assume... And only, too, in parts... That's what's so distorting and upsetting and utterly unfair. (*BA*, p. 184) (Woolf's ellipses)

Instead of the glorifying reflection that magnifies the moral or intellectual stature of the British folks (and this magnification would be expected of a national history), the pageant's last act exposes the shortcomings and moral failings of "ourselves." As if the mirrors might be too subtle a device to promote self-knowledge in a group hardened by centuries of self-magnification, the history pageant ends with an admonishment from an anonymous voice:

> [L]*et's talk in words of one syllable, without larding, stuffing or cant . . . Don't hide among rags. Or let our cloth protect us. Or for the matter of that book learning; or skillful practice on pianos; or laying on of paint . . . Consider the gun slayers, bomb droppers here or there. They do openly what we do slyly.* (*BA*, p. 187) (Woolf's emphasis)

But even as Woolf deconstructs the dominant class's self-aggrandizement through historical mirroring, she demonstrates that the mechanics of group identification through repudiation are multifaceted and difficult to dislodge because of the ambivalences brought about by the interiority of the repudiated abject. Bhabha links this ambivalence to the "doubleness" of the nation's narration of itself, arguing that a "tension between the pedagogical and the performative . . . in the narrative address of the nation, turns the reference to a 'people' – from whatever political or cultural position it is made – into a problem of knowledge that haunts the symbolic formation of social authority."[70] Citing Freud's theories of ambivalence, Bhabha further argues that group cohesion among inevitably diverse people is facilitated by finding "outsiders" to hate. However, "the problem is, of course, that the ambivalent identifications of love and hate occupy the same psychic space; and paranoid projections 'outwards' return to haunt and split the place from which they are made."[71]

Following Butler, we can see that the queer abject is the ideal target of this ambivalence, for the queer is not only the difficult-to-assimilate outsider-within-the-realm, but the queer figure (or specter) is also the disavowed outsider within the psyche. It is not a coincidence, then, that the novel's two boundary figures, who shore up the village inhabitants' sense of themselves as innately British subjects, are William Dodge, the shamed gay man, and Miss La Trobe, the lesbian playwright who stands on the sidelines of historical production, then disappears from view. Giles reacts with rage, for example, to Dodge's appreciation for Isa's fine English china:

His expression, considering the daggers, coming to this conclusion, gave Giles another peg on which to hang his rage as one hangs a coat on a peg, conveniently. A toady; a lickspittle; not a downright plain man of his senses; but a teaser and twitcher; a fingerer of sensations; picking and choosing; dillying and dallying; not a man to have straightforward love for a woman – his head was close to Isa's head – but simply a— At this word, which he could not speak in public, he pursed his lips; and the signet-ring on his little finger looked redder, for the flesh next it whitened as he gripped the arm of his chair. (*BA*, p. 60)

As if aware of the rage projected at him, Dodge later remembers a shaming incident from his childhood that becomes constitutive of his identity and thinks:

At school they held me under a bucket of dirty water, Mrs. Swithin; when I looked up, the world was dirty, Mrs. Swithin; so I married; but my child's not my child, Mrs. Swithin. I'm a half-man, Mrs. Swithin; a flickering, mind-divided little snake in the grass, Mrs. Swithin; as Giles saw; but you've healed me. (*BA*, p. 73)

Woolf's particular use of the metaphor of a "snake in the grass" links Dodge conceptually to the violence that Giles enacts in order to assert his own masculinity. The action of crushing the "monstrous inversion" of the snake in the grass "relieves" Giles of his anxiety about being suffocated by polite, "effeminate" society during a time of political crisis:

There, couched in the grass, curled in an olive green ring, was a snake. Dead? No, choked with a toad in its mouth. The snake was unable to swallow; the toad was unable to die. A spasm made the ribs contract; blood oozed. It was birth the wrong way round – a monstrous inversion. So, raising his foot, he stamped on them. The mass crushed and slithered. The white canvas on his tennis shoes was bloodstained and sticky. But it was action. Action relieved him. He strode to the Barn, with blood on his shoes. (*BA*, p. 99)

There is not a necessary link to the image of the snake and Dodge, or inversion, or birth. The snake might be choking because of its own gluttony, its overzealous performance of what a snake routinely does.

However, this image of undigested-ingestion evokes the ambivalent, interior place of queer abjection that Butler considers central to the consolidation of the subject. In mustering hate or repulsion for the queer other, the disavowal of a lost attachment is reiterated and on some level uncomfortably recalled.[72] It is significant, then, that Giles reads the snake as a symbol of "inversion," a term that alludes to the sexological description of homosexuals as "inverts," whose gender performances purportedly coincide with those of the "opposite" sex.[73] Giles' interpretation of the snake as "birth the wrong way round" also carries the suggestion of illegitimate or unnatural penetration, an allusion that links his violent stamping-out of the snake to his previous aggressive impulses toward Dodge. Crushing the snake appears temporarily to relieve Giles of the psychic threat posed by Dodge's homosexuality. This action, in turn, momentarily satisfies his impatience with England's lack of military action on the continent, which is "bristling" with aggression like a "hedgehog."

La Trobe, too, serves as the target of the villagers' repudiation. She is the un-English, unfeminine, unliked persona who is able to bring about the villagers' performance of themselves as British subjects. From the moment she is introduced in the text, her origins and sexual orientation are suspect:

> But where did she spring from? With that name she wasn't presumably pure English. From the Channel Islands perhaps? Only her eyes and something about her always made Mrs. Bingham suspect that she had Russian blood in her . . . She had been an actress. That had failed. She had bought a four-roomed cottage and shared it with an actress . . . Outwardly she was swarthy, sturdy and thick set; strode about the fields in a smock frock; sometimes with a cigarette in her mouth; often with a whip in her hand; and used rather strong language – perhaps, then, she wasn't altogether a lady? (*BA*, pp. 57–58)

Several critics have made note of both La Trobe's lesbian outsidership and her seemingly authoritarian propensities as the "dictatorial" director of the historical pageant.[74] Patricia Klindienst Joplin, for example, suggests that La Trobe "embodies the author-as-tyrant" who "in her finer moments . . . becomes the author as anti-fascist."[75] This apparent contradiction may be explained by her position as the bearer of the ambivalence inherent in what Bhabha calls the tension between the "pedagogical" and the performative. When her pageant stresses the "pedagogical" recitation of British history to the passive audience – the object of historical discourse – La Trobe is controlling, "bossy" (*BA*, p. 63). When her pageant is most performative – interpellating her audience as active subjects of British history – she relinquishes her control, allowing events – such as the

Woolf's resilience

chance occurrences of "ten mins. of present time" – to unfold without her direction (*BA*, p. 179). She most significantly relinquishes her directorial control when she allows, indeed insists, that the audience become the subjects of the play in the final scene, then refuses to come forth as the "author" of the pageant: "Whom could they make responsible? Whom could they thank for their entertainment? Was there no one?" (*BA*, p. 195).

La Trobe's disappearance as the author of the historical pageant is central to Woolf's focus on the performative as a way to deconstruct the problematic reifications of the pedagogical recitation of "memory and tradition." Ultimately, although La Trobe enables the discourse of history to be produced as the spectacle of national identity, she does not have the agency to author discourse; she must merely cite it and redeploy it differently. Hence her production is a parody of existing literary and historical stories. As Farfan notes, "Woolf provides an example of the potential impact on individual spectators of the parodic repetition of familiar materials in provocative juxtaposition and of the power of theatre to subvert, through its re-enactment of conventional dramatic plots, some of the long entrenched ways of seeing and patterns of interaction that help legitimate patriarchal authority."[76] It is not only through a repetition of plots, however, that La Trobe's parody works subversively, but also through her dramatic reenactment of the consolidation of national identity through citation. This distinction may seem subtle, yet it is important, for theatrical performance, where an actor, pre-existing a role, takes up that role and then resumes her "real" identity after the show is over is not the same thing as everyday performativity, where the "doing" or acting constitutes the doer.[77] La Trobe's pageant, however, is both a performance and performative. As a theatrical staging of the performativity of history-making, the pageant is performative. That is, this performance, like the parodic performance of drag, makes the audience conscious of the performative construction of identities that are assumed to be "natural."[78]

La Trobe's staging of British history therefore draws on available historical discourse, but it does so in a way that demonstrates how powerful figures consolidate their authoritative identity through the spectacle of their power. Eliza Clark's performance of Queen Elizabeth therefore half-convincingly mimics (and hence exposes) the monarch's assertion of royalty through the performance of royalty:

From behind the bushes issued Queen Elizabeth – Eliza Clark, licensed to sell tobacco. Could she be Mrs. Clark of the village shop? She was splendidly made up. Her head, pearl-hung, rose from a vast ruff. Shiny satins draped her. Sixpenny brooches glared like cats' eyes and tigers' eyes; pearls looked down;

her cape was made of cloth of silver – in fact swabs used to scour saucepans. She looked the age in person. (*BA*, p. 83)

The imposing spectacle of the strong-armed Eliza in her silvery garb calls to mind Elizabeth's own performance of drag, when she donned a suit of armor in order to inspire her troops at Tilbury. So too, Eliza's "pearl-hung" image, obviously an illusion brought about by La Trobe's stagecraft, nevertheless calls to mind the class identifications that are maintained through similar props and inferences. Mrs. Swithin, for example, is considered "batty" but is still granted deference by the villagers who do all of the work at Pointz Hall: "Snobs they were; long enough stationed that is in that one corner of the world to have taken indelibly the print of some three hundred years of customary behaviour. So they laughed; but respected. If she wore pearls, pearls they were" (*BA*, p. 27). The meaning of the last sentence is ambiguous. Are Mrs. Swithin's pearls fake, but the villagers overlook this fact because of her upper-class standing? Or do Mrs. Swithin's pearls confer respect on her, because they are emblems of class standing? In either case, she, unlike Eliza, can naturalize her pearl-hung performance because of her class, because she can cite tradition and confidently assert that "the Swithins were there before the Conquest."[79] Such social distinctions, taken for granted and yet ceaselessly maintained through cultural citation, are at the root of traditional historiographic distinctions between historical "actors" and the undifferentiated masses.

La Trobe's refusal to be recognized as the author of the historical performance is a significant critique of the agency attributed to those who make history (in both senses of the phrase). She relinquishes the illusion of control over her production by acknowledging that accident influences the unfolding of events. Not satisfied with the "pedagogical" presentations of history, she riddles her pageant with uncomfortable moments where theatrical verisimilitude breaks down. During her experiment with "ten mins. of present time," for example, La Trobe agonizes, "This is death, death, death . . . when illusion fails" (*BA*, pp. 179, 180). Considered a comment on the director's desire for control over the outcome of events, this statement can be read as an admission of La Trobe's crushed egotism.[80] Yet as a comment on the performative consolidation of identity, La Trobe's statement is both more humble and philosophically unflinching, for if performing makes the subject, then the cessation of performing signals the end of the subject. "This is death . . . when illusion fails," for identity is impelled precisely by our illusion of its coherence.

The uncomfortable sense of dispersion that accompanies La Trobe's "mirror-staging" at the end of the pageant, then, acts as a philosophical counter to the identity-producing spectacle of the Lacanian "mirror stage," with its reliance on the illusion of a coherent identity.[81] Woolf's rhetorical move here is prefigured in her remarks on Sarah Bernhardt's memoirs:

> Yes – one must dine and sleep and register one's life by the dial of the clock, in a pale light, attended only by the irrelevant uproar of cart and carriage, and observed by the universal eye of sun and moon which looks upon us all, we are told, impartially. But is not this a gigantic falsehood? Are we not each in truth the centre of innumerable rays which so strike upon one figure only, and is it not our business to flash them straight and completely back again, and never suffer a single shaft to blunt itself on the far side of us? Sarah Bernhardt at least, by reason of some such concentration, will sparkle for many generations a sinister and enigmatic message; but still she will sparkle, while the rest of us – is the prophecy too arrogant? – lie dissipated among the floods. (*BP*, p. 207)

The inward contraction of attention upon the "actor" in the spotlight makes her an individual who stands out from the masses. The outward turn of the mirrors in the pageant, on the other hand, signals the inevitable failure of such a consolidating vision of identity. Instead of concentrating focus on the unified subject, the mirrors highlight the fragmentation of the onlookers who "lie dissipated among the floods."

La Trobe's rejection of the spectacle of coherent identity in favor of a partial vision of "ourselves" acting in the present time is a significant alternative to the logic of repudiation that consolidates identity, for the actor's usual prominence is achieved at the expense of the dispersed and undifferentiated masses. In this sense, *Between the Acts* is a continuation of the antifascist philosophy of *Three Guineas*, suggesting that the very logic of dialectical repudiation must be challenged if we are to "think peace into existence." As the queer figure who exposes the workings of dominant discourse, La Trobe, alone among all the more entitled inhabitants of the village, has the audacity to point this out.

We may be tempted to think of La Trobe's ambitious effort to interpellate a community of self-reflective subjects, capable of the cooperation necessary to rebuild "civilization," as a failed cause. In the long term, however, *Between the Acts*, as a cultural production and a philosophical argument, works to question and reconfigure the way "memory and tradition" construct national subjects who, like Giles, think of war as a necessary and logical expression of heroic character. War, as Scarry argues, may be a frighteningly effective means of conferring reality on the conqueror's version of events.[82] As Butler notes, however, power retains its material force through its repeated citation.[83] Although our capacity to bring about change is limited by the kinds of performances power makes available or intelligible to us at a particular discursive moment, we may, nevertheless, work to bring about change in the future by attempting performatively to alter the pedagogical scripts that present exclusionary nationalistic identification as inevitable.[84] Presenting an ironic history that undermines the "naturalness" of the abstract concepts over which wars are fought (nationality, racial superiority, sovereignty), La Trobe rearticulates the old cultural scripts discordantly and differently. When the curtain rises on the new scene that ends the novel, history may be set in motion to repeat itself. Woolf leaves the scene unacted, however, suggesting that the course of the drama that ensues will depend on the willingness of her audience, "ourselves," to imagine a "new plot" (*BA*, p. 215).

CHAPTER 2

Stein's shame

SACRED MONSTER

In *Virginia Woolf Icon*, Brenda Silver analyzes the function of the "icon" of Virginia Woolf, arguing that tracking the meanings attached to her representation gives us insight into cultural formations that trouble our present age.[1] Few female writers approach the iconic status of Woolf, but Gertrude Stein certainly does. Catharine Stimpson and Brenda Wineapple address the "challenge" of Stein's iconicity directly, arguing that Stein's iconic status tempts readers to recirculate caricatures of Stein already available in popular culture, rather than engaging meaningfully with her work.[2] In another context, Stimpson notes that there is a long tradition of associating Stein's body with "monstrosity," arguing that among her detractors, Stein's body is read as a sign of sexual, feminine, or egotistical excess, and among her admirers her girth grants her the status of a "sacred monster."[3]

This image of the "sacred monster" is apt if, along the line of Silver's analysis, we take into consideration Stein's iconic association with shame, or what Eve Kosofsky Sedgwick calls "the double movement shame makes: toward painful individuation, toward uncontrollable relationality."[4] To explain this "double movement," Sedgwick describes a "thought experiment" where she asks her listeners to imagine a "misbehaving man" doing something socially unacceptable (in her example, urinating) in their midst. "I pictured the excruciation of everyone else in the room: each looking down, wishing to be anywhere else yet conscious of the inexorable fate of being exactly there ... at the same time, though, unable to staunch the hemorrhage of painful identification with the misbehaving man."[5] If shame exerts an identificatory/repulsive force, then the icon of Stein works apotropaically to ward off shame by representing it. Because Stein's multifaceted identity intersects with so many shame-producing conditions – she is not heterosexual in a world where queerness is stigmatized, she is

53

fat at a time when thinness is the fashion, she is Jewish in a time of intense anti-Semitism, she is gregarious and egotistical when women should be demure, she speaks about sex when she should be silent – she threatens to become the spectacle of the "misbehaving [wo]man" whose shame, if Sedgwick is right, is potentially contagious.

Moreover, Stein's association with the "hemorrhage of painful identification" demonstrates in specific a more general disquiet that accompanies the persistence of modernism. Stein's life and works generate "painful identifications" which migrate from the texts of the early twentieth century to the (con)texts of the twenty-first. But for the reservations I note below, this migration might be described as a form of modernist "postmemory," infused with the "uncontrollable relationality" and "painful individuation" of shame. Marianne Hirsch, who coined the term, explains that

Postmemory characterizes the experience of those who grow up dominated by narratives that preceded their birth, whose own belated stories are evacuated by the stories of the previous generation shaped by traumatic events that can be neither understood nor recreated. I have developed this notion in relation to children of Holocaust survivors, but I believe it may usefully describe other second-generation memories of cultural or collective traumatic events and experiences.[6]

James Young similarly links "postmemory" to the vicarious nature of memories passed on from one generation to the next. Postmemory, for Young, is an open, ongoing process. Describing the "postmemory" of contemporary artists and architects who are second-generation survivors of the *Shoah*, Young observes that

By portraying the Holocaust as a "vicarious past," these artists insist on maintaining a distinct boundary between their work and the testimony of their parents' generation . . . Yet by calling attention to their vicarious relationship to events, the next generation ensures that their "post-memory" of events remains an unfinished, ephemeral process, not a means toward definitive answers to impossible questions.[7]

Both Young and Hirsch use "postmemory" to describe the second-generation trauma experienced by children of survivors of the *Shoah*. It therefore may not be appropriate to use the term to describe the compulsive attraction of Stein's apotropaic icon for readers whose relations to Stein are wholly vicarious (and not familial). Instead, with a nod to the theorists who analyze the generational transmission of affect through postmemory, I will call the shame mobilized by Stein's iconic representation "vicarious compunction."

Vicarious compunction haunts (to use the ghostly language of Gordon) present-day understandings of modernism's past. Facing similar pressures, would we have behaved better than Stein? This is not merely a "thought experiment" for many in the USA who, in the current historical moment, wrestle with the specter of identification with a national government that advocates pre-emptive war, the indefinite detention of "alien unlawful enemy combatants," "secret detentions," and "'alternative' interrogation techniques" that violate the spirit (and for many commentators the letter) of international human rights law.[8] The "painful individuation"/ "uncontrollable relationality" mobilized by vicarious compunction might prove to be less paralyzing than liberal guilt or defensive self-righteousness. As Butler notes, recognizing our relationality as well as our vulnerability is a prerequisite for an ethics that would respond to violence effectively (PL, pp. 22–27). "Is there a way that we might struggle for autonomy in many spheres, yet also consider the demands that are imposed upon us by living in a world of beings who are, by definition physically vulnerable?" asks Butler (PL, p. 27). The "precariousness" of life for Butler, following Levinas, is the beginning of ethics – an ethics that requires recognizing our ability to harm as well as our vulnerability to harm, our ability to kill as well as our susceptibility to murder (PL, pp. 134–35). In this context the apotropaic "sacred monster" provides an important reminder of our duality, our relationality and autonomy. Its shame-producing toxicity invites awareness of one's own potential to harm as well as to be harmed. As a "sacred monster," Stein invites identification with its negativity: are we like Stein? And if so, are we like her in her potential to suffer at the hands of unjust power, or are we like her in her capacity to be complicit with that power? Charting Stein's attraction/repulsion provides insight into the mechanisms with which we manage the ethical contagion of those whose actions in a time of crisis are morally ambiguous. Can we like Stein without being like her? The stakes of understanding the double move of individuation/relationality are especially pronounced when one is dealing with modernist writers who may have flirted with fascism. From a backshadowing perspective, this flirtation is morally repugnant, knowing as we know the disastrous consequences of fascist rule in Germany and Italy. From a sideshadowing perspective, however, we might see how that complicity was banalized in the early twentieth century among writers who might never have agreed with the historical consequences of fascist rule.

In what follows, I analyze the boundary confusion that is represented through metaphors of contagion and intimate transgression in critical treatments of Stein's Jewishness, her flirtation with fascism, her lesbianism, and her odd and disturbing pronouncements about race and gender. I arrive at this analysis after a brief interlude on H.D.'s painful negotiation of her intimacy with Ezra Pound, a very toxic figure for someone (like H.D.) who finds fascism repulsive. I then read *The Making of Americans* and Stein's later "detective" stories as examples of "forensics." Forensics, for Stein, has a double connotation, being a form of persuasive writing associated with Harvard's "forensic" writing seminars (what we would call composition today) and the process of criminological evidence gathering. Through her forensic investigations, Stein examines how history, as a written record, is constructed in language, and how history, as public consciousness of important things that happened in the past, is constructed through the repetition of stories about "interesting" events or persons. While it may be too much of a stretch to say that Stein is an early proponent of sideshadowing, her anti-metaphorical writing nevertheless challenges the recuperative gesture of historiography, and provides a method for "detecting" the significance of seemingly banal events. Her method counteracts the "redemptory" pull of history that Young's proponents of "postmemory" contest through their contemporary artistic productions.

CONTAGIOUS METAPHORS – H.D.'S TORMENT AND STEIN'S DIFFICULTY

The fascists of the early twentieth century used the language of contagion to describe members of the groups they targeted for their hate. Jews, sexual "deviants," Gypsies, communists, and the mentally ill were considered unclean, degenerate, and infectious elements that lurked within the social body and damaged its health. Describing the rhetoric of Ezra Pound's radio broadcasts, for example, Robert Casillo notes that Pound's "hatred and fear of Jews finally reduces them in his mind to the demonic status of germs and bacilli, invisible 'carriers' of plague and disease, a swamp, an enormous 'power of putrefaction' and profanation preying invisibly on the body of the West."[9] The germ – the gamete – was to be regulated and feared as a powerful eugenic or degenerative agent. In Hitler's notorious formulation, for example, Jewish men willfully "poison" the blood of the next generation, participating in a covert version of biological warfare against German (Aryan) society by inseminating Aryan women.[10] As if caught up by the rhetoric of contamination, antifascists study the germs of fascism, too – charting its historical incubation, diagnosing its symptoms, identifying pockets of reinfection and outlining prophylactic and educational measures designed to prevent the outbreak of further epidemics.[11] Woolf, therefore, likened the threat of fascism to an "embryo" or "egg" that she could "shake out from our most respectable newspapers any day of the week":

There, in those quotations, is the egg of the very same worm that we know under other names in other countries. There we have in embryo the creature, Dictator as we call him when he is Italian or German, who believes that he has the right, whether given by God, Nature, sex or race is immaterial, to dictate to other human beings how they shall live; what they shall do. (*TG*, p. 53)

Woolf's redeployment of the fascist rhetoric of antiseptics – of health and infection – calls attention to the boundary confusion that motivates fascism's paranoid logic.[12] The tropes of infection, disease, inoculation, and insemination signal a fear of invasion by the other into interior spaces where the "me" and the "not me" commingle within the blood.

Familiar with Pound's Rome Radio broadcasts, H.D. takes up the tropes of infection and inoculation to describe the painful process of reevaluating her own intimacy with Pound in *End to Torment*.[13] H.D. begins this brief memoir (written in 1958, the year that Pound was released from St. Elizabeth's hospital), by resisting the specter of her identification with Pound. Describing her psychoanalyst Erich Heydt's attempt to give her a copy of *The Cantos*, she comments, "The face, full-face, bronze against the dark background, looked at me, a reflection in a mental mirror. 'No,' I said and handed the book back."[14] Ultimately, she does confront her troubling relationship with Pound, using the metaphor of inoculation to describe the incubation of her memoir: "When I came, the second time, summer 1953, after an operation in Lausanne, he [Heydt] jabbed an injection needle into my arm. It was perhaps the second or third time that I had seen him – or was it the first? He said, 'You know Ezra Pound, don't you?' This was a shock coming from a stranger. Perhaps he injected me or re-injected me with Ezra."[15] A few pages later H.D. reiterates, "Dr. Erich Heydt injected me with Ezra, jabbing a needle into my arm, and 'You know Ezra Pound, don't you?' This was almost five years ago. It took a long time for the virus or the anti-virus to take effect. But the hypodermic needle did its work or didn't it?"[16] For H.D., the work of remembrance is like the work of immunization; memory is an antibody, but a dangerous one – for she can't tell whether she has been injected with a virus or an "anti-virus."

H.D.'s inoculation metaphor is a response to the dis-ease of her identification with Pound, whose image she has just described as "a reflection in a mental mirror."[17] The person this "mental mirror" reveals is troubling precisely because his mental image may be contagious. Mixing metaphors of infestation and insemination, H.D. suggests that "[Pound] is far from lost. He is centralized and accessible. A thousand Ameisen [ants], ant hill upon ant hill of provincial colleges, have had a curious insemination."[18] Among those who visited Pound at St. Elizabeth's were teachers such as Norman Holmes Pearson and the influential Hugh Kenner, who went on to describe modernism as the "Pound Era." But also among those swarming Pound at St. Elizabeth's were people like racist activist John Kasper. In a letter to H.D., Pearson describes Pound's protégé thus:

Kasper comes from New Jersey, but organized a white supremacy group . . . Is now on bond awaiting trial. Meanwhile has shifted his ground to Florida where he is giving violently anti-Negro and anti-Semitic speeches. His bookshop in Washington is now called the Ezra Pound Bookshop. I am sick about it. Ezra sent me a copy of his newspaper with some semi-flattering remarks about Kasper, and hopes I can keep Kasper's press going.[19]

Is Pearson "sick about this" development because of moral repugnance, or because he fears that Kasper's antics will jeopardize Pound's release from St. Elizabeth's by indicating the contagiousness of Pound's ideas? (When Pound was released, he was declared still insane, but not a danger to others.)[20] Pound's influence apparently is not an issue for Pearson, who suggests that his own teaching methods will make Pound safe for students:

I don't approve, as you know, of what Ezra says about the Jews . . . But I think I know perhaps even better than Pound does what he is really talking about, and I have no problem in teaching *The Cantos* to Jews, when they understand him through me.[21]

This is an odd comment for many reasons – among them, the suggestion that a teacher can know what a poet is "really talking about," or that he can sanitize Pound's comments by filtering them "through" himself. But the strangest thing about Pearson's comments are his suggestion that he needs to be the conduit of understanding Pound to Jews, who are arguably the least likely to become "infected" with Pound's anti-Semitism. Or perhaps he is suggesting that Pound's noxious politics are a kind of poison that makes him "sick" but to which he has the proper methodological antidote, so that he can, like a good apothecary, dispense Pound's words safely to the students who might be most damaged by them. In any case, Pearson's pedagogical filtering techniques are representative of what has become a long-standing New Critical practice of separating Pound's poetry from his political beliefs.

Pearson's predicament highlights the dynamics of vicarious compunction that can accompany the toxic politics of a writer. As in the case of shame, the reader/critic negotiates the "double movement" between individuation (Pound the man must be separated radically from Pound the poet in order for his poetry to be safe for consumption) and "hemorrhage of painful identification" that can make the reader "sick about it."[22] If, as Said says, the past cannot be "quarantined from the present," and, as Gordon notes, the past may be "powerfully present" as the uncanny that haunts us, then the New Critical practice of radically separating the poet from the poetry begins to look like the disavowal Adorno decries in his critique of "cultural criticism."[23] On the other hand, conflating the poet with the poetry is not helpful either, for this practice underestimates the "capacity for self-extension" implicit in the creative process.

The predicament of vicarious compunction is important to acknowledge when writing about Stein, for although she is no Ezra Pound, she is a *difficult* writer, not only because of the complexity and obscurity of her works, but also because her political and ethical life is maddeningly inconsistent. One can but pity the poor biographer who attempts to create a seamless narrative of her life as an avant-garde-expatriate-Jewish-lesbian who lived through World War II unscathed in the French countryside largely because of her associations with fascist collaborators such as Bernard Fäy and Maréchal Pétain. She was, as Gordon would say, endowed with "complex personhood."[24]

VICARIOUS COMPUNCTION AND STEIN'S CULTURAL LEGIBILITY

Because Stein exhibits "complex personhood," she makes her critics uneasy. Stein's lesbianism and Jewishness do not seem to fit well with her conservatism and early support for fascism. Her masculinity, too, stimulates a font of speculative criticism that does more to reveal her critics' presumptions than her own. An early example of biography that sees identity coherence where it wishes to find it is Arthur Lachman's "Gertrude Stein as I Knew Her," an undated manuscript in the Stein Papers of the Yale Collection of American Literature, since published by Linda Simon. "I knew Stein during her chrysalis stage when we both belonged to a small group of earnest young people at Harvard University," writes Lachman. "At this time she was about twenty-four years old. She was a heavy-set, ungainly young woman, very mannish in her appearance. Her hair was cut short at a time when this was by no means the fashion among the fair sex."[25] Simon points out the inaccuracy of Lachman's remark about her short hair.[26] (She had her hair cut short in 1926, twenty-eight years after she graduated from Harvard.)[27] Expecting her to exhibit "masculine" characteristics because of her later self-presentation, Lachman alters his memory in order to produce a historical continuity of Stein's perceived gender attributes. Such descriptions of Stein's physical appearance fit into what Stimpson argues is a larger pattern of aversive attitudes expressed towards Stein's "monstrous" body.[28]

Moreover, as far back as 1979 lesbian feminist critics preferred Woolf, who lived most of her adult life in a heterosexual marriage, to Stein, who lived her most of her adult life in a committed partnership with a woman. Blanche Wiesen Cook helped to construct the image of Stein as a reactionary, misogynist lesbian, suffering from male-identified false consciousness in her article "'Women Alone Stir My Imagination': Lesbianism and the Cultural Tradition." "It was, I think, no accident that Gertrude Stein, for example, was far more available to us," Cook argues. "Heterosexist society is little threatened by a relationship that appeared so culturally determined. Stein wrote and slept while Toklas cooked, embroidered, and typed. Few feminist principles are evident there to challenge the ruling scheme of things."[29] Stein's gender performance is thus linked to her conservative politics: "her politics, though not simple, seem on the balance impoverished," writes Cook. "Stein was not a radical feminist. She was Jewish and anti-Semitic, lesbian and contemptuous of women, ignorant about economics and hostile toward socialism."[30] Shari Benstock makes a similar equation between Stein's "mannishness" and her politics ("Paris Lesbianism," pp. 340–42). In a more recent article in *The Gay and Lesbian Review*, Jean E. Mills even goes so far as to suggest that "Stein's psychic survival against the backdrop of the Nazi witch hunt . . . can only be explained, in my view, with reference to her identity as a transgendered person."[31] Because transgendered identity is already embattled, argues Mills, Stein was psychologically prepared for life in Vichy France: "But for Stein very little changed during the war, because she was always at war with herself anyway, which somehow cancelled external events."[32] While Mills' appraisal of Stein appears to be sympathetic, insofar as it acknowledges the possibility of Stein's transgendered subjectivity, it is far from comforting to think that a transgendered subjectivity prepares one to be especially insusceptible to the suffering of others, or to be oblivious to violence outside one's psyche simply because one is "at war with [one's self] anyway."[33] It is just as likely that someone with a painful history of psychic distress would be *more* likely to empathize with the misery of others, or to react emotionally to painful "external events."[34] While gender performances are always articulated *in* discourse, and therefore in the political, it does not follow that one can predict a seamless relation between one's gender performance and one's political allegiances.[35] Nor is it the case that gender automatically trumps all other social considerations, even in non-normatively gendered persons.

To be fair, those who recuperate Stein as a model or "subversive" butch lesbian employ a similar logic of seamless relation between gender, sexuality, and political affinity. However, in this case Stein's gender performance is read as an indication of her progressive politics. Leigh Gilmore, in a Butlerian reading of the Stein/Toklas relationship suggests that the couple's "role playing" enacts a butch/femme parody (and hence deconstruction) of normative heterosexuality.[36] While Gilmore's reading is more compelling than Cook's simple dismissal of Stein as suffering from false consciousness, her recuperation of the Stein/Toklas relationship in a celebratory mode is not necessarily a more "accurate" representation of Stein and Toklas' coupling, but another way to make meaning of their relationship through now established modes of lesbian representation. Gilmore herself suggests that "lesbians can act in certain stylized ways toward each other through a discourse of signs and gestures in which they become knowable as lesbians against tremendous cultural pressure toward invisibility and neutralization."[37] Stein's "mannishness" is read now as a sign of butch identity rather than false consciousness. It's difficult to imagine, however, Stein in her corduroy skirts, sandals, and floppy hats walking into a butch/femme bar in Buffalo of the late 1940s or 1950s and presenting a gender performance that would be culturally intelligible to the working-class butch or femme patrons of the establishment, or walking on to the set of the *L-Word* and being recognized as a self-styled butch.[38] It is difficult, even, to imagine Stein as an "invert" in the style of Radclyffe Hall or Romaine Brooks. As Stimpson argues, "a popular icon of the lesbian, which *The Well of Loneliness* codified – that of a slim, breastless creature who cropped her hair and wore sleek, mannish clothes did little to reinforce an association between the ample Stein and deviancy."[39] In other words, there were models for performing female masculinity available to Stein, but it is not clear that she patterned her gender after them.[40] Even so, Gilmore's casting of Stein's relationship with Toklas in a butch/femme model grants it cultural intelligibility as a legitimate form of same-sex relationship, and rescues it from the charge, leveled by earlier feminist critics such as Cook, that Stein selfishly lorded over a cowering and mistreated Toklas.[41] In the process of defending Stein from false consciousness, however, butch/femme is drained of its cultural specificity and its particular stylizations of gender performance. It is important to note, as Gilmore does (following Butler), that butch/femme relationships are not simply copies of heterosexual relationships. By the same token, not all presentations of masculinity and femininity in a same-sex relationship are copies of butch/femme.

The recuperation of Stein as a butch figure has other perlocutionary effects, especially when the terms "butch/femme" – which connotes a *difference* structural to the relationship – and "lesbian" – which connotes, for many theorists, a *sameness* upon which the relationship is built – are conflated. In this instance, Stein and Toklas are presented as a unified entity whose differences are really a stylized formal presentation of their fundamental sameness. Central to this reading, as Gilmore notes, is a doodle "Gertrice/Altrude" that Wendy Steiner discovered in the margins of the manuscript of Stein's "Lend a Hand."[42] The melding of identity that this doodle seems to suggest is taken as a sign of the strategy of *The Autobiography of Alice B. Toklas*, which, according to this reading sets up the lesbian couple as the autobiographical subject. "The puzzles and the pleasures – figurative and literal – of lesbianism are figured in the autobiographical signature ['Gertrice/Altrude'] as the intermingling of syllables across a penetrable border," writes Gilmore. "Gertrude Stein revises the subject position of autobiography by replacing the solitary I bound by the conventions of realist narrative and historical accountability – the terms of the autobiographical pact – with the lesbian couple evoked through the signature 'Gertrice/Altrude.'"[43]

In a similar move, Sidonie Smith reads a Man Ray photograph of Stein and Toklas and the insignia "rose is a rose is a rose is a rose" as a symbol of "the erotic union of Alice B. Toklas and Gertrude Stein," and suggests that the *Autobiography of Alice B. Toklas* is one more such symbol.[44] "Like the rose insignia," Smith argues,

the photograph and title page confuse the notions of self and other, identity and difference, narrator and narratee, "I" and "you," and they visualize in their semiotics, as the ring does, the lesbian couple, going in or coming out of the writing closet. The pleasures of the text (that is, of writing) and the pleasures of the body (that is, of lesbian coupling) are here foretold.[45]

Stein's shame 63

The duplicitous autobiographical "I" of the *Autobiography* "is an 'I' of two-ness" for Smith: "There is a 'we-ness' to the textual 'I.'"[46] Smith goes on to suggest that the "resistance to identity" figured by Stein's autobiographical strategy "has everything to do with Stein's troubles with sexual identity."[47] These troubles, as Smith explains, have to do with "male-identification."[48] Like Gilmore, Smith argues that Stein's "male-identification," signifies a butch gender role, and through a Butlerian reading Smith suggests that the *Autobiography* undermines the naturalness of heterosexual coupling.[49] Using the metaphor of a "host," associated with Alice as the exemplary "hostess," Smith suggests that

> Stein enters the mouth of her lover and takes up lodging in the body of 'Alice' for the purposes of writing the autobiography. 'Alice' in turn enters the mouth of her host writer through whose body she speaks. This commingling of subjects in the text is thus an act of erotic union, signed by the wedding band/vaginal image on the cover.[50]

The lesbian coupling that is celebrated in this passage is synonymous with boundary dissolution. Smith alludes to the "sacrificial," "Eucharist[ic]" connotation of the term "host," suggesting that Stein has deconstructed the traditional story of female self-sacrifice because Stein is a woman playing the role of "husband": "Alice's performance of the wife's role is a travesty through which Stein is displacing the heterosexual couple and heterosexual coupling, resituating in its stead, in its textual homestead, the lesbian couple and lesbian coupling."[51] The slippage from parody to travesty here is troubling. Butch/femme is no longer a denaturalizing performance of gender difference, but rather the recuperation of the social equation of "wifeliness" with self-effacement and self-sacrifice. The equation of "femininity" with selflessness, a cultural logic that many femme gender performances seek to denaturalize, is left unchallenged.

Ultimately Smith recuperates both Stein's autobiographical act and her relationship with Toklas for radical politics, concluding, "the cultural radicalism of Stein's modernism and her lesbianism invigorate one another. The text's eroticism and its radical disruptiveness are one and the same."[52] This recuperation is a refreshing alternative to the previous equation used to dismiss Stein: masculinity in a woman = male identification = bad politics. Nevertheless, the effects of this recuperation of butch/femme/lesbianism call for elucidation. Smith's reading, tellingly titled "'Stein' Is an 'Alice' Is a 'Gertrude Stein,'" conflates the (perceived) lack of discrete psychic boundaries between women with lesbian eroticism. As I noted above, for Smith the "wedding band" symbol "confuse[s] the notions of self and other, identity and difference, narrator and narratee, 'I' and 'you.'" Butch/femme/lesbianism has thus become another place where the "me" and the "not me" commingle. While it would not be helpful to reanimate the paranoid reading of boundary confusion that I outlined at the beginning of this chapter, neither does it seem promising to privilege butch/femme/lesbianism as a site of idyllic boundary dissolution. A lack of psychic boundaries between people in a romantic couple is something that would be seen as worrisome in a heterosexual relationship. Why a similar dissolution of boundaries between women would be celebrated as erotic, subversive or empowering is a puzzling question.

As important as that question is, it is even more important to attend to the relationships that are still ongoing – not those between Stein and Toklas or H.D. and Pound, but rather between reader and text or critic and author. These relationships do produce intimacies, especially if we remember that to be intimate with something is to know it well. However, they are not exclusively identificatory, nor exclusively bounded by the alterity of the text, but rather made up of complex networks of identifications, counteridentifications, and disidentifications. How else to explain our (literary critics') occasional irritations with the subjects of our work for being obscure, for making stupid jokes, for being on the wrong side of political arguments, in short, for producing embarrassing moments of vicarious compunction? It is helpful to avow such intimacies if we are to understand their effect.

The pain of identification with Stein is especially pronounced when the subject is Stein's racism, particularly as it is articulated in her 1909 story, "Melanctha." In the last two lines of the story – the textual space where, in a more traditional female *Bildungsroman* one would expect some version of "reader, I married him" – the protagonist Melanctha is abruptly carted off to die in obscurity: "Melanctha went back to the hospital, and there the Doctor told her she had the consumption, and before long she would surely die. They sent her where she would be taken care of, a home for poor consumptives, and there Melanctha stayed until she died."[53] Is this ending a recirculation of the "tragic mulatta" stereotype, or a parody of the genre? Although Marianne DeKoven suggests that the characters in the story "simultaneously embody and contradict racial stereotypes," Sonia Saldívar-Hull argues that Stein expediently kills off the racialized, stereotyped body of her protagonist once she has been used up for narrative purposes.[54] Critics eager to celebrate Stein, writes Saldívar-Hull, are in danger of replicating her racist gesture: "The reader loses consciousness of the racism and classism because s/he is encouraged to think only of an aesthetic category, urged to remember that Stein wrote at a specific time, in a particular culture. But these embarrassments that feminist scholars do not discuss at any depth are at the center of 'Melanctha.'"[55] Jamie Hovey continues this critical trajectory, contending that "even the critics who do attempt to address and unravel the elaborate racial taxonomies that structure Stein's early narratives seem to fall into the trap of the racial categories as Stein sets them up, replicating the very illogical equivalences which form the core of discursive racial 'knowledge' in texts such as *Q.E.D.* and 'Melanctha.'"[56] The racist representations in "Melanctha" are in this sense viral – self-replicating and ultimately toxic.

Within the logic of the text, Melanctha herself is toxic, a dangerous person because of her mixed race and sexual promiscuity. Her dangerousness is highlighted by her tuberculosis, which in 1909 was incurable and highly contagious. Moreover, as Susan Sontag notes, the disease was thought to symbolize and expose consuming passions: "TB is the disease that makes manifest intense desire; that discloses, in spite of the reluctance of the individual, what the individual does not want to reveal."[57] Melanctha is consumed, too, by melancholy, the "black bile" which is etymologically linked to her name.[58] The text begins and ends with her profound melancholy. On the second page we are told that "Sometimes the thought of how all her world was made, filled the complex, desiring Melanctha with despair. She wondered, often, how she could go on living when she was so blue."[59] The "consumption" that ends Melanctha's life thus stands in for the suicide she desires, coming in its place at the end of the story:

> But Melanctha Herbert never really killed herself because she was so blue, though often she thought this would be really the best way for her to do. Melanctha never killed herself she only got a bad fever and went into the hospital where they took care of her and cured her.
>
> When Melanctha was well again, she took a place and began to work and to live regular. Then Melanctha got very sick again, she began to cough and sweat and be so weak she could not stand to do her work.
>
> Melanctha went back to the hospital, and there the Doctor told her she had the consumption, and before long she would surely die.[60]

Given that Melanctha's character is based in part on Stein's ex-lover, May Bookstaver, her unfortunate end can also be read as a revenge fantasy – killing off the ex with a disease associated with excessive desire.[61]

In this case, memory, melancholy, and "complex" desiring are safely contained by the abrupt ending of Melanctha and her narrative.

Melanctha's fascinating allure in the text is her willingness to flout convention and "wander" with "break neck courage" after "wisdom" in places that blemished her character with the taint of impurity.[62] For similar reasons, Stein is simultaneously fascinating and repulsive to present-day readers who feel compelled to conduct background detective work about her personal life and her political affiliations. Who would want to be in the embarrassed position of finding out from others, after spending years getting to know Stein, that she was less than naïve about Bernard Fäy's role in persecuting thousands of Freemasons during his time in the Vichy government, or that Stein had joked about nominating Hitler for the Nobel Prize, or that she fancied Otto Weininger's racist, misogynist sexological theories?[63] As several scholars have noted, Stein championed the collaborationist government of Pétain in her memoirs of World War II.[64] Stein's comments on war range from flippantly insensitive to fearfully aware of the dangers facing herself and Toklas. In a frequently cited posthumous essay, Wanda Van Dusen argues that Stein's praise for Pétain "raises both ethical and theoretical questions . . . how much she may have collaborated with the Vichy regime to protect her and Alice Toklas' lives as Jewish American lesbians in the French countryside at Bilignin par Belley."[65] Phoebe Stein Davis and Barbara Will complicate Van Dusen's claim that in translating Pétain, Stein was engaged in "performing a redemptive fetishistic ritual that denies the existence of racism in the so-called free zone (*zone libre*) administered by Pétain."[66] Davis contends that Stein engaged with political events through her experimental aesthetics in her World War II "autobiographies" *Wars I Have Seen* and *Mrs. Reynolds*.[67] Will, in a careful assessment of Stein's Vichy translations, concludes that Stein's "passive" and overly literal translations indicate that she was writing under duress: "Stein may well have decided to undertake the Pétain translation project largely as an insurance policy to guarantee her and Toklas's survival. And to this extent, Stein's voice in the translations could be seen as that of a petrified subject, of a Scheherazade, writing as literally and hence as faithfully as possible in order to save her own life."[68] In a later essay on Stein's ambivalent (but not self-loathing) engagement with Zionism, Will sounds a cautionary note, arguing that "While we should not overstate the degree of Stein's wartime collaboration, or underestimate her personal vulnerability during this period, it remains disturbing to consider that Stein could have lent any support at all to a profoundly antisemitic movement."[69]

Janet Malcolm, whose *New Yorker* articles are among the most serious discussions of Stein in the popular press, is perhaps the most transparent about both her detective work and her feelings of betrayal upon learning less than savory details about Stein and her acquaintances. In the first of two articles on Stein's World War II activities, "Gertrude Stein's War," Malcolm begins with a pleasant reverie about her food-stained *Alice B. Toklas Cookbook*:

> More than a cookbook and memoir, it could almost be called a work of literary modernism, a sort of pendant to Stein's tour de force "The Autobiography of Alice B. Toklas," published in 1933. The similarity of tone of the two books only deepens the mystery of who influenced whom. Was Stein imitating Toklas when she wrote in Toklas's voice in the "Autobiography," or did she invent the voice, and did Toklas then imitate Stein's invention when she wrote the "Cook Book"? It is impossible to say.[70]

Intrigued by the title of one chapter, "Food in the Bugey during the Occupation," Malcolm begins the detective story that will ultimately lead to her discovery of Bernard Fäy's close connections to Stein and Toklas, his persecution of Freemasons, his links to the Gestapo, and his escape from his war-crimes prison in 1951 with the financial assistance of Toklas.

Part of the mystery for Malcolm is Stein's closetedness, both about her sex life and her Jewishness: "When I had occasion to read this [cookbook] chapter a few months ago, I was struck by its evasiveness no less than by its painfully forced gaiety. How had the pair of elderly Jewish lesbians escaped the Nazis? Why had they stayed in France instead of returning to the safety of the United States? Why did Toklas omit any mention of her and Stein's Jewishness (never mind lesbianism)?"[71] In a recent article, Malcolm goes over the same ground, this time reporting exculpatory information received via an interview with one of Stein's neighbors in Culoz. There is a tone of relief in Malcolm's writing: evidently Stein was not as closeted about her Jewishness as it at first seemed, and was even consulted in 1944 about the adoption of a Jewish boy who had been hidden from the authorities in an orphanage for Spanish refugees. Stein, according to Malcolm's source, insisted that he be adopted by a Jewish family after the liberation.[72] There is something uncanny about the way Malcolm hinges her reappraisal of Stein's wartime behavior on the story of the boy, who was apparently safely adopted. It seems symbolic of the dis-ease of her earlier article, and out of place in her current essay, which focuses mainly on Toklas' conversion to Catholicism and the difficulty of her life after Stein died in 1946. Only in light of the first story of betrayal does the second story of relief make sense, in part because it mitigates the charge of collaboration that Malcolm so agonizingly considers in the first. Such a charge cannot be made lightly. As Judith Butler notes, "No label could be worse for a Jew. The very idea of it puts fear in the heart of any Jew who knows that, ethically and politically, the position with which it would be utterly unbearable to identify is that of the anti-Semite" (*PL*, p. 103). It is also possible that the story of the adopted boy evokes an identificatory response, perhaps connected to "postmemory," from Malcolm, whose own family escaped Czechoslovakia in 1939 when she was a child.[73] Under different circumstances – an unlucky chance, a connection gone awry – the boy's fate could have been her own.

"DEAD IS DEAD": STEIN'S FORENSICS

Stein herself may provide an antidote to the painful identification of vicarious compunction in her own "psychological" work, especially *The Making of Americans*, the massive book Stein considered a "history of every one and every kind of one and all of the nature in every one and all of the ways it comes out of them."[74] In her analysis of *The Making of Americans* as a narrative of immigration and Americanization, Priscilla Wald argues that Stein's mammoth novel "emblazons the violence inherent in the forgetting" of the immigrant's severed attachment to the "old world" that must be repressed if "Americanization" is to be successful.[75] The process of "forgetting," Wald explains, is "at once analogous to and predicated on an act of violence, the figurative annihilation of one's ancestors tantamount to the 'self'-mutilation implicitly evinced by Antin and Riis. It is a violence, moreover, endemic to a nationalist discourse."[76] Wald makes clear that the repression of the violence that precedes national identity is not unique to assimilationist projects, although there may be more pressure for that repression to be seamless in immigrant narratives.[77] Indeed, according to Butler, internalizing the violence of the state makes subjectivity possible. As Butler explains in *The Psychic Life of Power*, "The process of forming the subject is a process of rendering the terrorizing power of the state invisible – and effective – as the ideality of conscience."[78] Because she makes the troping and incorporation necessary to subject-making visible, Stein opens up conscience (and perhaps bad conscience)

Stein's shame 69

to our inspection. Hence in a move similar to Woolf's deconstruction of national *assujetissement*, Stein "remembers" the violence inherent in the process of national identification, and in her tedious prose renders what is repressed in the production of national subjects. In addition, if Butler accurately describes the melancholic "rage" that accompanies dominant forms of *assujetissement*, then Melanctha's long struggle against the "consumption" of being "so blue" links that toxic text to the simultaneously written *The Making of Americans* (*Three Lives*, p. 147).[79] As a long, comprehensive collection of repeating events and relentless, often formless narrative, *The Making of Americans* records the tedious "historicity" of subject-making.

If identification is, as Butler suggests, the "historicity of loss," then "successful" identity formation is achieved through surrogation.[80] Diana Fuss further examines the metaphorical logic of identification, contending that "every identity is actually an identification come to light."[81] To understand identification, moreover, one must understand metaphor. "Freud's scientific theory of identification," Fuss argues:

is entirely predicated on a logic of metaphoric exchange and displacement. Metaphor, *the substitution of the one for the other*, is internal to the work of identification. Freud's concept of self–other relations fundamentally presupposes the possibility of metaphoricity – of iterability, redoubling, translation, and transposition. The Greek *metaphora*, meaning transport, immediately implicated the transferential act of identification in the rhetorical process of figuration. Psychoanalysis, at least where its theory of identification is concerned, can actually be understood as a scientific discourse on the very problem of metaphorization.[82]

The subject of metaphor is not new to studies of Stein, for her prose is famous for refusing the metaphorical turn. Her phrase "Rose is a rose is a rose is a rose" first appears in "Sacred Emily" but, like an errant (or industrious) piece of DNA, it replicates itself in many of Stein's later works. As Thornton Wilder explains in his introduction to *Four in America*, Stein considered the phrase an antidote to the dead metaphor. Responding to a student's question about the (in)famous line, Stein remarked, "Now listen! I'm no fool. I know that in daily life we don't go around saying 'is a . . . is a . . . is a . . .' Yes, I'm no fool; but I think that in that line the rose is red for the first time in English poetry for a hundred years."[83] Refusing the metaphoric turn, Stein refuses the substitutive logic that transforms the rose into something else.

Stein's famous line, however, is not her first use of an antimetaphor. The phrase "dead is dead" appears and reappears throughout the latter half of *The Making of Americans*. A variation of this antimetaphor also occurs in one of her unpublished notebooks to *The Making of Americans*:

Describe the whole relation as I have lived it and then – but it's nice as are most things in this best of all possible worlds except death and taxes and those alas we can't escape and so we inevitably get mixed up with sadness.
This world is all. When I am dead I am dead.[84]

Stein emphasizes this theme in *The Making of Americans*, using the phrase to distinguish the two belief systems she was most acquainted with, the Judaism of her family and the Christianity of American dominant culture:

Dead is dead. To be dead is to be really dead said one man and there are very many men who really feel this in them, to be dead is to be really dead and that is the end of them. To be dead is to be really dead and yet perhaps that is not really the end of them. To be dead is to be really dead and yet perhaps that is not really the end of them, some men feel this in them . . . Dead is dead yes that is certain and they go on having their religion and are not believing and their religion is believing that dead is not dead, to be dead is to be not really dead.[85]

In her own belief system, death is not a turn or a trope (death as rebirth) but "to be dead is to be really dead."[86] In Christianity, where death is figured as rebirth, "to be dead is to be not really dead."[87]

Although making such crude distinctions based on the refrain "dead is dead" seems to belabor the obvious, Stein's insights were rearticulated a half-century later by Marcuse, who shows how such "obvious" observations are obscured in service to ideology. According to Marcuse, one's attitude toward death – whether it is treated empirically, as the technical limit to life, or metaphorically, as a moment of transformation – profoundly influences the meaning one gives to life. "In the history of Western thought," argues Marcuse:

the interpretation of death has run the whole gamut from the notion of a mere natural fact, pertaining to man as organic matter, to the idea of death as the telos of life, the distinguishing feature of human existence. From these two opposite poles, two contrasting ethics may be derived: On the one hand, the attitude toward death is the stoic or skeptic acceptance of the inevitable, or even the repression of the thought of death by life; on the other hand the idealistic glorification of death is that which gives "meaning" to life.[88]

If "dead is dead," then, as Marcuse states, "life is not and cannot be redeemed by anything other than life."[89] But if "dead is not really dead," then a "series of sacrifices" that negate the importance of empirical life ensues.[90] In this light, Stein's long discourse on these two fundamentally opposed belief systems elucidates the metaphorical process of "redescription," a process of verbal substitution that Scarry describes in *The Body in Pain*. In the extreme cases that Scarry analyzes – torture and war – those who inflict bodily pain intentionally misdescribe the process as "intelligence gathering," or redescribe slaughter with benign phrases such as "neutralizing," or "cleaning out."[91]

In a psychoanalytic context, the substitutive process of redescription defends the psyche against unpleasant reality. Freud, for example, analyzes this substitutive turn in "Thoughts for the Times on War and Death (1915)." For Freud, substitutive disavowal enables people to repress death's literal meaning (the end of life) and replace it with a transcendent one:

> It was beside the dead body of someone he loved that he ["Man"] invented spirits ... His persisting memory of the dead became the basis for assuming other forms of existence and gave him the conception of a life continuing after apparent death ... It was only later that religions succeeded in representing this after life as the more desirable, the truly valid one, and in reducing the life which is ended by death to a mere preparation.[92]

Repressing death's literal meaning "as the termination of life,"[93] Freud suggests, leads to the impoverishment of life.[94] The impoverishment of life, moreover, makes taking life or sacrificing life – the two chief activities of war – more palatable.

It may be that Stein's scientific studies at Harvard Annex and later Johns Hopkins University led her to think pragmatically about death as a "mere natural fact" rather than a "preparation" for something better to come.[95] Much has been made of the influence of William James, Stein's philosophy teacher at the Harvard Annex, on Stein's writing.[96] With the exception of B. F. Skinner, whose "Has Gertrude Stein a Secret?" attempts to connect Stein's undergraduate experiments on automatic writing to the cryptic style of *Tender Buttons*, few scholars have noted the importance of Hugo Münsterberg, her professor in the Harvard Psychological Laboratory, on Stein's work. Stein's understanding of the extreme variability of perception may have been directly influenced by Münsterberg, who conducted numerous experiments on the unreliability of perceptions. Münsterberg's book describing these experiments, *On the Witness Stand*, was published in 1908, when Stein was in the midst of writing *The Making of Americans*. During Stein's early years as a writer, Münsterberg enjoyed popular success as a proponent of forensic psychology in *McClure's* magazine. His success accompanied the rise of urban police forces and the "golden age" of detective fiction.[97] Not only did Stein take classes from Münsterberg, she was also a friend of muckraking journalist

Hutchins Hapgood, author of *The Autobiography of a Thief*. Perhaps these acquaintances sparked her interest in the budding science of forensics.

This interest is reflected in Stein's appreciation of detective stories. She describes them with great delight in *Everybody's Autobiography*, opening her reminiscences with an anecdote about a dinner with Dashiell Hammett: "I never was interested in cross word puzzles or any kind of puzzles but I do like detective stories. I never try to guess who has done the crime and if I did I would be sure to guess wrong but I like somebody being dead and how it moves along and Dashiell Hammett was all that and more."[98] Detective stories continue to be good stories even in the twentieth century, because "the hero is the dead man and so there can be no beginning and middle and end."[99] In a traditional detective story the main character, unlike the characters in *The Making of Americans*, is already realized. S/he doesn't change during the time of the novel. Detective fiction also functions as a wish fulfillment, a fantasy of justice and control over distressing circumstances. Maureen T. Reddy argues that:

> The classic crime novel begins in disorder or in violation of order and proceeds more or less linearly to order; it is therefore essentially reassuring, its message proclaiming that it is not only desirable, but actually possible, to banish or to destroy disruptive social elements, and that the greatly to be desired continuation of bourgeois, patriarchal society depends upon general acceptance of the control of a masculine authority figure who is alone capable of explaining the world satisfactorily.[100]

The satisfaction of the traditional detective story, then, is provided by its closure, a characteristic that runs counter to Stein's intellectual interest in the process of detection.

Far from providing the comforting closure of the traditional detective story, however, Stein's attempt at detective fiction, *Blood on the Dining-Room Floor*, does not provide neat resolutions. Instead it presents many autobiographical and historical incidents as unsolved mysteries.[101] In the middle of the story, Stein even makes an attempt to provide a definitive answer:

> You will say to me it has not happened and I will answer yes of course it has not happened and you will dream and I will dream and cream.
> It has not happened. She slept and it has not happened. He will have been unhappy and it has not happened. They will be dogs dogs and it has not happened.
> Prepare sunsets and it has not happened.
> Finally decry all arrangement and still, it has not happened.
> This is where I alone finish finally fairly well, I exchange it has not happened for it has not happened and it gives me peace of mind.[102]

Stein's shame

In this passage, the present perfective verb form ("it has not happened") emphasizes that the detective/writer seems to be finished, arriving at a final, comforting conclusion. But this moment takes place in the middle of the story, and is immediately undercut by one of Stein's many unsettling references to Lizzie Borden.[103] An American cultural icon, Borden represents the vengeful, murderous daughter. Her case, which ended up an acquittal, also represents an unsolved mystery, an unpunished crime. Simply repeating the mantra "it has not happened . . . it has not happened" does not ultimately lead to "peace of mind," since the Lizzie Borden case remains unsolved. As Stein admits, the open-endedness of her own narrative means that her detective story falls short of its generic mark: "on the whole a detective story has to have if it has not a detective it has to have an ending and my detective story did not have any."[104]

If Stein's approach, the process of "general detecting," is ultimately unsatisfying, it is because it refuses the comforting form of the whodunit. For a detective story to have an "ending," the detective must arrive at a solution and bring the guilty party to justice. "Crime stories," which Stein associates with the "real world," are not so easily solved, nor is justice so readily achieved. Stein discusses the difference between crime stories and detective stories in her further comments on "American Crimes and How They Matter," "I think a lot about American crime and about crime stories written by any one, they call them detective stories instead of crime stories and that is in a way the trouble with them they are detective stories instead of crime stories in real life they are crime stories instead of detective stories."[105]

This reflection is inspired by an evening Stein spent on patrol with a Chicago Police Department homicide detective in 1934. During the evening the detective seems quite confident of his ability to know who might be liable to commit a crime, why, and how. Only later in the conversation does he seem less sure of his abilities, when he tells Stein the story of an African American man who was found murdered on the street corner: "he was shot down dead, nobody saw it, nobody heard anything, nobody is interested, nobody will find out anything about it because it is of no importance to anybody."[106] Through this anecdote, Stein acknowledges that the social status of the victim is what will set in motion the detective's quest for discovery.

For Stein, puzzling connections, unrevealed secrets, and unsolved mysteries are the most "interesting" and "American" of crimes. Discussing the Lizzie Borden case once more, Stein suggests, "it was all so simple so evident so subtle and so open and nobody ever really came to know anything that is a kind of a crime that means something as an expression of the American character, yes if you know what I mean, yes it does if you know what I mean."[107] Stein's focus on the "American" character here is connected to her reconstruction of her own familial past as "*The Making of Americans.*" More generally, she is pointing out the contradiction between the presumed openness and equality in American culture that makes social situations seem predictable or mystery-free, and the flipside of such presumptions – the fact that "insignificant" crimes, like the murder of the African American man, go unremarked and unredressed. Stein's focus on unsolved mysteries and unanswered questions, her suggestion that an unsolved murder case is the "kind of a crime that means something as an expression of the American character," encourages an interrogative stance towards even seemingly self-evident renderings of the cultural past.

Stein continues to link history writing, detective fiction, and anti-metaphorical prose in *The Geographical History of America*. The text of *The Geographical History* begins with the distinction between "human nature," which roughly translates to the psyche, and "the human mind," which is akin to the intellect. Human nature denies the biological implications of death, while the "human mind" "can know this."[108] "If nobody had to die," writes Stein,

> how would there be room enough for any of us who now live to have lived. We never could have been if all the others had not died. There would have been no room.
> Now the relation of human nature to the human mind is this.
> Human nature does not know this.
> Human nature cannot know this.[109]

Stein's question seems schoolgirlish at first. Read with the "ideology of death" in mind, however, Stein's question refocuses our attention to space and physical factors rather than time, and social factors. "The species perpetuates itself through the death of individuals; this is a natural fact," writes Marcuse:

> Society perpetuates itself through the death of individuals; this is no longer a natural but an historical fact. The two facts are not equivalent. In the first proposition, death is a biological event: disintegration of organic into inorganic matter. In the second proposition, death is an institution and a value: the cohesion of the social order depends to a considerable extent on the effectiveness with which individuals comply with death as more than a natural necessity; on

their willingness, even urge, to die many deaths which are not natural; on their agreement to sacrifice themselves and not to fight death "too much."[110]

Stein's focus on geography, on the limits to the physical resources necessary to sustain human life, acknowledges the biological element of human life and death. "Human nature," according to Stein, disavows this element, while the "human mind" would prefer not to know it. "After all would do we like to live to have lived, then if we do then everybody else has had to die and we have to cry because we too one day we too will have to die otherwise the others who will like to live could not come by."[111] Furthermore, for Stein, this disavowal is what makes "religion and propaganda and politics" possible.[112] Ideology, Stein intimates, manufactures reasons for our physical deterioration, or, as Marcuse would say, gives a social meaning to death.

In the middle of Stein's ruminations on the biological and social aspects of death, she interjects a reference to "Madame Reverdy," the "wife of a hotel keeper," and the subject of the mystery in *Blood on the Dining-Room Floor*.[113] Stein distinguishes the social phenomenon of Madame Reverdy's death from the biological inevitability of death. Madame Reverdy (Pernollet in real life), as John Gill notes, may have been killed so that her husband's mistress could take over her place as the hotel keeper's wife.[114] Like the deaths of preceding generations, which make space on the earth for the next generation, Madame Reverdy's death clears a space for her successor. This socially engineered death is neither desirable nor necessary, however. "She is as much dead as much dead as if she had not lived longer," writes Stein, linking death from biological causes to "not liv[ing] longer."[115] "I feel that it is a failure not to live longer," Stein concludes, rejecting the social necessity of violent or untimely death.

Shortly after Stein makes this conclusion, she returns to the antimetaphor, this time in a more wistful mood, writing:

I wish I knew a history was a history.
And tears.
I wish I knew a history as a history which is not which is not there are no fears.[116]

In this passage, Stein rejects history as consolation or reassurance.[117] She does not wish history to be transformed, metaphorically, into "there are no fears." The wistful tone of her utterance, however, acknowledges the difficulty of this undertaking. Stein links this difficulty to the temporal difficulties that she discusses in *Narration*, suggesting that "what you say is not the same as what you write," and therefore, "we come to what is really what we write what we write is really a crime story."[118] The "crime story" is, as I noted above, the story of what happened in the past, but it leaves out the present moment, the story of detection. Stein attempts to write her history as a detective story, however, which means that her text will be both recursive – calling attention to the process of the writer in the present attempting to make sense of the past – and hermetic, for in her focus on the story of detection, the crime story drops from view. "This whole book now is going to be a detective story of how to write," Stein interjects in the middle of the text:

A play of the relation of human nature to the human mind.
And a poem of how to begin again.
And a description of how the earth looks as you look at it which is perhaps a play
  if it can be done in a day and is perhaps a detective story if it can be found out.
Anything is a detective story if it can be found out and can anything be found out. Yes.[119]

Here Stein links several of the historiographic concepts that she has been grappling with throughout her career. Her focus on "how the earth looks as you look at it" links her concern about differential perception to the process of detection and "forensics," the process by which "anything can be found out." The self-announcing form of Stein's story of detection emphasizes the constructed nature of all historical narratives, even those which leave out the story of their construction.

Stein suggests, too, that her detective story will be "a poem of how to begin again," a project that resists the teleological unfolding of historical progress. Stein's use of repetition is not simply word play; it is an acknowledgment that belief (in tradition, in progress, in the nation) is garnered through reiteration. Repetition, furthermore, is not the opposite of diachronic time, or "progress." The passage of time is marked by many "insignificant" repetitions, including the pulsing of the heart, the drawing of breath, and the myriad other mundane activities that keep us alive. Repetition, written into the prose of history, acknowledges the significance of these "non-momentous" occurrences. The bulk of history, for Stein, consists of events that happen over and over again, but seldom get recorded. Her focus on the everyday, the non-heroic, moreover, is culturally significant, for in the present tense we never know what occurrences will be deemed "momentous."[120]

As Stein notes in "American Biography and Why Waste It": "There is a way of recording an arbitrary collision but in inventing barbed wire and in inventing puzzles there is no arbitrary collision. Not at all."[121] In other words, there is a difference between intentionality and arbitrary occurrence. Like history, biography transforms the arbitrary into the intentional or portentous by its very narrative structure. American biographies "say there is coercion, cohesion and administration, then there are authentic dispatches, then there is recognition."[122] As an alternative to the traditional, cohesive rendering of the past, Stein offers us this:

A biography.
Eugene George Herald was refused because of his accentuation. We do not accentuate, we increase in regard to measure sound and sections. In this way we are united to stand.[123]

In the second sentence, "Eugene George Herald was refused because of his accentuation," Stein alludes to the discrimination he might face because he is an immigrant or cultural minority, like the women of *Three Lives*, whose "accentuation" signals that they will be deemed unimportant figures for traditional history or biography. Stein's focus on dispersal, rather than accentuation, refigures and refuses biography's traditional focus on "great men," individuals who do not speak with unpreferred accents, and who are "accentuated" in traditional history or biography by their stories of uniqueness. Stein herself explains, in her "Transatlantic Interview," that "to me one human being is as important as another human being, and you might say that the landscape has the same values, a blade of grass has the same value as a tree."[124] "In *The Making of Americans*," Stein explains, "I wanted each one to have the same value. I was not at all interested in the little or big men but to realize absolutely every variety of human experience that it was possible to have, every type, every style and nuance."[125] Regarding the distinction between important and insignificant people, Stein goes on to link her interest in giving each person the same "value" in a representation to her concern for the welfare of children:

I have no sense of difference in this respect, because every human being comprises the combination form. Just as everybody had the vote, including the women, I think children should, because as soon as a child is conscious of itself, then it has to me an existence and has a stake in what happens. Everybody who has that stake has that quality of interest, and in *The Making of Americans* that is what I tried to show.[126]

Stein's desire to give each element in her compositions equal "value" ultimately leads to her emphasis on the non-heroic quotidian in her World War II writings. As Malcolm especially points out, Stein's focus on daily living, even while recounting the national and international events of the early 1940s, makes her wartime writing seem provincial and insensitive to the fate of millions of people suffering at the hands of the Nazis. Even in her problematic World War II writing, Stein's focus on the details of everyday life during the war may be read as a continuation of her valuation of the non-momentous. Such a strategy is not, as Van Dusen has argued, a "rejection of history" but rather an assertion, much like her "Transatlantic Interview," that non-heroic, ordinary people too, have "a stake in what happens."[127] Stein acknowledges, too, that some people, like the many refugees that have fled to Culoz and the "young men who do not want to go to forced labor and they change their town" are compelled by the circumstances of war to have a greater "stake in what happens."[128] The small details of daily living described in *Wars I Have Seen* – procuring food, negotiating public space without drawing the attention of Nazi soldiers, and creating support networks among neighbors are not inconsequential to the story of World War II.[129] They are, rather, a sign of resiliency and resistance to the dehumanizing purpose of war, an insistence that daily life is worth living and preserving. There is nothing heroic in Stein's accounts of village life during the war, but they do tell the story of survival. In her interest in the particulars of everyday life during, or rather despite, the privations of war, and her reluctance to use metaphor to describe war in heroic terms, Stein is like Woolf, who refused to make myths from the deaths produced by the war. Echoing the sentiment of Stein's "dead is dead," Woolf remarks in her diary, "So if one dies, it'll be a common sense, dull end – not comparable to a days walk, & then an evening reading over the fire" (*D-V*, 15 May 1940).

In one of her last works, *Reflection on the Atomic Bomb*, Stein, too, focuses on the "dullness" of death, writing, "I could never take any interest in the atomic bomb, I just couldn't any more than in everybody's secret weapon. Sure it will destroy a lot and kill a lot, but it's the living that are interesting not the way of killing them."[130] Stein's emotionally flat description of this agent of mass destruction has the effect of reducing its glamour by describing it precisely – a killing machine – "the atomic [bomb] is not at all interesting, not any more interesting than any other machine."[131] This nonchalant description of such a destructive weapon may seem like callous indifference at best or moral stupidity at worst, but an understanding of Stein's antimetaphorical prose can help us better appreciate her insistence that "it's the living that are interesting not the way of killing them." Through her flat description, Stein refuses to redescribe the primary activity of war. As Scarry argues, one "path by which injuring disappears [as an acknowledged goal of war] is the active redescription of the event: the act of injuring, or the tissue that is to be injured, or the weapon that is to accomplish the injury is to be renamed."[132] The atomic bomb, for Stein, is not a special kind of weapon because it is more efficient at killing larger numbers of people than other kinds of weapons. If this were the case, the act of granting special status to the atomic bomb would grant legitimacy to other, less efficient methods of killing. Stein's flat description emphasizes that the purpose of a weapon, inefficient or efficient, is killing. The efficiency of the atomic bomb may interfere with our ability to believe that it has any purpose ("neutralization," "cleaning out," or "cleaning up" as Scarry notes) other than killing, but this is a purpose shared by all weapons.[133] If "dead is dead," then killing is killing. This realization should not be used to trivialize the horror of nuclear war, but rather encourage us to take a more attentive look at how the killing that takes place in so-called conventional war has come to be socially sanctioned.

Stein's refusal to redescribe the atomic bomb as something monstrous, or glorious, or apocalyptic, is consistent with the rejection of metaphoric substitution in her earlier work. For history writing, this rejection is significant, for it precludes the identification with the lost other of the past (even if that other is one's younger self) that allows "history" to be perceived as the seamless and completed story of what happened. Rather than that seamless story, Stein advocates instead "forensics," the present-tense collection of information about what happened in the past. Forensics are plodding; they are methodical; they require attention to the actions of the detective in the present moment collecting data; they require persistent questioning and a refusal to take "insignificant" details for granted; they acknowledge that some evidence may be missing, or destroyed, or unrecognizable. Through inference, forensics can tell us a lot about what happened in the past, but they require persistence and legwork rather than icons or "sacred monsters" to make that past useful for the present day.

CHAPTER 3

H.D.'s wars

When H.D.'s novel *Pilate's Wife* was published in 2000, it seemed more of a posthumous supplement to the *oeuvre* of an important modernist poet than a novel with something relevant to say about political unrest in the Middle East and the imperialistic reach of the world's sole military superpower. In the "patched" present, however, *Pilate's Wife* can be read as a war novel concerned with the fate of diasporic subjects living in the "contact zones" of a vast, military empire. This is only fitting, given the novel's genesis in conversations that H.D. had with D. H. Lawrence, most likely when he and his wife Frieda sought refuge with H.D. during World War I.[1]

Similarly, H.D.'s World War II long poem, *Trilogy*, has a different resonance in the United States in the twenty-first century than it did in the late twentieth century. Selections from "The Walls Do Not Fall" circulated on electronic discussion lists in response to the September 11 attacks as early as 13 September 2001.[2] More generally, modernism, because of its historical context – spanning two world wars, the Russian and Irish revolutions, the *Shoah*, and the only atomic bombings to have taken place in human history – gives us many models for writing about devastation and loss. Some of the most beautiful aesthetic forms are perhaps the most problematic because they transform suffering into "terrible beauty" so successfully that we might begin seeing beauty in suffering and violence rather than seeing its repulsive effects.

It would be callous to suggest that H.D.'s poem offered no comfort in the immediate aftermath of the attacks. With its redemptive, resilient message, the poem provides a powerful example of public mourning. The compelling, apocalyptic language of *Trilogy* is not without its costs, however, for in its redemptive turn, the poem redescribes loss as something triumphant, character-building, transformative. Similar tropes dominated US discourse in the wake of the September 11 attacks.[3] Judith Butler discusses the *de facto* censorship that results from such imperatives to mourn properly, arguing that calls to remember the fallen were too often transformed into injunctions against any criticism of the official US policy: "In a strong sense, the binarism that Bush proposes in which only two positions are possible – 'Either you're with us or with the terrorists' – makes it untenable to hold a position in which one opposes both and queries the terms in which the opposition is framed" (*PL*, p. 2). When dissent is automatically assumed to be disrespect, non-nationalistic responses to devastation are muted by mourners' desire to act with propriety. Imperatives to mourn "properly" (that is, in accordance with nationalistic ideology) transform the deaths of victims into *sacrifices* that can only be redeemed through nationalistic heroics. This rhetoric fosters what Michael S. Roth describes elsewhere as a vicious cycle of trauma, where "memory of trauma in the past is constructed in the present as a cause of abhorrent behavior or as a reason for political or military strategies that would otherwise be morally repugnant."[4]

Are there ways to respond to trauma differently, without falling prey to uncritical patriotism, or the cynicism that Roth calls "the ironist's cage,"[5] or the stunned helplessness that Cathy Caruth describes as "belatedness"?[6] In what follows, I analyze the logic of sacrifice in the apocalyptic resonances of H.D.'s *Trilogy* and T. S. Eliot's *Four Quartets*, juxtaposing the poems' redemptive logic to the style and method of H.D.'s prose – her "Madrigal" trilogy (*Paint it Today, Asphodel, Bid Me to Live*), her World War II memoir (*The Gift*), and the posthumously published *Pilate's Wife*.[7]

Like the elegy, which helps to manage loss on the individual scale, apocalyptic rhetoric can help a culture cope with catastrophic loss by suggesting that such losses happened for divine reasons that will be revealed in the future. As Michael André Bernstein argues, "we try to make sense of a historical disaster by interpreting it, according to the strictest teleological model, as the climax of a bitter trajectory whose inevitable outcome it must be."[8] This tragic emplotment – what Bernstein calls "backshadowing" – retrospectively creates categories of people who were doomed to die. Within this narrative structure – available only to those whose future survival affords them the benefit of historical hindsight – individuals' efforts to resist their impending fate are always futile, and doomed persons who misunderstand the danger of their predicament are deemed naïve, even foolish, fatally unable to recognize the warning signs of their future doom. Even when the doomed victims are scripted heroically, their deaths and therefore their foreclosed futures are usurped into the meaning-making apparatus of redemptive historiography, making it difficult, if not impossible, to imagine the open and unpredictable future – the unwritten script – that faced them on the day before their death.[9]

Often read as a sign of H.D.'s feminist difference from male modernists, *Trilogy* shares many of the conservative features of her contemporaries' attempts to create the "new" from the scattered remnants of the old.[10] The redemptive turn of *Trilogy*, for example, echoes Yeats' elegiac transformation of slaughtered Irish rebels into a "terrible beauty," a symbol of hope for Ireland.[11] So too, Yeats' "rough beast" that "slouches towards Bethlehem to be born," although a more sinister figure than the child of *Trilogy*'s nativity scene, prefigures *Trilogy*'s use of the "second coming" story to manage and provide justification for the bloodshed of World War II.[12] *Trilogy* bears even more striking similarities to Eliot's *Four Quartets*, a poem whose apocalyptic rhetoric anesthetizes the bloody casualties of the war.[13] Like Eliot's poem, *Trilogy* represents the destruction of the war as cleansing, an alchemy that brings about new hope. Although *Trilogy* is inspired by H.D.'s hope for a future where the "word" replaces the "sword," the poem deflects our attention from unpleasant reality – the annihilation of people who were killed in their bombed homes, or the millions of people who were murdered in Nazi death camps.

The consequences of *Trilogy*'s redescriptive turns are made more evident when the poem is read against *The Gift*, a childhood memoir that is haunted by the fear of sexual violence and the uncanny death of girls. Through its repetition of the image of burned girls, *The Gift* presents the story of a daughter who is not seen, but who has a knack for seeing the everyday perils of girlhood, and for seeing connections between private, familial, personal traumas and the publicly acknowledged traumas of war.[14] The child narrator thus sees the significance of supposedly useless, inglorious deaths, such as that of the "girl who was burnt to death at the Seminary" who confronts us in the very first line of *The Gift*. The death of a girl – associated with the particularity of the body, individual attachments to home, community, or family – cannot be rescripted into the story of national glory with the same ease with which the deaths of "good fighting men" are recuperated "usefully" for the state.[15] To focus on the useless death of the burned girl rather than that of the "good fighting man," or the triumphant culture reborn from the flames of war thus questions the notion of a "useful death" altogether. Telling the story of the unrecognized daughter, H.D. ultimately suggests that "the gift" is precisely this knack for seeing others, recognizing the stories of past wounding and connecting them to the apprehension of present dangers. *The Gift* thus proposes an empathetic approach to reading and translating the texts of trauma.

While *The Gift* temporizes *Trilogy*'s apocalyptic turn, H.D.'s interwar prose presents an even greater challenge to the logic of redemption that fuels "the ideology of death." In the three *romans à clef* of her "Madrigal cycle," stories of heroism and battles at the front are conspicuously absent. Instead, H.D. describes the hardships confronted by those left at home during the war, and questions the sacrifices exacted of young men as well as "patriotic" mothers in Britain during World War I.[16] H.D.'s most overt resistance to the ideology of death is articulated in *Pilate's Wife*. According to Susan Stanford Friedman, the novel is part of a set of novels that "'ghost' for H.D.'s state of mind in the early to middle 1920s when she was particularly preoccupied with a conflicted desire to forget and remember the events of the war years."[17] H.D.'s interwar prose thus remembers without redeeming, a process that evokes Bernstein's concept of "sideshadowing" – "a gesturing to the side, to a present tense with multiple, and mutually exclusive possibilities for what is to come."[18]

THE "TERRIBLE BEAUTY" OF APOCALYPTIC MODERNISM

Yeats' "The Second Coming" and its philosophical counterpart, *A Vision*, present history as a closed system, evolving according to a predetermined hourglass shape into periods of expansion and contraction, chaos and order, bloodshed and peace. Even Yeats' "Easter 1916," which is at first a very ambivalent elegy, asking – "Too long a sacrifice / Can make a stone of the heart. / O when may it suffice?" – answers its own question with an appeal to divine authority, and the imperative to mourn properly and publicly: "That is Heaven's part, our part / To murmur name upon name." As an elegy that transforms capital punishment into a nationalistic symbol, "Easter 1916" partakes of "the ideology of death" – "the idea of death as the *telos* of life."[19] At the heart of the ideology of death is the myth of transcendence, of an outside to time from which God plays the ultimate backshadower, arranging the accidents and catastrophes of our lives into coherent, triumphant narratives.

God the backshadower plays a part in Eliot's *Four Quartets* as well, redeeming the time of bombed-out London. Given the focus on redemption within a culture that ascribes to the "ideology of death," it is not surprising that Eliot devotes *Four Quartets* to the subjects of personal renunciation and "redeeming the time." "Burnt Norton," the only section of *Four Quartets* written before the onset of World War II, was composed in 1935 and originally planned for *Murder in the Cathedral*, a play about a martyr's contemplation of his own sacrificial death at the hands of political/religious enemies.[20] Eliot suggests that without a transcendental understanding of temporal unfolding – the ability to see the kernel of the future in the past, or the remnants of the past in the future, "all time is unredeemable" ("BN," line 5).[21] Moreover, consciousness, for Eliot, entails an escape from or conquering of time, a retreat to the "still point of the turning world" ("BN," line 63) attained through the "abstention from movement" ("BN," line 126). "Burnt Norton," then, suggests that "redeeming" the time necessitates the renunciation of desire ("appetency") and a suspension of our "time sense":

> Internal darkness, deprivation
> And destitution of all property,
> Desiccation of the world of sense,
> Evacuation of the world of fancy,
> Inoperancy of the world of spirit;
> This is the one way, and the other
> Is the same, not in movement
> But abstention from movement; while the world moves
> In appetency, on its metalled ways
> Of time past and time future.   ("BN," lines 119–28)

In his gentle, comforting language, Eliot heralds self-sacrifice as the way to make meaning out of the flux and confusion of the present moment. This logic of personal renunciation sets the tone for the larger cultural renunciations that the remainder of *Four Quartets* will chronicle and "redeem."

Written during World War II, a "present" whose horrors even now seem especially unredeemable, the remaining three sections of *Four Quartets* present an elaborate attempt to make sense of the brutal senselessness of mass violence. The "redemption" that *Four Quartets* does finally achieve is less than comforting:

> Whatever we inherit from the fortunate
> We have taken from the defeated
> What they had to leave us – a symbol:
> A symbol perfected in death.
> And all shall be well and
> All manner of things shall be well
> By the purification of the motive
> In the ground of our beseeching.

> IV
> The dove descending breaks the air
> With flame of incandescent terror
> Of which the tongues declare
> The one discharge from sin and error.
> The only hope, or else despair
> Lies in the choice of pyre or pyre –
> To be redeemed from fire by fire.   ("LG," lines 193–207)[22]

Here the poem offers consolation, pointing the reader in the direction of hope – if s/he chooses the right way, the right pyre. Brutality is transformed into benevolence: the German bombers, that "break the air / With flame of incandescent terror," have become doves, ancient and obvious symbols for peace. In a rhetorical maneuver that parallels what Scarry describes as "the structure of war," the dead bodies of the "defeated" become "symbols perfected in death."[23] These symbols, moreover, are meaningful only according to the terms set forth by the victors.

If, as Walter Benjamin notes, "there is no document of civilization which is not at the same time a document of barbarism,"[24] then Eliot's text is one in which the barbarity is effaced, or rather burned out. The story that remains is the story of those who prevail. Loss becomes a remnant or trace, like the ash and dust of "Little Gidding":

> Ash on an old man's sleeve
> Is all the ash the burnt-roses leave.
> Dust in the air suspended
> Marks the place where a story has ended.   ("LG," lines 54–57)

As in much apocalyptic writing, Eliot's "story" that "has ended" does not end, but rather gestures to new beginnings:

> What we call the beginning is often the end
> And to make an end is to make a beginning.
> The end is where we start from . . .   ("LG," lines 215–17)

To call an end a beginning is, on the one hand, a defiant consolation, a refusal to feel defeated in the face of great loss. On the other hand, it is a troubling redescription. If, to quote Stein, "dead is not really dead," if the end is really a new beginning, then we might be persuaded to compliantly endure, even desire, our endings and overlook, even welcome, actions that result in the ends of others.

The transcendental vantage point of *Four Quartets* – achieved through the renunciation of desire "on its metalled ways / Of time past and time future" – presents time as a closed system, unfolding according to a divine order whereby the seeds of the future are knowable in the past. The insularity of this system is typical of apocalyptic writing, which "presumes a unity framed by a moment of origin and a moment of end,"[25] or "implies a closed universe in which all choices have already been made, in which human free will can exist only in the paradoxical sense of choosing to accept or willfully – and vainly – rebelling against what is inevitable."[26] Understanding time to be unfolding according to a teleological plan allows for the reassuring resolution of the poem:

> And all shall be well and
> All manner of things shall be well
> When the tongues of flame are in-folded
> Into the crowned knot of fire
> And the fire and the rose are one. ("LG," lines 255–59)

This ending, according to the logic of apocalyptic thinking, is reassuring because, as Elinor Shaffer reminds us, "'The End of the World' as traditionally understood is the end of others, the enemy, the unworthy, the present oppressors – but not of ourselves."[27] The apocalyptic thinker never really imagines that it is s/he who will be the object of the fire's purifying, purging blaze. Eliot's poem consoles with the message that "All shall be well and / All manner of things shall be well." But for whom? Certainly not for those who perished in the flames.

H.D.'s citations from the Book of Revelation in "Tribute to the Angels" clearly mark the text as apocalyptic as well. Allusions to "purifying" fire occur even earlier, in the very first section of "The Walls Do Not Fall":

> pressure on heart, lungs, the brain
> about to burst its brittle case
> (what the skull can endure!):
>
> over us, Apocryphal fire,
> under us, the earth sway, dip of a floor,
> . . .
> the bone-frame was made for
> no such shock knit within terror,
> yet the skeleton stood up to it:
>
> the flesh? it was melted away,
> the heart burnt out, dead ember,
> tendons, muscles shattered, outer husk dismembered,
>
> yet the frame held:
> we passed the flame: we wonder
> what saved us? what for? ("WDNF," lines 34–38, 43–51)

The "what for?" turns out to be a contemporary version of the "New Jerusalem," which H.D. invokes several times in "Tribute to the Angels." The first allusion comes in section 2 of the poem:

> Your walls do not fall, he said,
> because your walls are made of jasper;
> . . .
> for the *twelve foundations*,
> for the *transparent glass*,
> for *no need of the sun*
> nor the *moon to shine*;   ("TA," lines 21–22, 27–30)[28] (H.D.'s emphasis)

H.D.'s reference to the "New Jerusalem" of the Book of Revelation is especially problematic given the context of the *Shoah*, since it was precisely Jews who were being systematically exterminated by the Nazis. H.D., who witnessed Nazi anti-Semitism firsthand during her analysis with Freud in Vienna in 1934, who knew of Freud's forced exile to London in 1938, whose partner Bryher participated in efforts to aid Jewish refugees during the war, would have, in 1942, been more aware of Nazi atrocities than most British residents.[29] It is therefore troubling that H.D. uses the language of the Book of Revelation – with its emphasis on Christian righteousness and avenging judgment – to rescript the losses of the war as triumphal. As Victoria Harrison argues, H.D.'s Christian mysticism overwrites the particular plight of European Jews during World War II: "The poem's vision overcomes the world-erasing realities of bombed-out neighborhoods, incinerated Jews, and the terror of daily life under attack, by creating its alternative vision – its 'spiritual realism' – 'on papyrus of parchment.'"[30] The transcendence that such apocalyptic rhetoric promises thus overwrites the story of suffering.

It may be that the desire to re-script the story of loss as the story of triumph-over-loss is fueled by the wish "not to see" one's lost attachments. The Book of Revelation, notably, promises the cessation of mourning: "He will wipe every tear from their eyes. There will be no more death or mourning or crying or pain, for the old order of things has passed away. He who was seated on the throne said, 'I am making everything new!'"[31]

We can understand the comfort of this function of apocalyptic rhetoric better by looking at the work of mourning that is done on a smaller scale by the elegy. Although the elegy and apocalyptic writing may seem to be distinct, the two forms are quite similar in their insistence on renunciation and their promise of transcendence to those who submit dutifully to the authority of a higher power. In both cases, loss or devastation is deemed an inevitable setback that must be overcome – denied as loss and reconstituted as gain. According to Sacks, one function of the elegist's performance is the "need to draw attention, consolingly, to his [sic] own surviving powers."[32] Apocalyptic writing, too, is ultimately a production for the survivors of cataclysm. In both forms it is through the act of figuration – troping or turning – that the survivor renounces the lost object and therefore manages loss. Sacks explains that "the story of Apollo and Daphne itself exemplifies the dramatic relation between loss and figuration."[33] Apollo invents "a consoling substitute for Daphne."[34] "Daphne's 'turning' into a tree matches Apollo's 'turning' from the object of his love to a sign for her. It is this substitutive turn or act of troping that any mourner must perform."[35] By renouncing the particularity of the lost love object, the elegist gains the aesthetic symbol for it. Moreover, by showing him/herself willing to perform this renunciation and "transcend" loss, the elegist shows him/herself worthy of being an inheritor (one might even say a producer) of culture.[36] As [Aranye] Louise O. Fradenburg argues, this imperative is political in nature, both a demand for submission to cultural norms and a renunciation of particular attachments.[37]

Resisting the link between "healthy" mourning and renunciation, Fradenburg reimagines Freud's "fort-da" game, emphasizing relationship rather than mastery:

The child throwing out his spool of thread and reeling it back in is thought of as mastering absence by means of its representation – a representation that recalls the absent through a substitutive figure and through the substitute of language. But the thread surely might be read instead as a link between the *fort* and *da*. And if so, what if *fort* and *da* are not so much alternating oppositions but particularities linked by this thread?[38]

The *fort-da* game thus provides a way to acknowledge the important connection between the bereaved and the lost object without implying that the loss can be transcended through substitution. As I mentioned in the previous chapter, Freud argues that the logic of transcendence is fueled by disavowal, the transvaluation of death's literal meaning as the end of life.[39] That transvaluation impoverishes life by "reducing the life which is ended by death to a mere preparation" for the supposedly better life to come.[40]

"FATHER, DON'T YOU SEE I'M BURNING?": THE "GIFT" OF WITNESS

Read through the lens of trauma theory, the survivor's story produced by the elegy is akin to the father's story in Freud's much-analyzed "dream of a burning child." The dream is a key to understanding "belatedness" for Caruth. In *The Interpretation of Dreams*, Freud recounts the dream thus:

> A father had been watching beside his child's sick-bed for days and nights on end. After the child had died, he went into the next room to lie down, but left the door open so that he could see from his bedroom into the room in which his child's body was laid out, with tall candles standing round it . . . After a few hours' sleep, the father had a dream that *his child was standing beside his bed, caught by the arm and whispered to him reproachfully: "Father, don't you see I'm burning?"* He then woke up, noticed a bright glare of light from the next room, hurried into it and found that . . . the wrappings and one of the arms of his beloved child's dead body had been burned by a lighted candle that had fallen on them.[41]

Reading the dream through Lacan, Caruth suggests that the father's awakening tells the story of what it means to survive trauma. The child's words form an "address" that awakens the father to the reality of the child's death: "To awaken is thus to bear the imperative to survive: to survive no longer simply as the father of a child, but as the one who must tell *what it means not to see*, which is also what it means to hear the unthinkable words of the dying child."[42] The dream, then, represents the troubling story of survival. Privileging Lacan's analysis of Freud's interpretation of the father's dream, Caruth argues "that the shock of traumatic sight reveals at the heart of human subjectivity . . . an *ethical* relation to the real."[43] But what does it mean that the story of survival – a story "at the very heart of subjectivity itself" – is at the same time the story of a death, or, more precisely, the story of "not seeing" death until it is too late? For Caruth, the particular story of the father's awakening to the fact of his child's death has become the universal story of "trauma as the very origin of consciousness and all of life itself."[44] Read with Sacks' interpretation of elegy in mind, the stakes of this move from the particular to the universal are high indeed, for now not only is the survivor's cultural inheritance dependent on his or her ability to mourn properly, but consciousness itself depends on negotiating this trauma successfully.

How would the dream of the burning child be changed if it were the story of a child confronted with the imperative to survive?[45] Butler argues that subjectivity takes on just such a trajectory – where survival is achieved through submission to the very authority figures that threaten the child's autonomy: "The desire to survive, 'to be,' is a pervasively exploitable desire. The one who holds out the promise of continued existence plays to the desire to survive. 'I would rather exist in subordination than not exist' is one formulation of this predicament (where the risk of 'death' is also possible)"[46] (*PL*, p. 7). In a brief aside, Butler mentions that the sexual abuse of a child by a primary caretaker is a particular manifestation of the child's general vulnerability to exploitation:

This is one reason why debates about the reality of the sexual abuse of children tend to misstate the character of the exploitation. It is not simply that a sexuality is unilaterally imposed by the adult, nor that a sexuality is unilaterally fantasized by the child, but that the child's love, a love that is necessary for its existence, is exploited and a passionate attachment abused.[47]

This aside is telling, because it suggests that sexual abuse is situated at one (negative) end of a continuum of traumatic, integrity-dissolving experiences that are constitutive of subjectivity/subjection. Butler's observation offers an interesting alternative to popular beliefs that sexual abuse is a special "monstrous" or "unnatural" category of trauma that shatters an originally "whole" subject.[48] This popular formulation is problematic because it validates a "whole," transcendent subject by suggesting its inverse – the shattered subject robbed of wholeness and childhood innocence through the experience of abuse. (Wholeness is figured here as the rightful inheritance of the child.)

If the child's vulnerability to abuse were instead considered a particularly glaring example of the subject's originary subjugation, lack of autonomy, fragility, exploitable "desire to survive, 'to be,'" then acknowledging that vulnerability in "ordinary" families would serve as a reminder – for all subjects – of the subject's "founding subordination or dependency [which] is rigorously repressed."[49] This may account for the vehemence, disbelief, and even disgust, with which listeners respond to survivors' stories. The subject desires to repress its frailty, exploitability, and subjection. Therefore childhood sexual abuse, as a reminder of that frailty, must be denied. The compulsion to deny in this case gives new significance to figuring the father-survivor "as the one who must tell *what it means not to see.*"[50]

Belatedness, however, is not an inevitable given but rather the result of what, as I mention in Chapter 1, John Berger calls a habit of "looking beyond ... that which is before the eyes."[51] To look, as Berger would have us do, squarely at representations of suffering entails a different sort of ethical awakening to the "face of horror" presented by the victim of trauma.[52] The ethical imperative to look upon "the face of horror" thus requires a commitment to see and acknowledge the *particularity* of suffering without redescribing it as necessary, "strategic," or inevitable. To see in this way necessitates resisting the comforting logic of transcendent narratives that redescribe physical loss as spiritual gain, terror as cleansing, pain as edification. While such narratives provide hope, even insight, for those who live in the aftermath of trauma, they occlude our recognition of the particularity of suffering, and thus circumvent the ethical response called forth by that suffering – to resist the forces that brought it about.

The figure of the burned girl who confronts us on the first line of H.D.'s memoir brings us back again to the father's story of the burning boy. H.D., who was an analysand and "student" of Freud's would likely have been familiar with the dream as it is recounted in Freud's work.[53] The image of the girl in flames suggests a parallel "address" to the survivor of trauma. While the father's story of confronting trauma is of awakening to the imperative to "tell *what it means not to see*," *The Gift* tells the daughter's story of what it means *to see* and to be *unseen*. As both Friedman and Edmunds note, H.D. uses filmic metaphors for describing the function of memory.[54] The desire to "see" and apprehend the past is further linked to "the gift":

> Because it had once been like that, it would be possible with time and with the curious chemical constituents of biological or psychic thought processes – whatever thought is, nobody yet knows – to develop single photographs or to develop long strips of continuous photography, stored in the dark-room of memory, and again to watch people enter a room, leave a room, to watch, not only those people enter and leave a room, but to watch the child watching them . . . Though maybe at times we are motivated by the primitive curiosity of the proverbial tiresome child who "wants to see the wheels go round," yet even so, there must be a beginning, there is a Gift waiting, someone must inherit the Gift which passed us by. Someone must reveal secrets of thought which combine a new element; science and art must beget a new creative medium. (*Gift*, p. 50)

The "proverbial" child is "tiresome" precisely because she wishes to see, and yet is continually slighted because her family members do not recognize that she is "gifted." This "gift," moreover, is associated with the ability to see, translate, and transmit texts that have been effaced by the texts of "civilization." H.D. receives confirmation of her "gift" from her grandmother, "Mamalie," in a scene that highlights the potential dangers of the gift of translation. In a moment of delirium, Mamalie tells the child Hilda the "Secret" of *Wunden Eiland* (Isle of Wounds), a meeting between early Moravians and Native Americans who were connected with the *Gnadenhuetten* Indians. (Two settlements of *Gnadenhuetten* Indians, as H.D. notes, were massacred – the first by an enemy Native American tribe, and the second by a band of white settlers and soldiers [*Gift*, pp. 271–74]). The conversation between grandmother and child reveals that Mamalie's first husband had come across a text describing the meeting, written in musical code. Mamalie received "the gift" upon decoding the text, but then apparently lost or repressed it: "Well, where had Mamalie's gift gone then? I did not ask her but I sense now, that she burnt it all up in an hour or so of rapture" (*Gift*, p. 168). In the child's narration, the burning gift quickly becomes the fear of burning, for the knowledge offered by the text is forbidden: "Maybe she was afraid they would burn her for a witch (like they did at Salem, Massachusetts)" (*Gift*, p. 170). She then remembers that Mamalie did "burn" with a fever after translating the text, which was also destroyed by fire (*Gift*, p. 179). H.D. links this fire, which has destroyed both *Gnadenhuetten* and the evidence of *Wunden Eiland*, with the fire of the present-day London air raids, "the *Storm of Death* . . . storming in my ears now" (*Gift*, p. 182).

The air raids, moreover, are explicitly linked to the image of the burned girl: "But enough – this is one small earth, our earth not yet in itself, psychically projected; here the forces of evil and the forces of good are struggling; the whole structure of civilisation may go down at any moment like the Christmas-tree in the Seminary that caught fire when the girl in the crinoline was burnt to death" (*Gift*, pp. 121–22).[55] Although cataclysmic, this rhetoric is strikingly different from the rhetoric of redemption, where, for example, the burned girl might occasion the "rebirth" of civilization. Rather, when the burned girl goes up in flames, the "whole structure of civilization" goes down with her.

Such scenes recounting the traumatic deaths of young girls are repeated almost obsessively in *The Gift*, and this precipitates an early and acute awareness of gender difference for young Hilda. "Why was it always a girl who had died?" she asks, and then, through association, suggests that "the gift" is somehow frozen in her along with her ability to mourn for the dead girls in her family:

> The crying was frozen inside of me but it was my own, it was my own crying. There was Alice, my own half-sister, Edith, my own sister, and I was the third of this trio, these three Fates, or maybe Fanny was the third. The gift was there, but the expression of the gift was somewhere else.
> It lay buried in the ground. (*Gift*, p. 37)

Shortly after recounting this family history of dead girls, young Hilda questions what seems to be the gender exclusivity of "the gift." Confused about whether her femaleness might prevent her from inheriting "the gift," she asks her uncle if "ladies can be just the same as men"

(*Gift*, p. 43). Yes, her uncle replies, ladies can be "like Louisa Alcott and like Harriet Beecher Stowe" (*Gift*, p. 43). This assurance leads to Hilda's memory of attending, as a young child, a performance of *Uncle Tom's Cabin*. Significantly, it is through her reflection upon the play and the town pageant that accompanied it, that Hilda gains insight into the nature of "the gift" and her ability to possess it.[56]

Furthermore, H.D.'s "gift" is curiously obtuse about racial matters, as H.D.'s memoir is blind to the consequences of its own redeployment of representations of African American suffering as corroboration of the young Hilda's "gift."[57] The play's performance, so full of the stereotypes associated with minstrel shows, provides the occasion for Hilda's reflections on the distinction between reality and representation, and the impact of representation on one's understanding of reality.[58] As Hilda explains:

> We saw Uncle Tom. He sat on a bench before a wooden hut that was drawn in a cart. The wooden hut was his cabin and they told us that the book was called *Uncle Tom's Cabin* and that the play we were going to be taken to see, in a real theatre, on the other side of the river, was called Uncle Tom's Cabin but it was the book that started it or it was the real story, in the beginning, that started it, because Uncle Tom was a real darkie on a real plantation, *Way down upon the Swanee river*. (*Gift*, p. 43) (H.D.'s emphasis)

Here Hilda has layered several "realities" – the real theatre, the real book, the real story, all anchored by the presence of the "real darkie" on the "real plantation."[59] The fact that the "real darkie" would most likely have been played by a white man in blackface, or that the location of the "real plantation" is indicated by the lyrics of a popular song, seems inconsequential to Hilda, who suggests that by understanding this layering, she possesses a prerequisite for "the gift" – the ability to see into the spiritual reality of artistic representations. Contrasting herself to the rude and pretentious "University Boys," who disrupt the performance by whistling and heckling, she explains:

> Lots of people do not know the things we know and that Uncle Tom was seeing a vision like something in the Bible, when he saw Little Eva with a long night-dress and her golden hair, standing against the curtain that had wings painted on it, just where Little Eva was standing, so it made Little Eva look like the Princess in our fairy-book who had long gold hair, only the Princess hadn't wings, only maybe the University boys didn't have that kind of book or maybe they didn't know how to look at pictures, or to see things in themselves and then to see them as if they were a picture. (*Gift*, p. 47)

Reflecting on this newfound understanding of the gift of seeing things "as if they were a picture," Hilda explains that after the performance, "everything would always be different" (*Gift*, p. 47). "Well really," she notes, "there had been so much, you kept remembering bits of it; in the light of the play itself . . . everything came true" (*Gift*, p. 47). She continues:

I know it was only Little Eva in a jerry-built, gold chariot, and yet it was the very dawn of art, it was the sun, the drama, the theatre, it was poetry, why it was music, it was folk-lore and folk-song, it was history. It was all these things, and in our small-town, on the curb of the pavement, the three children – and maybe Tootie – who stood watching, were all the children of all the world; in Rome, in Athens, in Palestine, in Egypt, they had watched golden-chariots, they had seen black-men chained together and cruel overseers brandishing whips. It was Alexandria, it was a Roman Triumph, it was a Medieval miracle-play procession with a Devil who was Simon Legree and the poor dark shades of Purgatory, who were the Negroes chained together, and it was Pallas Athene in her chariot with the winged Victory poised with the olive-crown, who was coming to save us all. (*Gift*, p. 48)

Besides the shift in voice in this passage – where Hilda's childlike observations are supplanted by the adult H.D.'s ruminations on the transcultural universality of art forms – the other significant shift in this passage is from the historical to the allegorical. That is, the story of the "real darkie" (however dubiously founded) is evacuated to become the story of all stories, or more specifically, the story of the artist who can make something transcendent and redemptive through her rendering. The "poor dark shades of Purgatory, who were the Negroes chained together" will be saved through the work of the poet – through the work of H.D., more specifically, who identifies elsewhere with the figure of "winged victory." This is perhaps the salvific fantasy of academic liberalism *par excellence*. Moreover, at the crux of this fantasy, it is not "really" the "Negroes chained together" who will be saved, but the poet herself, who wrote her memoir in the midst of Nazi air raids while hoping that "the gift" would survive the terrible destruction of the war.

Although blind to the racist implications of her symbolic understanding of slavery as a human condition rather than a historical fact, H.D. is aware of the gendered dynamics of the "gift" of seeing trauma. H.D. highlights this gendered dimension by pairing the figure of the burned girl with that of the wounded father. While the girl goes up in flames in the proximity of fathers, however, the wounded father is saved by the attentive daughter. As Mamalie concludes her revelations to Hilda, H.D.

again connects the fires at *Gnadenhuetten* to the "*Storm of Death*" of the air raids, and then further connects these traumas to her experience of finding her father wounded after an accident:

Mamalie, don't get lost, I must go on, I must go on into the darkness that was my own darkness and the face that was my own terrible inheritance, but it was Papa, it was my own Papa's face, it wasn't the face of the Wounded One at *Wunden Eiland* though I got them all mixed up, but I will get them separated again and I will hold the cup in my hand that is a lily, that is a rose, that is . . . (*Gift*, p. 182)

In the next chapter, the small child Hilda finds her father wounded with a concussion and wandering outside the house late at night. Although no one recognizes her feat, it is she who guides him to the house and begins to bathe his wounds:

They did not ask, "Who found him?" They did not say, "But this is your father, were you alone with your father? Did you wash his face? Who got the basin? Who held the basin? Who washed his face?" . . . No one said, "but who found him?" They said, "run along, run along." (*Gift*, p. 193)

This theme of the daughter's rescue of the father is repeated in the Isis/Osiris story of *Trilogy*. Wounded girls, however, are far more prevalent in *The Gift* than the one scene of the wounded father, coupled as it is with the family's ignoring the daughter's saving actions. The Christmas-time death of the burned girl uncannily mirrors the end of *Trilogy*. As a mirror image of *The Gift*, one that begins with the saga of the wounded father (Osiris) and ends with a fantasmatic recuperation of the daughter, *Trilogy* symbolically resurrects the dead girls who haunt the text of *The Gift*.

The Gift, on the other hand, preserves the story of burned girls through identification. Fanny, the girl whose death opens *The Gift*, is unknown to the child Hilda, but H.D. identifies with her through a set of familial associations. First, the story of the burned girl is linked to H.D.'s grandfather (called "Papalie"), who is considered a second father to Hilda and her siblings: "There was a girl who was burnt to death at the seminary, as they called the old school where our grandfather was principal" (*Gift*, p. 35). As if by free association, the story of Fanny's death sandwiches a long digression outlining a child's struggle to understand the place of fathers' fathers in the family structure:

For a long time we were under the impression that we had two fathers, Papa and Papalie, but the children across the street said Papalie was our grandfather. "He is not," we said, "he is our Papalie." But Ida, our devoted friend, who did the cooking and read Grimm's tales to us at night before we went to sleep, said yes,

Papalie was our grandfather, people had a grandfather, sometimes they had two. The other grandfather was dead, he was Papa's father, she explained. But the girl who was burnt to death, was burnt to death in a crinoline. The Christmas tree was lighted at the end of one of the long halls and the girl's ruffles or ribbons caught fire and she was in a great hoop. (*Gift*, p. 35)

The story of Fanny is known to Hilda through anecdote, the story of her own mother's mourning for the burned girl:

"Why are you crying?" this is Mama and her younger brother, little Hartley. Mamalie finds them crouched at the turn of the stairs under the big clock that Mamalie's father had made himself . . .
  "Why are you crying?"
  Mama, who was older, said, "We are crying because Fanny died." Mamalie laughed and told us the story of Mama and Uncle Hartley crouching under the clock, which was our clock in our house now and our great-grandfather had made it. (*Gift*, p. 35)

As H.D. explains the family story, she makes it clear that Mama (H.D.'s mother) does not really know Fanny, and yet mourns for her because of her childhood capacity for empathy. H.D.'s grandmother (Mamalie) finds Mama's grief amusing – "Well, you see, they couldn't possibly remember Fanny. Fanny died before Hartley was born, and your own mama was just a baby, how could she remember Fanny?" (*Gift*, p. 36) But Hilda, who identifies with Fanny, finds it odd that Mamalie does not feel sadness for the dead girl, and that neither Mama nor Mamalie connect Fanny's death to Hilda's two dead sisters: "I wondered about that. Mama was crying about Fanny. Why did Mamalie think it funny? Mamalie did not seem to think of Fanny, Mama did not speak often of little Edith, and the other little girl was not mentioned" (*Gift*, p. 36).

Hilda's confusion discloses her gift for empathy. Seen from the child's perspective, the story of Fanny's demise is not amusing because Hilda is able to imagine herself in the place of the endangered girl. Just as Mama feels empathy for Fanny, Hilda feels empathy for all three dead little girls, whose fate seems somehow linked to their gender. Hilda even goes so far as to identify with the dead girl:

I was the inheritor. The boys, of whom there were so many . . . could not really care about Fanny; little Hartley had cried only because his tiny older sister was crying. I cared about Fanny. And she died. I inherited Fanny from Mama, from Mamalie, if you will, but I inherited Fanny. Was I indeed Frances, come back? . . . Why was it always a girl who had died? . . . There was Alice – my own half sister, Edith – my own sister, and I was the third of this trio, these three Fates, or maybe Fanny was the third. (*Gift*, p. 37)

The question, "why was it always a girl who had died?" – a question that indicates Hilda's gender consciousness at a very early age – is linked through another free association to the Grimms' fairy tales Ida reads her nightly:

> I can not say that a story called Bluebeard that Ida read us from one of the fairy tales, actually linked up in thought – how could it? – with our kind father. There was a man called Bluebeard, and he murdered his wives. How was it that Edith and Alice and the Lady (the mother of Alfred and Eric [H.D.'s half-brothers]) all belonged to Papa and were there in the graveyard? No, of course, I did not actually put this two-and-two together. (*Gift*, p. 39)

While the association between Bluebeard and Hilda's father is not a direct accusation of violence (H.D. is careful to include qualifiers), its inclusion in the memoir indicates the daughter's awareness of the potential for familial violence to be directed towards women and girls. Immediately after the Bluebeard allusion, young Hilda wonders what it would have been like to be in her dead sister Alice's place. Describing the way her father chose her name by running his finger down a list of names in the dictionary, Hilda asks, "What would I have been, who would I have been, if my initial had come at the beginning and he had put his finger on Alice? Had he put his finger on Alice?" (*Gift*, p. 40) In this disturbing string of associations, the father's Adam-like power to name, to assign identities, becomes the power to assign life or death.

Hilda's empathy with the dead girls moves on through another chain of associations, this time linking the body of a dead/sleeping girl to sexual violence and terrors that occur in the night. Again beginning the chain of associations with an allusion to Grimms' fairy tales, H.D. recounts the story of an old man on Church Street who invites her into his house because she is the only girl in her crowd of friends. The man gives her special favors, taking her for a ride in his sleigh and giving her a lily, which she puts on her grandfather's grave. While her encounter with the old man is depicted innocently enough, when Hilda attempts to recall the event, her mother denies that such a man ever existed:

> One day I said to Mama, "what has become of the old man on Church Street who sent me a sleigh?" Mama said there was no such man on Church Street who sent us a sleigh . . . Anyhow . . . when I came to think about it, this was the odd thing; the lily was flowering and the streets were full of snow. It could not be worked out. But it happened. I had the lily, in my hand. (*Gift*, p. 102)

The mysterious old man's gift of the lily is significant. In at least two other instances in H.D.'s writing, the lily is connected to scenes of undesired sexual aggression. The first instance occurs in *Palimpsest*, when the Roman soldier Marius penetrates his concubine Hipparchia, who takes no pleasure in the intercourse. Here the lily is clearly figured as a metaphor for female genitalia: "Plunge dagger into gold lily. What more was she, had she in her most intimate encounters given him? You might as well plunge dagger into the cold and unresponsive flesh of some tall flower."[60] The second instance occurs in *Helen in Egypt*. As Edmunds notes, Helen's vision of the lily is connected to her rape by Achilles and to Horus, the child who accompanies his father Osiris on his nightly journey through the underworld.[61]

Immediately after H.D. recounts the scene with the old man and the lily, the narrative flashes to another reference to H.D.'s father: "Now Papa's hand was in my hand. He called me *Töchterlein* and I couldn't help it. It made a deep cave, it made a long tunnel inside me with things rushing through" (*Gift*, p. 102). This cryptic paragraph is never explained. Instead, the narrative immediately moves to a long passage discussing Hilda's confusion about the meaning of the word "nightmare." She becomes acquainted with the term through a picture in a children's book called *Simple Science*. The book contains a disturbing picture, which H.D.'s mother eventually cuts out because it has made one of the children scream:

The picture was a girl lying on her back, she was asleep, she might be dead but no, Ida said she was asleep. She had a white dress on like the dress the baby wore in the photograph Aunt Rosa sent Mama. Mama tried to hide it from us . . . the baby looked as if it were asleep, the girl in the picture looked as if she were dead, but the baby was dead and the girl was asleep and the picture was called *Nightmare*. (*Gift*, p. 103)

Terrified by the thought of the nightmare, Hilda wonders what it is, but no one will explain it to her. She associates it with more images of dead girls and "something terrible with hooves rushing out to trample you to death" (*Gift*, p. 104). This description of the terrible "night horse" is followed by the sentence "He goes out in the night" (*Gift*, p. 104). At first it seems as if the "he" of the sentence refers to the "something terrible with hooves" or to death, but the next paragraph indicates that the narrative has shifted once again to discussion of H.D.'s father. The sentence's placement between the description of the nightmare and the description of her father's nocturnal activities renders the pronoun "he" ambiguous. This ambiguity heightens the sense that, through some chain of associations, the father's activities are linked to nightmares.

Not much later in the memoir, H.D. recounts an actual nightmare that she had as a child:

This is magic against the evil that stings in the night. Its voice wails at two, at three (it is called the "siren" or the "alert") but safe, "frozen" in bed, there is magic. It is simple, innocuous magic. But sometimes through sheer nervous exhaustion, we drop off to sleep. We are not so safe then.

The serpent has great teeth, he crawled on Papa-and-Mama's bed and he was drinking water out of a kitchen tumbler, the sort of tumbler that we put our paintbrushes in . . .

The thing is, there is another snake on the floor, he may want water out of a glass, too, there is nothing very horrible about this until the snake on the floor rears up like a thick terrible length of fire hose around the legs of the bed. Then he strikes at me . . .

The snake has sprung at me and . . . I shout through the snake-face, that is fastened at the side of my mouth, "Gilbert; Mama, Mama, Mama."

The snake falls off. His great head, as he falls away, is close to my eyes and his teeth are strong, like the teeth of a horse. He has bitten the side of my mouth. I will never get well . . . how ugly my mouth is with a scar, and the side of my face seems stung to death. But no, "You are not stung to death," says dark Mary, who is enormous and very kind. "You must drink milk," she says. I do not like milk. "You must eat things you do not like," says Mary. (*Gift*, pp. 112–13)

The dream, as Friedman notes, bears all of the markers of the Freudian "primal scene."[62] As a primal scene, the dream contains some intriguing parallels to Freud's "Wolf Man" case. Hilda's fear of the picture in *Simple Science* is comparable to the Wolf Man's fear of a wolf illustration in a book of Russian fairy tales.[63] The grandfather clock where Hartley and Helen hide while they cry over the fate of Fanny is also a feature – representing safety from the predatory Wolf – of the Wolf Man's analysis.[64] The animal phobia – in H.D.'s case phallic snakes rather than castrated/castrating wolves – and the significance of the beloved/potentially lethal Christmas tree are other intriguing shared elements of both narratives.[65]

Freud's somewhat vexed analysis of the Wolf Man case is notable for the coexistence of his trauma theory of neurosis with his later Oedipal theory. Contemplating the function of childhood fantasies in analysis, Freud remarks "The old trauma theory of the neuroses, which was after all built up upon the impressions gained from psycho-analytic practice, had suddenly come to the front once more."[66] While adhering steadfastly to his Oedipal theory, Freud never fully lets go of the trauma theory, as at least some of the Wolf Man's neurotic tendencies stemmed from his "seduction" at a young age by his older sister.[67] "[H]is seduction by his sister was certainly not a phantasy," Freud asserts, "its credibility was increased by some information which had never been forgotten and which dated from a later part of his life."[68] While Freud does not posit "seduction" as the sole cause of the Wolf Man's later neurosis, he does admit to the reality of the Wolf Man's experience and the importance of that experience in the child's later development.

H.D.'s reminiscences can be interpreted with a similar awareness of the possible coexistence of traumatic memories with traumatic fantasies. After recounting the "primal scene" dream, H.D. free-associates and recalls a memory from childhood:

> This is the python. Can one look into the jaws of the python and live? Can one be stung on the mouth by the python and utter words other than poisonous? Long ago, a girl was called the Pythoness; she was a virgin.
> "What is a virgin, Mama?"
> "A virgin is – is a – is a girl who isn't married."
> "Am I a virgin, Mama?"
> "Yes, all little girls are virgins."
> All little girls are not virgins. The python took shape, his wings whirred overhead, he dropped his sulfur and his fire on us. (*Gift*, p. 115)

In the context of her sexual and violent dream, the surety with which young Hilda knows that "All little girls are not virgins" is startling. How does she receive such knowledge? *The Gift*'s earlier example of empathy for the losses of others should persuade us not to foreclose a reading that admits the possibility of Hilda's sexual endangerment.

For example, in a moment of identification, H.D. interrupts the narration of rescuing her wounded father, who may have been injured falling off a moving streetcar, with a scene of her own unnoticed, secret, falling – this time from a moving milk cart. This scene of having accepted a ride from a man in a milk cart shares none of the benevolent overtones of her ride with the old man in the sleigh. After climbing on board, the young Hilda looks over at the man only to see him presumably exposing himself, and, fearful of being abducted, she leaps from the cart while the horse is at a full run.

> I looked at the man and I saw he was . . . he had . . . and he said . . . but I said, "I get out here, I live here," but I did not live at the Fetters' Farm.
> I thought he might not stop the horse, so I slid out and I jumped over the wheel that was going fast and I stood by the switch and I saw Mr. Fetters was driving some cows out of their front field and Mrs. Fetters was shelling peas, on the porch.

I could pretend to go in, at the Fetters' gate, if the man looked to see where I was going, but he did not stop. (*Gift*, p. 205).

Daily rural life goes on in Bethlehem in the midst of the girl's endangerment and bravery. Unlike the father, whose misadventure creates a family emergency, the daughter must rescue herself and continue home with her experience of trauma and survival unnoticed.

DEAD GIRLS AND WOUNDED FATHERS: IDENTIFICATION AND RE-MEMBERING

The lesson of H.D.'s juxtaposition of the Fetters' Farm scene with that of her father's wounding seems to be that the girl is responsible for the public rescue of the father as well as her private, unacknowledged self-rescue. This message is echoed in the Isis/Osiris mythology of *Trilogy*. As many scholars have noted, *Trilogy* is concerned with imagining triumphant rebirth.[69] However, traces of *The Gift*'s burned girl are preserved in *Trilogy*, and can be read as remnants of unrelinquished attachments – unmourned losses – through an understanding of what Abraham and Torok call "endocryptic identification."[70] For Abraham and Torok, endocryptic identification is conservative, a way of denying loss and being lost at the same time. Attempting to cope with painful reality, a person might psychologically bury the "memory of an idyll experienced with a prestigious object that for some reason has become unspeakable, a memory thus entombed in a fast secure place, awaiting its resurrection."[71] The hidden painful memory "whose unutterable nature dodges all work of mourning" compels the psyche to "encrypt" an unspoken identification with the lost object.[72]

The process of encryption retains the lost object by incorporating it. That is, the ego changes places with the lost object, disavowing its loss by becoming its surrogate. In order for disavowal to be maintained, this exchange takes place secretly, in an unrecognizable form:

The shift itself is covert, since both the fact that the idyll has taken place and its subsequent loss will have to be disguised and denied. Such a situation leads to the setting up within the ego of a closed-off place, a crypt, as the consequences of a self-governing mechanism, a kind of anti-introjection comparable to the formation of a cocoon around the chrysalis, which we have called *inclusion*.[73]

Abraham and Torok developed their theory of endocryptic identification by returning to Freud's "Wolf Man" case. The "idyll" they describe as both denied and preserved in this case is incest – the Wolf Man's "seduction" by his older sister. Endocryptic identification, therefore, may be a way of simultaneously concealing and communicating that "unspeakable" traumatic experience. Abraham and Torok's mention of the cocoon or chrysalis is fortuitous, for H.D. herself uses such imagery to discuss the mechanics of signification – the way that meanings get covered up even as they are exposed:

> I know, I feel
> the meaning that words hide;
> they are anagrams, cryptograms,
> little boxes conditioned
> to hatch butterflies . . .   ("WDNF," lines 790–94)

Friedman reads H.D.'s cocoon imagery autobiographically, suggesting that the butterfly hatched from the cocoon is Psyche, a double for H.D., who is "reborn" as a poet after the dialectical process of analysis and contention with Freud.[74] H.D.'s allusion to the cocoon, however, highlights multiplicity and the problem of interpretation. Words hide as well as hatch meanings. The meanings that are hatched are plural ("butterflies") and ambiguous, puzzling ("anagrams, cryptograms"). This passage would suggest that H.D. is at least aware of the possibility of encryption and the potential for meanings to be hidden by the redemptive thrust of her poem.

That H.D. includes this passage just before launching her exploration of the Isis/Osiris myth is instructive for what the myth conceals and reveals about fatherhood, or, more precisely, daughterhood. Read alongside the story of traumatic girlhood in *The Gift*, *Trilogy*'s Isis/Osiris allusions offer an example of "endocryptic" role-reversal.[75] In *Trilogy*, Osiris is conflated with Amen-Ra. He is the "world-father,/father of past aeons,/present and future equally" ("WDNF," lines 364–66). According to Lewis Spence, whose 1915 study of *Ancient Egyptian Myths and Legends* was probably known to H.D., Osiris is also the god of the dead.[76] Isis, the sister/daughter of Osiris/Ra, must travel the world in order to piece together his murdered and dismembered body. Her own birth has been facilitated (against the wishes of Ra, the jealous father) by the creativity of Thoth, author of *The Book of the Dead* and the god of writing and several sciences, including astronomy.[77] (The allusion to Thoth and the link between Osiris, "O-Sire-is," and "the star Sirius" ["WDNF," lines 796, 798] call to mind H.D.'s own father, a professor of astronomy.) The myths

H.D.'s wars

of Ra, Nut, Thoth, Osiris, Isis, Set, and Horus are multifaceted, but they all tell the story of a family beset by murderous rages, jealousy, encrypted evidence (Osiris' body is encased within a casket, covered over with molten lead, thrown in the Nile and then enclosed within the trunk of a tree), intra-family alliances and fantastic/heroic recuperations of family equilibrium.

Most of the fantastic recuperations are brought about by the daughter/sister Isis, whose ability to grieve profusely is linked to her ability to recover the remains of Osiris. In one version of the myth, Isis locates the body of Osiris by asking some children if they had seen the casket containing Osiris' body. Only they are able to place her on the right track, and, according to Spence, "From that time children were regarded by the Egyptians as having some special faculty of divination."[78] Isis traces the casket to Byblos, where she disguises herself as a nursemaid to Queen Astarte's son. Her nightly mourning ritual – placing the child in the burning fireplace, then changing herself into a swallow to "twitter mournful lamentations for her dead husband" – alarms the Queen, who discovers her identity and allows her to take the body of Osiris back to Egypt.[79] In this version, the child is figured as a sacrificial figure, his placement on the pyre leading to the recovery of the father/husband.

Trilogy's reference to Osiris suggests that the father/brother is wounded, and he must be healed by the fantastic recuperative powers of the daughter/mother/sister figure of Isis/Mary/Mary Magdalene.[80] "The Flowering of the Rod," the title of *Trilogy*'s final poem, refers to the tamarisk tree in which the dead body of Osiris is encased. The tree undergoes several transformations – first a small bush, then a magnificent tree, a living crypt and pillar in the palace of Queen Astarte.[81] After her successful rescue mission to Byblos, Isis has the tree cut open to reveal the casket containing Osiris.[82] From the body of Osiris (later dismembered and scattered by Set) corn grows, representing a form of resurrection, or vegetative regeneration. Spence notes that "The accompanying legend [to a statue of Osiris] sets forth that 'this is the form of him whom one may not name, Osiris of the mysteries, who springs from the returning waters' . . . this personification was the kernel of the mysteries of the god, the innermost secret that was only revealed to the initiated."[83] The phrase recalls *Trilogy*'s:

> we know our Name
> we nameless initiates,
> born of one mother,
> companions

> of the flame.
> . . .
> dragging the forlorn
> husk of self after us,
>
> we are forced to confess to
> malaise and embarrassment;
> we pull at this dead shell,
> struggle but we must wait
>
> till the new Sun dries off
> the old-body humours   ("WDNF," lines 307–11, 314–21)

In H.D.'s version of the myth the "initiates" are identical to Osiris – "him whom one may not name." The "husks" which they drag around allude to Osiris' personification of corn, seed which must await germination in the "new Sun." The boundaries between the "scribe" who tells the story and the dismembered god have become blurred.

Additionally, the father/brother in H.D.'s account is not simply the wounded one. He is one who wounds. Through word play similar to that which takes place in psychoanalysis, Osiris becomes "O-sir-is or O-Sire-is," an authoritarian or father figure, and "Sirius" the Dog Star, reputed to watch over times of strife and unrest ("WDNF," lines 796–98). Finally, he becomes the "Zrr-hiss" ("WDNF," line 849) of the bombs which have exposed the "skeleton" ("WDNF," line 45) of London. The psychological transformation of the father from one who is wounded to one who wounds explains why *Trilogy* ends not with the reconstruction of the dismembered father-Osiris, but with the recuperation of the daughter, figured through a lost object, the jar of myrrh that Mary Magdalene/Isis recovers from the patriarch Kaspar. This jar is identical to the one she persuades him to give to the Christ child. But the child, in this case, turns out to be a "bundle of myrrh" in the mother Mary's arms ("FR," line 172). The Christian telos of *Trilogy*, ending with a nativity scene, suggests a traditional conclusion to the redemptive trajectory of the poem. The nativity scene that ends the poem, however, also enacts a uniquely female exchange, with the patriarch Kaspar as the go-between. Mary Magdalene/Isis, through her fantastic recuperative powers, has convinced him to give the myrrh to Mary/mother. But the bundle of myrrh in Mary's arms *is* Mary/Isis, who has promised previously:

> I am Mary, a great tower;
> through my will and my power,
> Mary shall be myrrh;

H.D.'s wars

> I am Mary – O, there are Marys a-plenty,
> (though I am mara, bitter) I shall be Mary-myrrh;   ("FR," lines 332–36)

The recuperated object, then, is not the father, but the child. Through the logic of endocryptic identification, the wounded child "becomes" the dismembered father, whom the daughter/sister attempts to heal. But the recuperative efforts, it turns out, have been directed all along toward the daughter/sister, who must persuade the father to give up his hold on the priceless Mary-myrrh that is herself. She must convince him to give Mary back to Mary.

The rescue of the child is very similar to a scene in the "Princess" dream H.D. recounts in *Tribute to Freud*:

> I, the dreamer, wait at the foot of the steps . . . I am concerned about something, however. I wait below the lowest step. There, in the water beside me, is a shallow basket or ark or box or boat. There is, of course, a baby nested in it. The Princess must find the baby. I know that she will find this child. I know that the baby will be protected and sheltered by her and that is all that matters.[84]

In analysis with Freud, H.D. interprets the dream as a wish to be "the founder of a new religion"; that is, Moses, the baby found in the bulrushes.[85] Moses, for Freud, represents the father figure, a "great man" who lends his subjects a share of his paternal authority in exchange for their submission.[86] The religious father figure, Freud further explains, represents an archaic memory of the brute patriarch, possessive over "his" females and violent toward his sons. "This patriarchal system came to an end," writes Freud, "through a rebellion of the sons, who united against the father, overpowered him, and together consumed his body."[87] H.D.'s analysis with Freud during the time that he was developing these ideas would have encouraged her to connect the baby in the boat with the figure of the wounded father, an Osiris figure, dismembered by jealous family members.

But what if H.D.'s question, "Am I, after all, in my fantasy, the baby?" were taken literally? Even in Freud's etymology, Moses is derived from the Egyptian "mose," meaning "a child."[88] In this case, H.D.'s identification would not be with the father, or "founder of a new religion," but with the abandoned and endangered child. In her dream, there are only three figures – the baby, "perhaps, the child Miriam" looking on, and the "Princess" who "must find the baby."[89] This scene, like the ending of *Trilogy*, represents a fantasy of female rescue. The Princess, like Isis/Mary Magdalene, must recover the Mary/myrrh/child and bring it back into the secure fold of maternal protection.

While the recuperation figured in the fantasy of female rescue is a desirable one, we must nevertheless ask what has been lost in the story. In figuring the story of the child's rescue as the story of Osiris (the story of re-membering the father) *Trilogy* has forgotten the story of the wounded girl. Her plight is overwritten by the story of the father's rescue and the triumphant Christmas story, which redescribes the story of *The Gift*'s burned girls in the acceptable language of spiritual rebirth. Celebrating this rebirth as a triumph, we may approach the fantasy of transcendence and an end to mourning promised in the apocalyptic rhetoric of the Book of Revelation. The promised end to mourning, however, is a form of denial, of turning one's face away from the particularity of loss and wounding. Ultimately, as a reading practice, the celebration of *Trilogy*'s transcendence is a rejection of the "gift" of sight, a refusal to hear the address of the child: "Father, don't you see I'm burning?"

SIDESHADOWING IN THE MADRIGAL TRILOGY AND *PILATE'S WIFE*

H.D.'s Madrigal trilogy, unlike *Trilogy*, does not overwrite losses, but rather questions them. Each of the three novels attempts to bring unspeakable or unacknowledged experiences of loss to discourse. *Paint It Today*, for example, depicts the pain and loneliness the closet brings to bear on H.D.'s relationship with Frances Gregg. *Asphodel* and *Bid Me to Live* continue to tell the story of relationships crushed by social conventions, war, betrayal. The midpoint of *Asphodel*, for example, describes the inexplicable suicide of Margaret Cravens – a senseless death that troubles Hermione (H.D.) deeply. Both Hermione and Shirley (Cravens) remain isolated because neither is able, or willing, to communicate her pain:

> It was Hermione who had killed her. Hermione on May-day might have reached her. Shirley looking wan and odd, seeing that Hermione was unhappy. Shirley had seen this. Hermione might have reached across, said simply, "I am so unhappy." Hermione hadn't done this. Hermione had killed her.[90]

This scene presents a curious reversal of expectation, for one would expect a woman who just learned that her friend committed suicide to wonder "why didn't she tell me she was so unhappy?" Hermione's response suggests that the expression of one's own vulnerabilities, more than a polite regard for the feelings of others, might lead to a compassionate connection between isolated individuals. The Madrigal trilogy's "anti-apocalyptic" method of rendering personal history is, importantly, riddled with vulnerabilities and presented without a seamless narrative to manage ambivalence and incomprehensibility.

Narrative, because it imposes a sense of time – beginning, middle, end – on one's words, makes it difficult to express notions of simultaneity. H.D.'s experimental prose admits this difficulty. In *Paint It Today*, for example, H.D. attempts to represent her own childhood (Midget is her name for herself in this text). The opening of the novel exhorts the writer to "paint" a self-portrait. But this exhortation is posed as a question – "A PORTRAIT, a painting?" – rather than an imperative.[91] Repeating that question four times in the ensuing three pages, the artist concedes that a rendering will not produce a complete picture of her former self, only a temporary vision soon eclipsed by others: "Find her, differentiate her, carve her from dark cypress wood, only to lose her again, her valiant outline blurred in the process of civilizing, of schooling, of devitalizing."[92] Recognizing the inadequacy of narrative representation, the writer falls back to a vocabulary of artistic rendering. This rendering, moreover, is somehow connected to a sense of loss or destruction in childhood, as if the acquisition or language itself breaks the "flawless shell" of coherent identity:

> Yet a beautiful thing, a perfect thing is inevitably broken. The small bird, fallen from its nest was so hideous, so wormlike with a repellent gruesomeness the smooth, clean, snakelike angle-worms or the flat garden grubs never had. The egg was so pretty with flecks of brown and vermilion on its Nile-green shell. The small bird was an uncanny monster. Perhaps the Midgets of this world would become curious, misshapen things if they were not captured early. What is the use of mourning for the broken egg shell when there is some hope in a small monster of flight or gift of singing?[93]

Repeating, going back to the same period of time and emphasizing different elements of that past, is a way to break down the hierarchy of importance imposed by traditional historical narratives. In H.D.'s retelling of the history of World War I, for example, the stories of heroism, of battles that take place at the "front" are conspicuously absent, except for a momentary reverie when Hermione questions both the sacrifice exacted of young men by the war, and the hypocritical discourse of patriotic motherhood so prevalent in Britain during World War I.[94] Richard Aldington's preoccupation with "going over the top," too, is described as a conformist's preoccupation with destroying "Fritz," the German enemy: "Why be démodé, it wasn't à la mode any more to be witty, it was Fritz and Fritz and such vile repetition."[95] Instead of tales of heroism, H.D. foregrounds what is usually considered the backdrop to histories of the war – life at home amid food and coal shortages, the single-mindedness of public discourse, war's shattering influence on relationships, and the primacy of death in the public imagination. Rather than soldiers and statesmen, she details incidents in the life of artists and poets, who are no longer considered "useful" to a society at war.

Like *Asphodel*, *Bid Me to Live* questions the renunciation that war makes necessary. Both novels acknowledge the sacrifices that war exacts from its "non-heroic" non-participants and trace the disillusioning effects of the war on those left at home:

Everybody was waiting for everything to be smashed. Why pretend that life could possibly be the same, ever? Why pretend, here in this room, in this house, that this was her room, this is my bed. Nothing belonged to anybody . . . The watch was the same watch, but time was different. Months, days were smashed. There was no continuity. She had given up pretending.[96]

More than disillusioned, those left at home are valued less because their lives are not directly linked to the war effort. Rico (D. H. Lawrence) takes refuge at Julia's (H.D.'s) home because the government, fearful of his pacifism and his wife's German nationality, has forced him to move from his home in Cornwall: "There was Rico, with incipient T.B., his little house of life come bang down, swept away by the war-tornado."[97] Impoverished by wartime economics and government censorship of his books, Lawrence eventually did succumb to tuberculosis in 1925. He died in 1930. Although his death does not "count" as a wartime casualty, H.D.'s history remembers his expulsion, poverty, and stigmatization as effects of the war.

H.D.'s deployment of writerly *passage* – her foregrounding of seemingly "private" details (like the stillbirth of her child) in her history of the years 1911–1919 – makes the Madrigal trilogy a good example of Foucauldian "genealogy." Lee Quinby explains that genealogy, a decidedly anti-apocalyptic discourse, is "an analytic approach that does not establish truth through the temporal and spatial narratives of the origin and the end of history but rather through attention to the intricate details of discourses and practices and their inscriptions on bodies."[98] In a similar vein, Jennifer Terry argues that genealogy, or "effective" history, "allows us to theorize a counterdiscursive position of history-telling which neither fashions a new coherence, nor provides a more inclusive resolution of contradicting 'events.' It is *not* an alternative narrative with its own glorious tumescence peopled by previously elided but now recuperated Others."[99]

Genealogical history, then, offers an important alternative to apocalyptic histories, which tend to naturalize barbarity, sacrifice, and violence as instrumental to linear "progress" and historical coherence. H.D.'s Madrigal trilogy, which depicts many accounts of the same time period in her life, presents us with an "effective history," admittedly incomplete, but attentive to the "intricate details of discourses and practices and their inscriptions on bodies." This effective history questions traditional notions of foreground and background in historical production. By detailing the tales of barbarity that are relegated to the inconspicuous background of traditional historical accounts, effective history suggests that the process of foregrounding itself enables the perpetuation of everyday, overlooked injustices. Our ability to consider such tales of barbarity in childhood memoirs like *The Gift*, or to question the sacrificial logic that determines which losses "count" as losses in historical renderings of traumatic times, might depend on our ability to hear polyphonic voices, or to see several facets of a story simultaneously. It may be that history is reshaped each time we go back to it, as it was for H.D. in her Madrigal trilogy. Different relationships may need to be highlighted at different times and in different contexts. A rendering which acknowledges this complexity may be more confusing than a history that proceeds as if its elements were causal links in a necessary chain of events. But such linear histories select their elements retroactively, cutting out or suppressing chains of associations that do not lead to the historian's vantage point, which is identical to the history's endpoint. This practice of excision is a rhetorical violence done in the name of "progress." A rendering of the past which acknowledges the "ends of others" as unacceptable would resist the urge to apocalyptically rescript losses as gains. The Madrigal trilogy thus provides us with one example of a historiography which resists this urge to redeem the time. *Pilate's Wife* offers an even more powerful critique of apocalyptic endings.

As Joan Burke and Susan Stanford Friedman note, *Pilate's Wife* is H.D.'s variant of a story that D. H. Lawrence tells in *The Man Who Died* – where Jesus is brought down from the cross alive, awakens in his tomb and escapes to the world of embodied life.[100] Burke explains that H.D. and Lawrence had most likely discussed the parallels between the Isis myth and the story of Jesus' resurrection: "When H.D. first learned from friends that Lawrence had worked on this theme, she thought, 'Now he has taken my story.'"[101] *Pilate's Wife*, as Burke suggests, offers a female perspective of the resurrection/Isis story.[102] It also imagines the world-changing potential of collective action and coalition across class, caste, gender, and ethnicity. While in Lawrence's story, Jesus wakes up in the tomb alone, alive because of a chance mistake (the Romans cut him down from the cross too soon), in H.D.'s variant, the prophet/poet Jesus is rescued through the collective intervention of women and men of both high and low social statuses. Ultimately, H.D.'s variant is instructive for its insistence on the value of the body (something that Lawrence does as well), and of interdependent networks of people brought together by contingency and shared purpose – something that Lawrence is less interested in, as his protagonist is likened to an escaped cock who must break the fetters of domesticity and servitude that have kept him literally henpecked. H.D.'s story, on the other hand, values both the sensuous, physical world and the political efficacy of love, suggesting that the greatest gift that we have to give each other might be our mutual survival, rather than our sacrifice.

It is precisely this logic of sacrifice that Marcuse seeks to problematize for its transvaluation of life and death. Marcuse traces a philosophical genealogy of this transvaluation from Plato's suggestion in the *Phaedo* that death brings about the "release" of the soul from the shackles of the body, to twentieth-century "philosophical morality" which is marked by its conflation of happiness with renunciation, and "the glorifying acceptance of death, which carries with it the acceptance of the political order."[103] In this system, the meaning of life is to be found in the manner of one's death. A good life is one in which life is not valued over much, and death is to be desired as a release from the unfreedom of life. In the *Phaedo*, Socrates demonstrates that he has lived a good life (the life of the philosopher seeking truth in ideal forms) through the manner of his death – unafraid, even willing, to drink the poison that will end his life because his death will "release" his soul from his body.[104] For Marcuse, this is a troubling development, but he suggests that in Platonic philosophy:

> the ideology of death is not yet an indispensable instrument of domination. It came to assume this function when the Christian doctrine of the freedom and equality of man as man had merged with the continuing institutions of unfreedom and injustice. The contradiction between the humanistic gospel and the inhumane reality required an effective solution . . . How can one protest against death, fight for its delay and conquest, when Christ died willingly on the cross so that mankind might be redeemed from sin? The death of the son of God bestows final sanction on the death of the son of man.[105]

Submission to death, in this case, seems less like the freedom that Socrates demonstrated, and more like a concession to powerful institutions. If one's own death can be given in the service to a higher power – indeed if the mark of one's goodness (as a citizen, subject, follower) is one's willingness to die for a cause – then by extension, others' deaths, too, can be taken in the name of the cause. Thus the soldier can die the good death on the battlefield, or take the lives of countless enemies, while others (those wishing physician-assisted suicide, for example) are sentenced to live, even if death would bring them a sense of freedom. It is the state, or the nation, that defines a good death, a proper sacrifice.

Both Lawrence and H.D. question the logic of sacrifice that is embedded in the traditional crucifixion story. In *The Man Who Died*, the protagonist walks away from the lure of renunciation, what he calls the compulsion to love chastely, with the "corpse of my love."[106] The man who died's affirmation of life is in the body (when he says "I am risen" he means it in a physiological as well as spiritual sense) but it is of a body alone and unfettered by social ties.[107] Lawrence's protagonist is Nietzschean in his contempt for slave morality (he literally chastises a young slave in the text) and his desire to be alone suggests an investment in the fantasy of radical autonomy. His freedom, one suspects, is the freedom to have sex without moralism, and although there is nothing wrong with this goal, he obtains this freedom through exile. By saying yes to sex, as Foucault would say, Lawrence's hero has not necessarily said no to power, just managed to stay outside of its punitive reach.[108]

H.D.'s critique of the logic of sacrifice is more complex, depending less on *Übermensch* individualism, and more on a shared sense of vulnerability and a revaluation of life in its particular incarnations. *Pilate's Wife* focuses on the spiritual awakening of Pontius Pilate's wife, called Veronica, to "sister love" through the cult of Isis and "brother love" through Mithraism and early (Gnostic) Christianity. In H.D.'s story, Jesus does not escape by accident, nor is his rescue an individual feat. Rather, Veronica, an Etruscan, must coordinate the rescue attempt by negotiating with Pilate, the Egyptian statesman Memnonius, the Roman captain Fabius, the Cretan priestess Mnevis, and a number of townspeople who help to bring off the escape. Motivating the rescue effort is Veronica's awakened appreciation for the value of love and life in its particularity – an awakening that she connects to Jesus' teaching that even the seemingly insignificant entities – the lilies in the field and the sparrows in the sky – have value in themselves. Jesus' gift, according to the novel, is to affirm the divinity in all living things: "By this argument," Mnevis explains, "this Jesus affirms the cult of mere humanity. Each man, he claims, is a priest and, since no bird can fall without the knowledge of the supreme Diviner, so no man, with like cognizance, can falter" (*PW*, p. 65).

It is no accident that the woman who awakens Veronica to the value of love and its creative mysteries is named Mnevis – a name associated with the Greek root for memory.[109] The name Mnevis evokes the memory, the angry memory, of the mother in ancient Athenian society. (Mnevis is paired with Menis here.) Nicole Loraux suggests that the Athenian Metroon, or temple to the mother, transforms the divine mother's vengeful anger into civic justice.[110] That is, in order to appease the anger of the wronged mother, the Athenians were instructed to build the Metroon, which then served to "protect the written memory of the city."[111] Ultimately, the structure of the Metroon serves to "domesticate feminine excess" for Loraux, but that very domestication calls attention to the threat of maternal vengeance, "another justice – terrible" that boils beneath the surface of injunctions to mourn properly.[112] In times of war, mourning mothers are disruptive to the ideology of death, for there is always the chance that they will cling to the particularity of their loss, forgetting, as it were, to translate their loss into a noble sacrifice for the state. (Consider the powerful appeal of Lila Lipscombe, the mourning mother in Michael Moore's *Fahrenheit 9/11*, for example.)[113] "When it comes to human mothers," writes Loraux, "everyday and domesticated, civilized by marriage and carriers of paternal writings, the citizens seem to have determined that they nevertheless still had enough of a potential for excess in the depths of their grief that they had to enclose their mourning within the narrow limits of regulations."[114] From this perspective, we might consider the Isis figure (central to both Lawrence's and H.D.'s revisions of the crucifixion story) as a woman who refuses to mourn properly. She won't be domesticated – instead wandering ceaselessly in search of her lost husband/brother – and she seeks literally to re-member Osiris – to put back together the pieces of his body.

The Isis of *Pilate's Wife*, in distinction to the Isis figure of *Trilogy*, attempts to save the brother/lover figure before his death. This links the novel to H.D.'s critique of patriotic discourse in her Madrigal trilogy, where the sacrifices exacted of young men and the sacrificial discourse of patriotic motherhood are shown up as strange, even cruel. In *Asphodel*, for example, the H.D. character, Hermione, notices a young deserter across the room who is being sheltered by one of her friends, Merry (Bridgit Patmore). This leads Hermione to question the moralism of those who would disdain Merry's sheltering of the young man. "She didn't believe in it, didn't believe in those hard lipped women (O God forgive me) who worked like that not knowing what love was, not knowing what life was."[115] In an imagined continuation of a previous argument with the

H.D.'s wars

"hard lipped women" she takes the side of the young soldier, whom she addresses alternatively in her rejoinder:

You have lost sons but what have they lost, what have *we* lost? Sweet life, sweet life that was over sweet, life, life, life . . . is life so light a treasure? . . . Life, life, life, they wore it like a white flower to be tossed away. O but you gave them life. I know, mothers, mothers, mothers. But I am a mother. I mean I am not.[116]

The "sweet life that was over sweet," is an echo of the saying made famous in Wilfred Owen's antiwar poem "Dulce et Decorum est [Pro Patria Mori]" – How sweet and fitting it is to die for one's country. *Life* is sweet, for H.D., not a "good death" for the fatherland.

If, in *Asphodel*, the hard-lipped women become lethal mothers, refusing to shelter the young man from the machinery of war, this may be because the state itself has usurped any other possible role for the mother except as bearer of soldiers. As Friedman notes, "The procreative politics of *Asphodel* is not a valorization of motherhood, but rather the basis for a pacifist critique of the patriarchal order."[117] "Both mother and soldier" writes Friedman, "are caught in a web they cannot control. Moreover, in producing sons that they send to war, mothers are complicitous in the production of war itself."[118]

H.D. explicitly rejects the ideology of patriotic motherhood in *Bid Me to Live*, recounting how her own life and the life of her stillborn child were deemed less valuable than the lives of the male youth who are sent to the front to toss away their lives like flowers. Arguably a "hard-lipped woman," her nursing home matron chastises her and tells her not to have another baby because the resources of the hospitals must be devoted to wounded soldiers:

Then 1915 and her death, or rather the death of her child. Three weeks in that ghastly nursing-home and then coming back to the same Rafe. Herself different. How could she blithely face what he called love, with that prospect looming ahead and the matron, in her harsh voice, laying a curse on whatever might then have been, "You know you must not have another baby until after the war is over."[119]

Although H.D.'s first child dies, the sacrificial logic of war deems this death unimportant, even inconvenient, while the death of soldiers is deemed consequential, heroic, because theirs are lives offered for the state.

Thus even within the discourse of patriotic motherhood, particular mothers do not seem to matter as much as the ideal of motherhood as universal provider of male sons for the war effort. Motherland supplants actual mothering. Butler, for example, describes the process of the state's usurpation of the mother's role:

the state intervenes in the family to wage war. The worth of the warring male youth is openly acknowledged, and in this way the community now loves him as she [the mother] has loved him. This investment is taken over by the community as it applauds the sons who have gone to war, an investment that is understood to preserve and consolidate the state.[120]

Lost in this universalization is the position of the daughter or sister, or lover, who mourns a particular man who can't be replaced through the cycle of patriotic reproduction. This is the Antigone position, and it's something of the position that H.D. found herself in after World War I, as her brother Gilbert was killed in action in France in 1918, and her father died less than a year later.[121] The young soldier whom Hermione imaginatively attempts to protect from the war therefore takes on a special resonance, for he is "An American fighting for France," much like her brother Gilbert:

Through the smoke, the cigarettes, the glasses ringed on the table and the glasses . . . on the carpet, one frail boy seemed to protest. He was a child really. He had had a nice mother, a young sister. He was too much a child – O God, let me not see . . . You saw it all, saw them all, Troy town and the flutes were playing. They were dancing on the walls of Athens; let the Spartans in, for what is life, sweet life that was over sweet?[122]

Rather than paying homage to the good death, this image suggests the vulnerability of young men caught up in the machinery of war. Recalling this image of the lost brother, as well as the loss of the stillborn child, H.D. becomes the unruly mourner/mother Loraux describes – returning again and again to her lament in her interwar prose, and uttering it in ways that are potentially corrosive to the ideology of the death-dealing state.

Pilate's Wife, if we read it alongside H.D.'s World War I fiction, provides an alternative to the story of Antigone, a narrative to which I will return in my epilogue. Antigone, though remembering her brother, seems to have forgotten that she has a sister who is still among the living. Mnevis, memory, thus stands for the memory of the forgotten sister, and the potential for coalition among the living. Through her relationship with Mnevis, Veronica remembers not only the divinity of small things but also the value of her relationships with, and obligations to, the living.

Veronica (the true-icon, and the comforter) is able to imagine a daring conspiracy to rescue a living leader, a victim of political retribution. This collective action is undertaken through networks of unlikely allies and its mission of rescue thwarts the ideology of death by suggesting that indeed it might be more sweet and fitting – perhaps sacred – to live than to submit to the lethal dictates of the state.

PART II

The modernist patch

CHAPTER 4

Pictures, arguments, and empathy

> In the form of a photograph, the explosion of an A-bomb can be used to advertise a safe.[1]

In *The Politics of Modernism*, Williams argues that modernism persists as an aesthetic form that has outlived its historical moment.[2] It is premature, however, to relegate modernism to the isolation ward of outdated formal experimentation. The remaining chapters of this book examine the "modernist patch," modernism's continuation into the twenty-first century, in the work of contemporary writers such as Susan Sontag, Pat Barker, and Hanif Kureishi. Sontag, the main focus of this chapter, made a point of drawing out the connections between the human-made catastrophes that plagued Europe during the early twentieth century and the deadly ethnic strife that plagued Europe at the century's close. Describing the death camps and mass executions that tore apart the former Yugoslavia in the 1990s, Sontag remarked, "Those of us who spent time in Sarajevo used to say that, as the 20th century began at Sarajevo, so will the 21st century begin at Sarajevo."[3] In this context, modernism has not outlived its moment.

OUTRAGE FATIGUE

The term "outrage fatigue" does not appear in dictionaries as of this writing, but given its frequency in recent political commentary (over 200,000 hits on Google and counting) it will most likely join its near twin "compassion fatigue" in our official lexica soon. The latter term, which is defined as "apathy or indifference towards the suffering of others or to charitable causes acting on their behalf," has, according to the *OED*, been used since 1968, but not commonly until, as Marjorie Garber notes, it entered the parlance of non-profit agencies in the late 1980s to describe diminishing volunteer activity or donor generosity after a quick succession of natural or human-made disasters.[4] The pseudo-diagnosis of "outrage fatigue" describes a similar numbness among media viewers whose responses to images of suffering, injustice, or abuse range from flash-in-the-pan indignation to flaccid apathy. "Outrage fatigue" provides one explanation for the capriciousness of empathy as an ethical motivator, at least on the large scale needed to bring about political change. Like "compassion fatigue," however, the term presumes that, if meted out in the right proportion, representations of suffering will produce identificatory, empathetic responses from all but the most misanthropic of onlookers, and that these responses will lead to action that will alleviate the suffering of others.[5]

Implicit in this presumption is a belief, dating back at least to the ancient Greeks, that the cultivation of appropriate feelings in subjects will lead to ethical behavior – that right feelings will produce right actions. Plato's *Republic* is a primer for cultivating the proper sentiments of citizen subjects, for example. Friedrich Schiller developed his theories on "aesthetic education" as a response to the terror of the French Revolution, arguing that "the way to the head must be opened through the heart."[6] Woolf, as I note in Chapter 1, advocated educational reforms designed to root out the "possessiveness ... jealousy ... pugnacity [...and] greed" that she linked to the violent nationalisms which precipitated the bloodshed of World War I and the Spanish Civil War (*TG*, p. 83). Adorno, in "Education after Auschwitz," suggested that the key to preventing yet another genocide would be to understand better the formation of subjects who were "cold," technophilic, detached, unable "to identify with others," or to love.[7] Berger argued that public dissemination of the "terrible images" in drawings by survivors of the atomic bombing of Hiroshima would "release an energy for opposing evil and for the lifelong struggle of that opposition."[8] And, in the present day, Martha Nussbaum argues for the "cultivation" of cosmopolitan subjects with a capacity for "compassionate imagination."[9] For Nussbaum, exposure to literature, especially drama, enables world citizens to develop "habits of empathy and conjecture [that] conduce to a certain type of citizenship and a certain form of community: one that cultivates a sympathetic responsiveness to another's needs, and understands the way circumstances shape those needs."[10]

But is it inevitable that cultivating a cadre of citizens who can feel for others will lead to justice? Lauren Berlant for example, suggests that "national sentimentality" might also work to displace consciousness of more banal, ubiquitous, and ambivalently felt forms of systematic inequity.[11] One might identify and empathize with suffering populations, and yet do little to change social formations (the distribution of wealth under global capitalism, for example) that exacerbate the suffering of many. Berlant explains that, "The public recognition by the dominant culture of certain sites of publicized subaltern suffering is frequently (mis) taken as a big step toward the amelioration of that suffering. It is a baby step, if that."[12] A further unintended consequence of sentiment-based ethics is that "right feeling" (a.k.a good intentions) can be used to justify or excuse clearly unethical actions. This of course is one of the points of Conrad's critique, in *Heart of Darkness*, of the missionary zeal of Belgian do-gooders who provided a "moral" cover for the colonization of the Congo.[13] Abuses or injustices perpetrated under the cover of "right feelings" would be described in sentimental rhetoric as aberrations, accidents, the actions of "a few bad apples" and not the predictable outcome of systems and policies. Consider President George W. Bush's appeal (in a *News Hour* interview titled, tellingly, "The Heart of Darkness") to compassionate feelings in his response to revelations of prisoner abuse at Abu Ghraib: "What took place in that prison does not represent America that I know. The America I know is a compassionate country that believes in freedom."[14]

Outrage is not sufficient to counter Bush's sentimental rationalization. What results is a rhetorical battle over the true character of the nation – you say we're abusive, I say we're compassionate – or a further call to empathize with the overworked and undertrained army reserves who didn't bargain on serving an unlimited tour of duty in extremely unpleasant conditions when they signed on for the medical benefits and college tuition they would receive for being "part-time" soldiers. As Berlant argues, "the important transpersonal intimacies created by calls to empathy all too frequently serve as proleptic shields, as ethically uncontestable legitimating devices for sustaining the hegemonic field."[15] Moreover, what gets lost in the call to be outraged, rather than to be principled (which would entail adhering to ethical precepts no matter how one *feels* about a situation), are less sensational, often tedious, examinations of policies and practices that make abuses such as those documented in the Abu Ghraib photos possible. Millions have seen the photos circulated in the media, but relatively few have read the reams of reports and government documents that provide an archive of the policies that made the unthinkable incidents documented in the photos not only thinkable, but apparently justifiable enough for the perpetrators to take, according to Joan Walsh, at least 279 photos and

19 videos documenting their actions.[16] Outrage may provide the incentive for slogging through this archive, but affect in itself cannot be the endpoint of ethics, even if it can provide motivation for principled conduct.

If this is a rather long preamble to a discussion of Sontag, Woolf, and Barker, it is intended to give context for understanding the present urgency of articulating the limits of "sentimental nationalism" at a time when national sentiment has been mobilized to justify actions and policies that are unprincipled and unjust. If national sentiment cannot be counted on as a platform for ethics, nor can cosmopolitan outrage. One can know that our responses to suffering are complex and overdetermined by political and cultural contexts, without falling prey to paralyzed cynicism or fatalistic *ennui*. This is a lesson that Woolf teaches us in her World War II writing, but one that Sontag does not fully appreciate in her engagements with such issues, particularly her use of Woolf's *Three Guineas* as the allegedly simplistic foil to her nuanced arguments about representations of suffering in her last book, *Regarding the Pain of Others*. Barker, on the other hand, takes up Sontag's skepticism about the self-evidence of representations of atrocity, but ends with a less skeptical vision of the artist's, the photographer's, and the reporter's articulation of the ambivalence of "regarding the pain of others."

RECOGNITION AND POLITICAL WILL

On 27 January 2005, in an event that received little attention in the North American press, the mayor of Sarajevo, Muhidin Hamamdzic, presided over a ceremony to rename the street in front of the city's National Theatre "Susan Sontag Theatre Square."[17] Sontag visited Sarajevo nine times during the 1992–95 Bosnian war, and in 1993 spent a month in the besieged city directing a production of Samuel Beckett's *Waiting for Godot* – an act that on the surface may seem an ineffectual form of intervention in a war-torn city, but was understood by many Sarajevans as an important contribution to the city's efforts to resist the dehumanizing and demoralizing impact of the siege. Hence the renaming ceremony honored not only Sontag, but a form of cultural resistance necessary to the city's survival as a multiethnic metropolis.

Sontag's meditations on visual and cultural representations of suffering sketch out many of the nodal points that are important to map if we are to understand better the larger contours of the terrain marked by witnessing, surviving, (re)cognizing, and remembering the atrocities and catastrophes of the early twentieth century that still resonate today like screen memories behind our perceptions and experiences of devastation in the early twenty-first century. I use the metaphor of a map of terrain deliberately, to displace the tendency to view our responses to trauma as points on the polar ends of a conceptual binary between speakability and unspeakability, voice and silence, action and paralysis. While it is important to acknowledge that extreme forms of trauma do have the effect of obliterating the conditions necessary for many victims to speak about their traumatic experiences – Primo Levi's description of the "those who did not return," or those whose "capacity for observation was paralyzed by suffering and incomprehension" so that they can no longer speak and bear witness to their own suffering is a prime example of this phenomenon – it is also important to recognize, and to listen to, those (such as Levi) who have survived trauma and have found ways to articulate their experiences.[18] In addition to creating conditions that might make witnessing more possible (e.g. survivors' testimony projects, international observer programs, post-traumatic stress disorder [PTSD] therapies, tribunals, and truth and reconciliation commissions), it is also necessary to examine social conditions that might dull or sharpen our ability to recognize atrocity when we see it, or see it represented. *To witness* implies a presence – "I was there; I saw; I heard; I felt" – while *to recognize* implies distance, even for a witness, who must take the additional cognitive step of categorizing the event as a murder, a hate crime, or part of a larger pattern of genocide. Recognition may also imply an absence, as in the case of an investigator who was not present at the scene of a crime, but comes across its evidence – a mass grave, for example – and recognizes that evidence as a sign that an atrocity has been committed.[19]

To speak in this way of recognition – as a cognitive activity of identifying and distinguishing patterns – is to lay stress on its transitive verb form *to recognize*. To do so reverses the tendency Paul Ricoeur charts, whereby increasing philosophical emphasis is placed on recognition in its passive form – *to be recognized*.[20] In this passive form, the desire *to be recognized* becomes an ontological claim,[21] while in its transitive verb form *to recognize* implies the cognitive activity of judgment and thus emphasizes ethical, over and above ontological, claims.[22] Recognition in the transitive sense therefore entails the act of interpreting signs, events, and evidence. A good deal of historical work in the late twentieth century has been devoted to providing contextual evidence that might lead to widespread public recognition of atrocities – the Armenian genocide, for example – that have previously been ignored. Recognition is thus also allied to public forms of remembering.[23] As Tony Judt argues, institutionalizing public memory through memorials has become something of an industry in post-1989 Europe, as a country or culture's willingness to memorialize atrocities and to acknowledge complicity in bringing them about (or failing to prevent them), has become requisite for belonging to the new "humane" and ethically responsible imagined community of twenty-first-century Europe.[24]

Sontag devoted much of her work to exploring the chasm between the first form of recognition – putting an event or evidence into cognitive context – and the second – civic, national, or cultural acknowledgment of an atrocity. She was intensely curious about what we recognize (or *if* we recognize) when we are confronted with images of atrocity. Early and outspoken in her condemnation of the Serbian genocide perpetrated against Bosnian Muslims, upon her return from Sarajevo in 1993 she wondered aloud at the "absence of any political will [in Europe or America] to end this suffering."[25] This lack of political will, for Sontag, was not the consequence of ignorance about the Serbian practice of "ethnic cleansing," for the news media had been covering the war "in extraordinary detail" since its inception.[26] "This is the first European genocide in our century to be tracked by the world press and documented nightly on TV," argued Sontag. "There were no reporters in 1915 sending daily stories to the world press from Armenia, and no foreign camera crews in Dachau and Auschwitz. Until the Bosnian genocide one might have thought . . . that if the story could be gotten out, the world would do something. The coverage of genocide in Bosnia has ended that illusion."[27]

One element of that "illusion" is the belief that the images of suffering distributed through international news outlets would inevitably elicit empathetic responses from viewers, who would then intervene to put an end to the atrocities. For Sontag, that illusion short-circuited not because consumers of news media are short on empathy, but because empathy in itself does not automatically translate to action. Writing two years before the Serbian massacre of approximately 8,000 Bosnian Muslims in Srebrenica, Sontag argued that, "It is the continuing coverage of the war in the absence of action to stop it that makes us mere spectators. Not television, but our politicians have made history come to seem like re-runs."[28]

And indeed to follow Sontag's career elicits that sense of historical repetition. In 1977, Sontag argued that, "A photograph that brings news of some unsuspected zone of misery cannot make a dent in public opinion unless there is an appropriate context of feeling and attitude . . . Photographs cannot create a moral position, but they can reinforce one – and help build a nascent one."[29] Over twenty-five years later, the technology of image-collecting and transmission has advanced, but the ethics of reception, for Sontag, seem to be stuck in a cycle of *déjà vu*. "[P]hotographs echo photographs," she argues in *Regarding the Pain of Others*: "it was inevitable that the photographs of emaciated Bosnian prisoners at Omarska, the Serb death camp created in northern Bosnia in 1992, would recall the photographs taken in the Nazi death camps in 1945."[30] What seems less inevitable, for Sontag, is the ethical content of a viewer's sense of recurrence and ubiquity of atrocity. Reacting to the pronouncements of theorists (among them "several distinguished French day-trippers to Sarajevo during the siege") Sontag contends that:

It has become a cliché of the cosmopolitan discussion of images of atrocity to assume that they have little effect, and that there is something innately cynical about their diffusion. As important as people now believe images of war to be, this does not dispel the suspicion that lingers about the interest in these images, and the intentions of those who produce them. Such a reaction comes from two extremes of the spectrum: from cynics who have never been near a war, and from the war-weary who are enduring the miseries being photographed.[31]

Countering the cynicism of those (including herself in 1977) who claim that the contemporary surfeit of media images of brutality and suffering short-circuits viewers' ability to empathize with the victims of violence, Sontag divides those with the potential to view images of atrocity into two groups – those who have been there and "understand" and those who "have the dubious privilege of becoming spectators, or of declining to be spectators, of other people's pain."[32] This is a curious resolution (or non-resolution) to the problem of the passivity of onlookers who should, in Sontag's (1993) view, respond to images of atrocity with actions and interventions.

The view that representations of the suffering of others should evoke, even compel, an ethical response, is in line with the position taken over twenty years ago by Berger. Although she does not engage Berger directly, Sontag suggests that viewers' responses to visual representations of suffering are less clear-cut than Berger would suppose. As Butler notes, Sontag had doubts about "whether a photograph can incite and motivate its viewers to change a point of view or to assume a new course of action."[33] Butler contends that, for Sontag, "photographs are transitive. They do not merely portray or represent – they relay affect."[34] Thus photography "frustrates" Sontag because it depicts "injustice that she does not know how best to oppose."[35] For Butler, however, Sontag's skepticism at least calls into question "the final narcissism of our habits of visual consumption."[36]

Although *Regarding the Pain of Others* seems to retract her earlier conclusions in *On Photography*, Sontag's position is less of a palinode (as Nancy Miller argues) than an example of her career-long oscillation between two standpoints – the first decrying the jaded sophistication of cosmopolitan elites ("a small, educated population living in the rich part of the world"), and the second upbraiding the politically naïve for their simplistic belief in the power of images to move us.[37] Rather than a sign of inconsistency, this oscillation is a form of navigation, as Sontag carefully tacks between a position that insists that photographic images "are a grammar and, even more importantly, an ethics of seeing" and a position that is skeptical about their ability to move us to action beyond prurient fascination, or even sadistic voyeurism.[38] Not wanting to situate herself in the position of the naïf who believes that human nature will facilitate the automatic translation of an image of atrocity to moral outrage and political action, Sontag places Woolf in that role – opening *Regarding the Pain of Others* with a direct critique of Woolf's *Three Guineas*. For Sontag, Woolf's purported reliance on the unmediated truth-value of photographic evidence of war's "horror and disgust" is problematic, because "photographs of the victims of war are themselves a species of rhetoric. They reiterate. They simplify. They agitate. They create the illusion of consensus."[39]

In her response to Woolf's assertion that "photographs are not an argument; they are simply a crude statement of fact addressed to the eye," Sontag suggests that "the photographic image, even to the extent that it is a trace (not a construction made out of disparate photographic traces), cannot be simply a transparency of something that happened."[40] Furthermore, the photographic image, which is presumed to stand in for the eyewitness as the quintessential recorder of reality, cannot provide the kind of interpretive consensus that one might hope for in response to atrocity. "In fact," Sontag argues,

> there are many uses of the innumerable opportunities a modern life supplies for regarding – at a distance, through the medium of photography – other people's pain. Photographs of an atrocity may give rise to opposing responses. A call for peace. A cry for revenge. Or simply the bemused awareness, continually restocked by photographic information, that terrible things happen.[41]

Insisting on a positivist relationship between representation and reality minimizes the role of ideology in determining conditions through which the "truth" might come to be considered valid or contestable, speakable or not. As Sontag notes in *On Photography*, "Without a politics, photographs of the slaughter-bench of history will most likely be experienced as, simply, unreal or as a demoralizing emotional blow."[42] Or, as she argues in "Regarding the Torture of Others," one group's slaughter-bench might be another's occasion for gleeful celebration – as in the case of white racists' collecting photos of lynching as "souvenirs" of the event.[43] This seems a realistic rebuttal to Woolf's assertion in *Three Guineas* that the medium of photography, because impartial, can provide the impetus for ethical agreement between two viewers positioned very differently because of their gender (and hence class) differences.

> These photographs are not an argument; they are simply a crude statement of fact addressed to the eye ... You, Sir, call them "horror and disgust." We also call them horror and disgust. And the same words rise to our lips. War, you say, is an abomination; a barbarity; war must be stopped at whatever cost. And we echo your words. War is an abomination; a barbarity; war must be stopped. For now we are looking at the same picture; we are seeing with you the same dead bodies, the same ruined houses. (*TG*, p. 11)

For Sontag, Woolf's imagined moment of consensus is impossibly naïve, although "brave."[44] "Not to be pained by these pictures," Sontag suggests, "not to recoil from them, not to strive to abolish what causes this havoc, this carnage – these, for Woolf, would be the reactions of a moral monster. And she is saying, we are not monsters, we members of the educated class. Our failure is one of imagination, of empathy. We fail to hold this reality in mind."[45] But, for Sontag, this imagined, empathetic consensus is presumptive on the part of Woolf. In direct response to this imagined consensus, Sontag asks, "Who believes today that war can be abolished? No one, not even pacifists. We hope only (so far in vain) to stop genocide and to bring to justice those who commit gross violations of the laws of war ... and to be able to stop specific wars by imposing negotiated alternatives to armed conflict."[46] Rather than invoking an empathetic response, Sontag argues, photographs of atrocity bear witness to the impossibility of "our" ever understanding the horror of events already so insufficiently depicted through any (even the most faithful of) representative media:

> We don't get it. We can't truly imagine what it was like. We can't imagine how dreadful, how terrifying war is; and how normal it becomes. Can't understand, can't imagine. That's what every soldier, and every journalist and aid worker and independent observer who has put in time under fire, and had the luck to elude the death that struck down others nearby, stubbornly feels. And they are right.[47]

These are the stunning last words of Sontag's *Regarding the Pain of Others*, but perhaps not the last words that can be said. While it is certainly the case that representations of pain and devastation can never adequately communicate what it is like to experience or eyewitness the kinds of suffering they purport to depict, such representations are only failures if we imagine that their main function in the first place is to give the viewer a vicarious sense of what it might be like to be there experiencing the events depicted. But even if we, the onlookers, "can't understand, can't imagine," the pain and devastation of war and atrocity, even if it would be impossible, not to mention arrogant, to imagine that one could know, understand, or identify with the suffering depicted in such representations, this encounter with otherness need not be futile. Woolf and Berger might even suggest that, if we want to respond to depictions of suffering ethically, we cannot afford to make the incommunicability, the unthinkability of horrific pain into an excuse to throw up our hands and passively spectate because we can't understand what it's like to be the person who is suffering. It is precisely because we are not that suffering person that we have an opportunity and obligation to take action.

Moreover, there are ethical ways to read the rhetoricity of photos without insisting that they are neutral, unmediated representations of reality. For starters, Sontag overlooks the work of many Woolf scholars, such as Diane Gillespie and Maggie Humm, who have shown that Woolf herself was not naïve about the rhetoricity of photography.[48] Woolf's great aunt, Julia Margaret Cameron, was after all one of the best-known Victorian photographers, noted for staging her subjects in literary tableaux.[49] As Gillespie observes, "Photography, then, like several painted renditions of the same model, undoubtedly reinforced Virginia Woolf's idea that any one perception is incomplete and that only multiple angles of vision can begin to suggest the complex person."[50] Humm notes that the photographs under question in Sontag's critique – the photos of "dead bodies and ruined houses" – are not present in the text of *Three Guineas*, unlike the five photographs illustrating masculine sartorial excess that Woolf did include in the text.[51] Extending Michèle Barrett's suggestion that the five photographs call attention to the patriarchal performances of military, judicial, and professional men, Humm argues that "it is the absent photographs or, rather, the narrator's memory of these photographs, that in a major way shape the narrative of *Three Guineas* and its dense visual plenitude."[52] What is curiously missing in Sontag's argument is attention to the outrage-producing potential of the five photos that Woolf does include in the text. Furthermore, Sontag does not catch the irony of Woolf's exclusively textual representation of the absent photos, even as she says "those photographs are not an argument; they are simply a crude statement of fact addressed to the eye" (*TG*, p. 11). Indeed, given that the entire text of *Three Guineas* is a carefully crafted rhetorical performance, it's hard to imagine that Woolf was naïve about the rhetoricity of her repeated invocations of these absent photos of "dead bodies and ruined houses" (*TG*, p. 33).

Depicting the atrocity photographs narratively, rather than including examples from any number of propaganda photographs circulating in Britain during the Spanish Civil War, Woolf subtly undermines the presumption of photographic realism. As Jeanette Winterson suggests in *Art Objects*, "The doctrine of Realism saves us from a bad attack of Otherness" – an otherness that "challenges the 'I' that we are," if we are willing to engage with art *as* other, rather than as an extension of self.[53] For Winterson, the otherness of art is not an unbridgeable alterity, but rather an imperative – demanding effort from its interlocutor. And this effort is transformative – it enables "the realization of complex emotion," and makes it "possible to live in energetic space."[54] Winterson is chiefly critical of realism as an *expectation of reception*, rather than a *strategy of representation* – "admire me is the sub-text of so much of our looking; the demand put on art that it should reflect the reality of the viewer."[55] This "narcissistic" closed circuit of reception forecloses what for Winterson is the grand potential of art – to connect people across otherness.[56] Extending Winterson's dynamic of reception from its focus on art to a more general understanding of representation allows one to focus on the ethics of representing the other *as* other. An understanding of one's own location within othering and privileging discourses demands that we be able to recognize a relationship with the other that is dependent upon neither identification nor the premise of absolute alterity. An ethics of reception begins with this recognition, and not with the elusive, sentimental promise of empathetic identification.

Winterson emphasizes the public, communicative function of art, even as she seeks to detach it from the narcissistic demand that the work of art reflect the viewers' reality back to them. Identification may not be the only, or the best, way to encounter a representation, and that is why empathetic identification (contemplating what it might be like to walk in another's shoes, to paraphrase Nussbaum) falls short; it is still channeled through the "I" of the spectator. As David Román argues in his work on the performance troupe "Pomo Afro Homos," the group's insistence upon sexed, gendered, and raced particularities prevents many audience members from making easy identifications with the staged representations of black gay men: "The Pomos seem to indicate that the spectatorial process – for all audiences – involves a certain self-positioning. *Fierce Love* [a performance] forces viewers to locate their own positionality with the material staged."[57] Precisely because it resists the allure of identification, the Pomo Afro Homos' performance creates a *space* for the viewers to do the work of tracing the relationship between a depiction on the stage and their own different, but connected, particularities. A theatrical performance, because it takes place in a clearly defined space and time, may be more amenable to the possibility of creating the kind of energetic space for self-positioning than the two-dimensional form of photography. However, the practice of viewing images of atrocity (whether in one of the many public memorials that are part of the process of civic recognition, or in news exposés depicting torture in Abu Ghraib or genocide in Darfur) also takes place in space and time – the space and time of the spectator. Precisely because of their otherness, representations of suffering demand "self-positioning" on the part of the spectator, and ethical spectatorship depends on recognizing this demand.

SEEING STRUCTURAL VIOLENCE BEYOND THE "ETHNOGRAPHICALLY VISIBLE"

Barker explores the necessity for self-positioning in *Double Vision* – the story of a shell-shocked war correspondent, Stephen, who retreats to Northumbria in order to regroup after witnessing atrocities in Bosnia and the death of his friend, Ben, a war photographer, in Afghanistan. Ben's widow, Kate, a sculptor who is commissioned to construct a huge statue of the "risen Christ" for the small church in the same Northumbrian village, must both cope with her grief and heal from a near-fatal car crash. Stephen resolves to write a book (something along the lines of *Regarding the Pain of Others*) on the ethics of photographing suffering and atrocity. He wonders about his own role in disseminating images of violence: when does witnessing become voyeurism? When does recording and reporting violent events (executions, wars) become complicity, feeding the spectators' desire for more killing, revenge, atrocity? When do photographs, ostensibly the "guarantor[s] of reality," purposely mislead?[58]

Like many of Barker's shell-shocked protagonists, Stephen is haunted by a horrible memory. While on assignment in Sarajevo, Stephen and Ben had come across the corpse of a young woman who was raped and left to die in a squalid downtown apartment building:

Pictures, arguments, and empathy 131

In the corner of the landing, away from the danger of flying glass, a girl huddled on a mattress. She didn't speak or cry out or try to get away. Ben swung the beam along the wall until it found her face. Eyes wide open, skirt bunched up around her waist, her splayed thighs enclosing a blackness of blood and pain.[59]

This image more than any other preoccupies Stephen, although he has witnessed a number of gruesome events, from the exhumation of mass graves, to war, to the smoke and dust of lower Manhattan on September 11: "nothing else had ever affected him in the same way, although he had seen many worse things."[60] One cannot know why certain experiences trigger post-traumatic stress and others equally disturbing do not. A possible explanation may be that the rape of the girl crosses too many boundaries for Stephen, between "crime and war," domestic and foreign, personal and political:

He sat back on his heels. No telling whether this was a casual crime – a punter wanting his money back, a drug deal gone wrong – or a sectarian killing linked to the civil war. Increasingly crime and war shade into each other, Stephen thought. No difference to their victims, certainly, and not much either in the minds of the perpetrators. Patriot, soldier, revolutionary, freedom fighter, terrorist, murderer – cross section their brains at the moment of killing and the differences might prove hard to find.[61]

Throughout the course of the novel, which is set approximately four years after the scene, Stephen learns to reconstruct the boundaries that have been gutted by his traumatic experiences – especially the boundaries between witness, victim, and perpetrator. Boundary confusion between witness and participant is one of the ethical dilemmas he contemplates in his book. One of Stephen's motivations for writing the book is a remembered conversation with Ben on September 11. Struggling with the ethical impact of his own role as a photographer who chronicles the events but also contributes to a media frenzy that he suspects is part of the terrorists' plan, Ben confesses to Stephen, "That was designed to be a photo-opportunity, and what have I done? I've spent the whole bloody day photographing it. Along with everybody else. Because we can't escape from the need for a visual record. The appetite for spectacle. And they've used that against us, just as they have used our own technology against us."[62] Later, while discussing Goya's sketches of wartime atrocities, Stephen relates the gist of this conversation and his subsequent decision to write his book to Kate:

It's that argument that [Goya's] having with himself, all the time, between the ethical problems of showing the atrocities and yet the need to say, "Look, this is what's happening" ... and I thought, My God, we're still facing exactly the same problem. There's always this tension between wanting to show the truth, and yet being skeptical about what the effects of showing it are going to be.[63]

Eventually, Stephen regains his ability to live with that tension, without feeling that his boundaries have caved in, in part because he has gone through the effort of articulating the tension in his book.

Two of the supporting characters in the novel, Adam, a young boy with Asperger's syndrome, and Peter, a young man with borderline personality disorder, define the poles of potential responses to the suffering of others. The indicators for Asperger's are, according to the Yale Developmental Disabilities Clinic: "a. paucity of empathy; b. naive, inappropriate, one-sided social interaction, little ability to form friendships and consequent social isolation; c. pedantic and monotonic speech; [and] d. poor non-verbal communication."[64] The first indicator, "paucity of empathy," seems of most concern in Barker's use of Asperger's as metaphor.[65] Adam, Stephen's nephew, has difficulty empathizing with others. Describing Adam's disability, Justine, Stephen's lover, explains that:

"It's basically a sort of difficulty in seeing other people as people. Like if you were looking at this" – she pointed to the trees his headlights were revealing – "there wouldn't be any essential difference between me and the trees. So you can't change your perspective and see the situation from another person's point of view, because you can't grasp the fact that they have their own internal life, and they might be thinking something different from you."[66]

In other words, Adam cannot self-position in relation to others because he cannot identify with them. He is not able to develop a "sympathetic imagination," as Nussbaum would put it.[67]

Peter, on the other hand, is apparently suffering from borderline personality disorder, which Barker (somewhat aslant of psychiatric descriptions of the diagnosis) likens to a surfeit of identification. He cannot respect boundaries between himself and others. So for Adam, the difficulty is too much distinction between self and other, and for Peter, the difficulty is not enough. Discussing Peter's disturbingly obsessive writing and behavior, Stephen asks Justine:

"Is that your impression? That he's got problems dealing with boundaries between people?"
She thought for a moment. "It's not the way he sees it. He thinks he's got exceptional powers of empathy. And he hasn't, of course. What he does is dump his own emotions on to the other person and then he empathizes with himself."[68]

Pictures, arguments, and empathy 133

Read in the context of the novel's concern with the pathos-producing effects of visual representation, this conversation suggests that, for Barker, the key to "regarding the pain of others" is to find the proper balance between empathy – the ability to imagine one's self in another's position and to feel for that person – and appropriation – projecting one's self onto another's experience and narcissistically using it in order to feel for one's self. Finding that balance, for Barker, involves recognizing our own capacity to do violence, and our own potential vulnerability to violence. We have to admit, as Sontag suggests in her last essay, "Regarding the Torture of Others," that the photos *are* us, in all of our capacity for cruelty and indifference. But it is equally imperative to take a stand, and insist that they are *not* us. They are rather a potential we must recognize if we are to keep our capacity for cruelty in check.

Barker hints at the necessity for this recognition through her re-examination of religious iconography. At the beginning of the novel, Kate, though an atheist, enters the church of her friend the vicar, Alec Braithewaite, to thank him for recommending Peter as an assistant. She looks up, as she has done since her husband's funeral, at the "Green Man" carvings on the ceiling:

Images of the Green Man were everywhere these days. A secular world sifting through pagan images, like a rag-and-bone man grubbing about for something – anything – of value. A symbol of renewal, people said, but only because they didn't look. Some of these heads were so emaciated they were hardly more than skulls. Others vomited leaves, their eyes staring, panic-stricken above the choking mouth. No, she thought, wincing with pain as she craned to look at them, they were wonderfully done – some anonymous craftsman's masterwork – but they were figures of utter ruin.[69]

For Kate, the carvings are apotropaic, figures meant to ward off evil by representing it. They are kin to her own version of Green Man carvings, a series of plaster representations of the September 11 hijackers:

They were part of a sequence she'd started after 9/11, not based on Ben's photographs, or anybody else's for that matter, because nobody had been there to photograph what chiefly compelled her imagination: the young men at the controls who'd seized aeroplanes full of people and flown them into sides of buildings. There they were, lean, predatory, equally ready to kill or die. She thought the figures might be rather good in the end. They certainly frightened her.[70]

Both sets of apotropaic images allude to the possibility for violence within each of us. Barker points out the ubiquity of this potential through the character of Alec, who grapples with his own impulses through the discipline of his vocation: "He'd never been a peaceful man, though over the years he'd fought hard to control his anger. And sometimes all that repressed aggression had paid dividends, enabling him to forge bonds with young men newly released from prison, some of them violent."[71] Alec must confront his repressed aggression anew after his daughter Justine is attacked: "The fantasies of revenge hadn't gone. They clung like bats to the inner walls of his skull, and no amount of prayer would dislodge them. His first sight of Justine, slumped in the chair like a broken and abandoned doll, had only reinforced them."[72]

Kate, who is in the process of finishing her statue of "the Jesus of history," a figure bearing the marks of his suffering, speculates on Alec's internal struggle, musing that "Alec had always thought of himself as a good man. That made him sound smug and horrible, which he wasn't, but he did tend to assume that in the great war of good and evil he'd always be on the right side, whereas Kate couldn't help thinking real adult life starts when you admit the other possibility. 'We're all a *bit* like that, aren't we?'"[73] For that reason, her Christ is "bruised, cut, swollen. Beaten up. Somebody with a talent for such things had given him a right going over. This was the Jesus of history. And we know what happens in history: the strong take what they can and the weak endure what they must, and the dead emphatically do not rise."[74]

Physician-anthropologist Paul Farmer describes the form of social organization where "the strong take what they can and the weak endure what they must" as "structural violence":

Structural violence is violence exerted systematically – that is, indirectly – by everyone who belongs to a certain social order: hence the discomfort these ideas provoke in a moral economy still geared to pinning praise or blame on individual actors. In short, the concept of structural violence is intended to inform the study of the social machinery of oppression. Oppression is a result of many conditions, not the least of which reside in consciousness. We will therefore need to examine, as well, the roles played by the erasure of historical memory and other forms of desocialization as enabling conditions of structures that are both "sinful" and ostensibly "nobody's fault."[75]

Kate's art, as a medium that traces the "historical memory" of suffering, but is not wholly defined by it, presents a visual acknowledgment of the structural violence that creates conditions conducive to widespread suffering. Stephen's creative work – his book on the ethics of war reporting – is similarly attentive to structural violence, and is aware of our potential, as consumers of images, to be complicit in systems of structural violence, even as we decry its symptoms.

In answer to Sontag's statement that "We don't get it. We can't truly imagine what it [is] like" to be in a situation of extreme violence, Barker and Woolf encourage self-positioning and introspection on the part of the spectator. Both insist that we must nevertheless investigate and respond to the causes of suffering. Woolf in particular is less naïve than Sontag suggests, for Woolf's imagined response to the photographs of "dead bodies and ruined houses" is at the very least embedded within an intricate rhetorical scaffolding that insists on both tracing our political investments in pain-producing practices, and acknowledging the particularities of power, class, gender, and nation that inform them. It may be the case that a representation of pain can't help us to know what it is like to suffer, to live through war or atrocity, but such images can inspire us to acknowledge the connections between our own locations within systems of structural violence and the atrocities depicted in ever more "photos of dead bodies and ruined houses."

CHAPTER 5

The promise and peril of metic *intimacy*

And so, for me, London became a kind of inferno of pleasure and madness.

– Hanif Kureishi[1]

At the end of Barker's *Double Vision*, Stephen regains a sense of emotional equilibrium through his intimate relationship with his young lover, Justine.[2] For Barker, helpful or healing intimacy involves a successful negotiation of borders, which must be permeable enough to allow a person who is "ec-static" or "beside oneself" (to use Butler's terms) to open up to another person's demonstration of shared humanity, but not so porous as to make one overwhelmingly vulnerable to destabilizing sensations or exploitation by others who do not or cannot respect boundaries.[3] While Barker explores the role intimacy can play as a remedy for the emotional numbness that accompanies what we now call posttraumatic stress disorder (PTSD), there are other, less therapeutically oriented functions of intimacy. "Intimate life," as Lauren Berlant and Michael Warner note, "is the endlessly cited *elsewhere* of political public discourse, a promised haven that distracts citizens from the unequal conditions of their political and economic lives, consoles them for the damaged humanity of mass society, and shames them for any divergence between their lives and the intimate sphere that is alleged to be simple personhood."[4] However, intimacy is more than a consolation prize for the indignity of submitting to dominant ideology. Warner and Berlant also suggest that certain forms of intimacy can provide the occasion for transforming public culture by exceeding normative constructions of identity and belonging.

Clearly, not all intimate counterpublics challenge exclusionary norms. The homoerotic intimacy cultivated in early twentieth-century German *Männerbünde* (avowedly antifeminist and anti-Semitic all-male youth groups) for example, led to a far different form of "world making" than the forms of intimacy celebrated by Berlant and Warner.[5] One can't presume in advance that the formation of intimate counterpublics will automatically lead to the "transformation of . . . social norms" that Warner and Berlant celebrate, but some forms of intimacy *do* open up the possibility for connections that test and transform exclusive social formations.[6] In what follows, I examine the productive intimacies and transformative counterpublics that Woolf and Kureishi depict in their early and late twentieth-century work, arguing that the fictional heterogeneous communities they create illuminate possibilities for fostering what Paul Gilroy describes as "conviviality," forms of "cohabitation and interaction that have made multiculture an ordinary feature of social life in Britain's urban areas and in postcolonial cities elsewhere."[7]

Because intimacy reminds us of our vulnerability and dependence on others, intimate alliances across multiple axes of difference can help convivial cohabitants to cultivate humane responses to the complex dynamics of national belonging and exclusion.[8] A sense of shared vulnerability may provide a starting point for shared ethics, if that vulnerability is experienced as a point of connection, rather than an occasion for defensive retrenchment. As Butler argues: "That we can be injured, that others can be injured, that we are subject to death at the whim of another, are all reasons for both fear and grief. What is less certain, however, is whether the experiences of vulnerability and loss have to lead straightaway to military violence and retribution. There are other passages" (*PL*, p. xii). The queer *metic* relationships that Kureishi and Woolf depict create models for imagining these "other passages" by providing examples of intimacies based on recognition of vulnerability, interdependence, and impermanence, rather than on domination or normativity.

Such alliances are "translocal" in the anthropological sense – forging affinities that connect groups of people who are geographically dispersed, yet who share a sense of community fostered by diasporic migration, shared media, and/or common extranational interests such as religious affiliation or same-sex desire.[9] Queer subjects, who in the early twentieth century often did not have standing as national subjects unless they disavowed the very qualities and desires that cast them as non-normative, may have formed such translocal connections as a way to counter their official non-recognition in national discourse. These translocal connections could be imagined as forms of "queer cosmopolitanism" (with an emphasis on "queer" as antiheteronormative, rather than an identity category).

Cosmopolitanism has undergone a critical reassessment lately, especially in the midst of escalated American imperialism, or what might be more accurately termed heightened American self-awareness of American imperialism. Beacon Press, for example, recently reissued Nussbaum's collection, *For Love of Country*, with a new (2002) introduction responding directly to the moral choices confronting Americans in the wake of September 11.[10] Citing Rabindranath Tagore's *The Home and the World*, Nussbaum suggests that "Only the cosmopolitan stance of the landlord Nikhil . . . has the promise of transcending these [caste, class, and religious] differences, because only this stance asks us to give our first allegiance to what is morally good – and that which, being good, I can commend as such to all human beings."[11] "Cosmopolitan," however, does not accurately describe queer, translocal intimacies because the term "world citizen" implies a mode of belonging to the imaginary community of the world *polis*.[12] Although the possibilities for non-heteronormative citizenship are putatively expanding in the early twenty-first century, in the early twentieth century, it would be more accurate to describe queer persons as *metics* – resident aliens of the *polis* who are vulnerable to the prevailing whims of political power. Dissenting *metics*, such as the ancient speechwriter Lycias, could have their patronage revoked and their goods seized.[13] *Metics* therefore, although often privileged and respected, remain in the city on sufferance.

It would be far too ambitious to suggest that the translocal intimacies depicted in Woolf's and Kureishi's work are *the* antidote to fascist or fundamentalist extremes of nationalism. However, in their writing, they describe *metic* intimacies that function as alternatives to the nationalistic bonds that can lead to war, racism, and fanatical violence. Both writers imagine the transformative potential (although Kureishi is aware, too, of the false idealism) of heterogeneous urban communities, such as the community that the Stephens created after their move from 22 Hyde Park Gate to the mixed society that Woolf describes in "Old Bloomsbury" ("OB"-*MB*, pp. 181–201). Woolf elaborates on the potential of heterogeneous intimacy further in her description of the air-raid-interrupted dinner party attended by arguably *metic* characters in the 1917 section of *The Years*.[14] That said, Woolf is far from the perfect anticolonialist: a simple comparison of the gatherings depicted in her novels with those depicted by Kureishi sixty years later is enough to demonstrate that the counterpublics she imagines are relatively homogeneous. And, as I note below, Woolf's flirtation with the Argentinian writer Victoria Ocampo further complicates any understanding of her commitment to truly global cosmopolitanism or translocal intimacy. Nevertheless, Woolf's depictions of non-violent, non-identitarian affiliations across difference illustrate the potential of queer *metic* discourse to traverse violent nationalisms. This is a discourse that Kureishi continues and complicates.

BLOOMSBURY AS *METIC* METROPOLIS

Woolf most conspicuously articulates her deep suspicion of what Butler calls "military violence and retribution" in *Three Guineas*. As I noted in my introduction, Woolf's declaration, "as a woman I want no country. As a woman my country is the whole world" transforms the negative condition of not-belonging (I have no country because marriage trumps nationality) into productive inspiration for affiliation across borders (I belong to the world, and therefore am accountable to it beyond the provincialism of my own borders) (*TG*, p. 109). Woolf also suggests that love of country might, too, provide the occasion for transnational accountability and generosity:

And when if, when reason has said its say, still some obstinate emotion remains, some love of England dropped into a child's ears by the cawing of rooks in an elm tree, by the splash of waves on a beach, or by English voices murmuring nursery rhymes, this drop of pure, if irrational emotion she will make serve her to give to England first what she desires of peace and freedom for the whole world. (*TG*, pp. 109–10)

Woolf's call for internationalism in this instance is sparked by pastoral memories – the sounds of birds and waves and nursery rhymes – that evoke the countryside, at St. Ives, perhaps. But later, in the midst of the Battle of Britain, it is her love for London that Woolf invokes in her diary (*D-V*, February 2, 1940). London is Woolf's "England" because of its cultural vibrancy, its pace, its beauty, and the abundance of humanity that one can survey from the top of an omnibus or a stroll through the park. It is also the setting, for Woolf, of world-expanding intimacies, honest conversation, and intellectual exchange.

Such intimacies were fostered by her move to Bloomsbury in 1904 after her father's death. Woolf credits this move with providing an "extraordinary increase of space" both literally and metaphorically ("OB"-*MB*, p. 185). In her memoir "Old Bloomsbury," Woolf carefully distinguishes physical proximity from the new world-expanding intimacies possible in 46 Gordon Square. She describes 22 Hyde Park Gate as teeming with family members "11 people aged between eight and sixty" whose main activity seems to be hoarding possessions and secrets ("OB"-*MB*, p. 182). Beginning her memoir where "22 Hyde Park Gate" left off, with George "fling[ing] himself on [her] bed," Woolf suggests that the claustrophobic Victorian mores that made intimacy across difference (of generation, gender, or class) difficult, did not prevent sexual encounters, but rather kept them hidden from public view ("OB"-*MB*, p. 182).

By contrast, the intimacy between men and women, straight and queer, in Bloomsbury shed "a flood of light" on the unspoken secrets of the previous generation. Woolf suggests that frankness about sexual matters, symbolized by Lytton Strachey's entering the room, pointing to a stain on Vanessa's dress and inquiring if it was semen, tore down barriers to intimacy and "revolutionized" "old sentimental views of marriage" ("OB"-*MB*, p. 196). "So there was now nothing that one could not say," Woolf writes, "nothing that one could not do, at 46 Gordon Square. It was, I think, a great advance in civilization" ("OB"-*MB*, p. 196).

Woolf again makes the connection between this sort of openness about sex, intimacy in conversation, and breaking down debilitating parochialisms in *The Years*, where the two most obviously "queer" members of the Pargiter family – Sara and Edward – are linked by their reading and translating of *Antigone* (*TY*, pp. 135–37). Antigone, as I noted in my introduction, describes herself as a *metic* after her defiance of Creon leads him to cast her out to be buried alive in a tomb outside the city walls.[15] In the 1907 section of *The Years*, Sara, who is outside heterosexual circuits of desire and exchange (her bodily deformity signifying her difference from her properly heterosexual sister), reads Edward's translation of *Antigone* while heterosexual couples from a late party next door dance and mingle in the courtyard below her flat.[16] She falls asleep imagining that she is being buried alive like the protagonist of the play – "She was buried alive. The tomb was a brick mound. There was just room for her to lie straight out. Straight out in the brick tomb" (*TY*, pp. 135–37). The sounds of heterosexual flirting from the courtyard and the subsequent entrance of her sister and mother (arriving home from a ball) wake Sara, who is curious about their evening out. Despite her attempts to talk with them about the spectacle, Sara is admonished to resume her Antigonean position: "'But you must go to sleep, Sal,' [her mother] protested. 'What did the doctor say? Lie straight, lie still, he said.' She pushed her back on to the pillows" (*TY*, p. 141).

Ten years later, in the 1917 section of the novel, Sara is shown again in a sepulchral space, but this time one that allows for movement and conversation among a gathering of *metic* characters who dine together in a London basement while taking refuge from an air raid. The intimacy between characters at the gathering is reminiscent of the scenes Woolf describes in "Old Bloomsbury," but the characters' recognition of shared vulnerability as the bombers pass directly overhead makes them even more acutely aware of the thing that makes them alike across their differences – the potentiality of death. As Eleanor observes of the casual dinner, "A little blur had come round the edges of things. It was the wine; it was the war. Things seemed to have lost their skins to be freed from some surface hardness" (*TY*, p. 287). Nicholas, whose foreignness and homosexuality mark him as a potential outsider to the group, explicitly voices their shared vulnerability, remarking, after the raid passes, "Ah, but we were frightened . . . Look – how pale we all are" (*TY*, p. 292).

Both Nicholas, the queer outsider, and Eleanor, the spinster (also outside heteronormative circuitry), articulate a desire to imagine a "new world" in response to the threat of the air raid. Stephen Barber analyzes the intimacies between gay men and spinsters in Woolf's work, suggesting that the "conspiracies" between them open up new possibilities for "a critically queer technology of self."[17] While this may be so, Woolf is also gesturing to something beyond the self, to the possibility of queer world making, as Berlant and Warner call it,[18] a resilient connectivity that exceeds subjectivity, and, in the words of Nicholas, "wishes to expand; to adventure; to form – new combinations" (*TY*, p. 296). The air raid scene thus suggests that the possibility of this "new world" depends upon the characters' ability to form intimacies that gesture to translocal, suprafamilial ways of being in the world. As if to reinforce this message, at the close of the air raid scene, Eleanor catches Sara and Nicholas, who have become queer intimates, exchanging telling banter:

"Cease to laugh at me for once, Sara," Nicholas was saying as he put on his coat.
  "And cease to lecture me," she said, opening the front door.
Renny smiled at Eleanor as they stood for a moment by the perambulator.
  "Educating themselves!" he said. (*TY*, p. 299)

Woolf indicates the limits of Sara's "education" in the final section of the novel, juxtaposing Eleanor's expansive, cosmopolitan vision (she has just returned from India) with Sara's anti-Semitic comments about her neighbor, "the Jew," with whom she shares a bathroom in her cramped London apartment building (*TY*, p. 339). Eleanor's class position (she is wealthy enough to live in a flat with a new "shower-bath" *en suite*) insulates her from the close proximity to others that occasions Sara's negative remarks about her neighbor, whom Sara and her cousin North can hear "coughing and clearing his throat" through the thin walls of her apartment (*TY*, pp. 308, 340).[19] As Maren Linett notes, Woolf associates Jewishness, through a chain of familial and political circumstances, with her own vulnerability and "imperiled" intellectual privacy.[20] Sara's reaction to the imagined invasion of privacy signified by the sounds of her Jewish neighbor's bathing calls to mind the phobic reactions to boundary crossing or mixing that, as I mentioned in Chapter 2, characterize fascist rhetoric. Woolf complicates this eruption of fascist allusion through Eleanor, who remembers fondly the expansive intimacy of the air raid dinner – "sitting round a wooden packing case, they had drunk to a new world" (*TY*, p. 329). Still basking in the reverie, Eleanor sees a newspaper with the image of a fascist dictator "gesticulating" and angrily tears up the story and flings it on the floor (*TY*, pp. 329–30). Sara's and Eleanor's attitudes don't cancel each other out, or make the anti-Semitic overtones of the bath scene less problematic, but rather they illustrate the coexisting promise and peril of *metic* intimacy, where vulnerability can inspire compassion or defensive contempt.

ON NOT COMING (TO ARGENTINA) WITH VICTORIA OCAMPO

As the above example suggests, Woolf was probably more ambivalent about challenges to normative behavior and belief than her many exquisitely articulated arguments against injustice would have us believe. Such is the case in Woolf's largely epistolary relationship with Victoria Ocampo, an Argentinian feminist intellectual with whom she corresponded in the 1930s. Woolf flirts with the potential of queer *metic* intimacy in her letters, but never quite follows through with the promise her flirtatious discourse intimates. Since Woolf's correspondence with Ocampo reads something like a case study of literary relationships between a *metic* woman at the center of empire and another on the outskirts of empire, the dynamics of that relationship reveal some of the limits of translocal affiliation, even between like-minded political subjects.

The scholarly treatment of their relationship reveals as well the traces of first-worldism in literary criticism today. It is still possible to be a Virginia Woolf scholar and know next to nothing of Victoria Ocampo, except perhaps that she was a wealthy South American ("the Sibyl Colefax of Argentina" Woolf says in a letter to Hugh Walpole [*L-III*, 5 Dec. 1934]), a beautiful woman "ripe & rich" "the colour of an apricot under glass" (*D-V*, 26 Nov. 1934). It is also fairly common knowledge among Woolf scholars that Woolf met Ocampo at an exhibition of Man Ray photographs in late 1934, and that Ocampo angered Woolf by introducing Gisèle Freund to Woolf in 1939 so that Freund could take her now iconic color photos of Woolf (*D-V*, 24 June 1939).[21] The "lesser-known" facts about Ocampo are that she was the founding editor of the literary journal *Sur*, that she persuaded Borges to translate two of Woolf's novels into Spanish, and that she maintained friendships with Rabindranath Tagore, Gabriela Mistral, José Ortega y Gasset, Adrienne Monnier, André Malraux, Albert Camus, and Igor Stravinsky. She was also the founder of the Argentine Women's Union, appointed to be an observer of the Nuremberg trials, imprisoned by Peron, and asked to be the Argentinian ambassador to India. The list of her accomplishments is impressive for someone who is, in Woolfian circles, known mainly for bringing Gisèle Freund round for tea and annoying photography.[22]

On the other hand, it is *not* possible to be a scholar of Victoria Ocampo and know nothing about Virginia Woolf. Ocampo considered Woolf a beautiful woman and interesting friend, but also thought of her as a formidable intellect, a fellow publisher, another "educated man's daughter" who might understand her own efforts to resist patriarchal domination (*TG*, p. 9). Ocampo not only wrote essays on Woolf's work, but oversaw Borges' translation and publication of *Room of One's Own* and *Orlando*. Both of her English-language biographers (Doris Meyer and Patricia Owen Steiner) include several-page sections on the importance of Woolf's intellectual influence on Ocampo, and Meyer even includes a translation of Ocampo's essay "Virginia Woolf in my Memory" in the appendix of her biography.[23]

"If there is anyone in the world who can give me courage and hope, it is *you*," Ocampo wrote to Woolf in early 1935:

By the simple fact of being who you are and thinking as you think. I would be ungrateful if I said that I had never been encouraged, etc. I have some friends (men) who think I am gifted to the point of genius and who have said so and written so. But these declarations have always left me cold and unbelieving in myself. They are impure. You understand what I mean . . . Men always (or almost always) judge a woman according to themselves, according to the reactions they experience in contact with her (even spiritually). Above all, if she is not deformed or unpleasant-looking. It is their particular fatality . . . They cannot *honestly* serve as guide marks.[24]

The misunderstanding over Freund's photo shoot notwithstanding, Ocampo makes it clear in her letter that, for her, Woolf was more than a celebrity with a photogenic face.

After they met in 1934, Woolf, on the other hand, immediately began a correspondence that figured Ocampo as the beautiful exotic suitor and rival to Vita Sackville-West for Woolf's affections. In a letter to Sackville-West dated 19 December 1934, Woolf goes so far as to profess that "I am in love with Victoria Okampo" [sic] and attempts to pique Vita's jealousy by mentioning Ocampo's gifts of orchids and roses in a postscript to a subsequent letter. Woolf's letters reiterate a thematic pattern that is familiar in her work from *The Voyage Out* to *Orlando* and *The Waves* – linking courtship with exotic otherness, risk, and the ultimate impossibility of requited passion. Perhaps recalling her childhood interest in butterfly collecting, Woolf infuses her flirtatious correspondence with repeated references to butterflies. Thanking her for a gift of orchids, Woolf writes, "You are too generous. And I must compare you to a butterfly if you send me these gorgeous purple butterflies. I opened the box and thought 'this is what a garden in South America looks like!'" (*L-III*, 27 Nov. 1934).

Ocampo doesn't immediately respond to the butterfly motif, and there are indications, noted by Meyer, that Ocampo may have unsuccessfully attempted to convey a less fanciful image of Argentina to Woolf. Her letters to Woolf tend to focus on writing, on language and creativity and the difficulty of expressing oneself as a woman. This is not to say that there are not seductive elements in Ocampo's letters, but that these moments have nothing to do with the muteness of the exotic and everything to do with Ocampo's "voracious" desire to be an agent of language, of creative production (and of love):

Please, Virginia, don't think for an instant that I am trying to flatter you. *I hate it.* When you spoke yesterday of K. Mansfield and I said you were not to be compared with her (or others, such as I know them) it is because, though I can perfectly see their charm, they *mean* very little to me. I don't like to eat and not be nourished. I am a very *voracious* person. And I believe *hunger* is all. I am not ashamed of being hungry. Don't you think love is our hunger to love? (I am speaking of love with a capital).
[And she continues in French]
 I mean to say that our hunger is a very important element. That things don't truly exist for us until, and because, we are hungry for them and then only in proportion to the intensity of that hunger. The secret of a Picasso is that he has a hunger (a lion's hunger) of painting.[25]

It is only later, in October 1935, that Ocampo indulges Woolf's butterfly fantasies, sending her a glass display case containing a number of preserved South American butterflies. In her thank you note, Woolf even admits to her tendencies to exoticize South America – "Every time I go out of my door I make up another picture of South America. And no doubt you'd be surprised if you could see your house as I arrange it. It is always grilling hot, and there is a moth alighted in a silver flower. And this too in broad daylight" (*L-III*, 29 October 1935).

As their correspondence continues, Ocampo is transformed in Woolf's prose from the bearer of butterflies and orchids to the fragile, beautiful insect itself. In a 1938 letter, Woolf writes, "Your butterflies hang over my front door, always brilliant; wings stretched, flying, like you: but pinned; unlike you" (*L-III*, 7 October 1938). The figure of the butterfly for Woolf is dual – the object of curiosity and cruelty – the child's wonder and the taxonomic zeal of the collector. There is something of this duality in Woolf's epistolary relationship with Ocampo, which is saturated with the rhetoric of invitation and refusal. In earlier letters, South America is invited, as a metaphorical setting to situate Woolf's attraction to Ocampo, but is literally refused, as Woolf admits to being too tied to England to actually go to South America and experience it (and Ocampo) in the flesh (*L-III*, 2 May 1936). Although Woolf figures Ocampo as the elusive one (always flitting, hard to pin down), it is Woolf who won't be caught.

This correspondence suggests the limits of Woolf's anticolonial, antinationalist vision, for even as she hints at intimacy with the South American other, she positions her rhetorically as a specimen to be collected and admired. With Ocampo, then, Woolf may be participating in the kind of colonizing gaze that Jane Marcus describes in her reading of Woolf's passing comment on "a very fine negress" in *A Room of One's Own*: "Woolf's eye and that of her narrator may be indulging that European visual lust to see and categorize the Other. As Ian Jeffrey puts it, 'the camera became a colonizer.'"[26]

The link between specimen collecting and an imperializing gaze is not all that far-fetched in Woolf. In *The Waves*, for example, the curiosity/cruelty of the butterfly collector is connected to other slippages between exploration and imperial conquest. Louis (acutely conscious of his Australian difference) likens the cricketing boys, who are always falling into step behind the likes of Percival, to little imperialists (and little sadists who rip the wings off of butterflies):

They are always forming into fours and marching in troops with badges on their caps; they salute simultaneously passing the figure of their general. How majestic is their order, how beautiful is their obedience! If I could follow, if I could be with them I would sacrifice all I know. But they also leave butterflies trembling with their wings pinched off, they throw dirty pocket-handkerchiefs clotted with blood screwed up into corners. They make little boys sob in dark passages. They have big red ears that stand out under their caps. Yet that is what we wish to be, Neville and I.[27]

There is an interesting oscillation between repulsion and desire in this passage, as if everything would be fine if Louis could only be one of the bullies making little boys sob in dark passages, instead of, presumably, one of the boys left sobbing, one of the butterflies left trembling with his wings pinched off.

This image of the butterfly with pinched wings is strikingly similar to an image that Woolf uses to refer to herself as a fifteen-year-old girl in Hyde Park Gate, awakening to a consciousness that is separate from her Victorian childhood but also to a consciousness of cruelty, suffering, and dashed expectations for happiness after the death of Stella so soon after her marriage, so soon after the death of Julia:

But I was thinking; feeling; living; those two lives that the two halves symbolized with the intensity, the muffled intensity, which a butterfly or moth feels when with its sticky tremulous legs and antennae it pushes out of the chrysalis and emerges and sits quivering beside the broken case for a moment; its wings still creased; its eyes dazzled, incapable of flight.

Anyone, whether fifteen or not, whether sensitive or not, must have felt something very acute, merely from what had happened . . .

All this [latent mourning for her mother in the background of Stella's death] had toned my mind and made it apprehensive; made it I suppose unnaturally responsive to Stella's happiness, and the promise it held for her and for us of escape from that gloom; when once more unbelievably – incredibly – as if one had been violently cheated of some promise; more than that, brutally told not to be such a fool as to hope for things; I remember saying to myself after she died: "But this is impossible; things aren't, can't be, like this" – the blow, the second blow of death, struck on me; tremulous, filmy-eyed as I was, with my wings still creased, sitting there on the edge of my broken chrysalis. ("SP"-*MB*, p. 124)

This image of herself as a bludgeoned butterfly on the edge of her broken chrysalis provides a clue to Woolf's attraction-avoidance behavior with Ocampo, especially if hope of "escape from gloom" carries with it the threat of being "violently cheated."

Robin Hackett, in her reading of "Sapphic primitivism," suggests that exoticism in Woolf's writing indicates displacement of lesbian desire. It "reflects a structure of imagination, for Woolf, in which lesbianism is consistent with a nonspecific colonial worldview and inconsistent with British middle-class whiteness."[28] Hackett reads the setting of *The Voyage Out* in South America as Woolf's early attempt to "experiment as a writer with the possibility of writing a young female protagonist out of a marriage plot. Woolf's experiment in *The Voyage Out* doesn't work: she still has to kill off Rachel to keep her out of a heterosexual marriage."[29] Unlike Woolf's protagonist, Ocampo did succeed in "writing herself out of the marriage plot" – not by killing herself or remaining in a chaste and restrictive marriage, but by obtaining a legal separation from her husband, Monaco Estrada. This was a difficult and scandalous thing to do at the time in Argentina, but Ocampo's life is a testament to the survivability of a woman who chose to be the author of her own escape strategy. And this perhaps is where Ocampo was an enigma for Woolf, for she was not only the socialite, not only the woman writer trying to find expression in a society where men were literally telling her that "Woman can't paint, women can't write" (*TL*, p. 48). She was an energetic organizer who arrived at solutions to gendered injustices. Nevertheless, one might say that the fantasy of Ocampo functions as a fetish for Woolf – preserving the *possibility* of desire, while warding off its *fulfillment* which, if we think back on the bludgeoned chrysalis, carries with it the threat of disaster – of happiness being snatched away just at the moment that it seems secured.

In this context, the flirtatious invitation-and-refusal structure of Woolf's correspondence with Ocampo is a way of keeping things alive, of staving off the end, the exhaustion of possibility. Following Adam Phillips we might say that flirtation serves as a form of rhetorical "tickling" – a way of giving/experiencing pleasure that does not have an end in mind.[30] "In the elaborate repertoire of intrusions, what is the quality – that is to say, the fantasy – of the experience?" Phillips asks of the "elaborate repertoire of intrusions" that constitute tickling.[31] He concludes that tickling involves

> often frenetic contact that so quickly reinstates a distance, only equally quickly to create another invitation . . . Does it not highlight, this delightful game, the impossibility of satisfaction and of reunion, with its continual reenactment of the irresistible attraction and the inevitable repulsion of the object, in which final satisfaction is frustration?[32]

Woolf engages in a "continual reenactment" of attraction and repulsion through her refusal of Ocampo's invitation to know her and to know Argentina, thus keeping her fantasy of the different, multicoloured, "ripe and rich" woman and land alive. In doing so, Woolf keeps the possibility of desire alive and, as an added enticement, her flirtation with Ocampo functions to stir the embers with Vita as well: "I had to stop Victoria Ocampo from sending me orchids," Woolf writes to Vita at the end of 1934. "I opened the letter to say this, in hope of annoying you" (*L-III*, 29 December 1934).

This brings us back to the story about Ocampo that most Woolfians know – her introducing Freund to Woolf so that Freund might ask Woolf to sit for her photographs. This scenario reverses the colonizing gaze described by Marcus. Ocampo, the colonial other, has come to London to collect multicolored images of the English writer in her native habitat. Woolf dislikes being collected as a specimen of European artists in Freund's photography. The tables have been turned, and the butterfly becomes the collector, a move that Woolf may resent – not simply because of the shift in power dynamics that this bespeaks – but because the reciprocity of Ocampo's gesture brings desire too close to home for its survival.

ENGLISHMAN BORN AND BRED . . . ALMOST

Kureishi takes *metic* intimacy even farther than Woolf, in ways that are potentially more troubling and transformative than Woolf's fictional and epistolary encounters. Central to his representation of this peril and potential is the multiethnic, postimperial contact zone of London. In *The Black Album*, for example, the protagonist, Shahid, lives in a crowded, thin-walled flat (much like Sara's) in a heterogeneous neighborhood that is similar to Sara's "Polluted city, unbelieving city, city of dead fish and worn-out frying-pans" (*TY*, p. 340). Shahid, although distressed by the poverty of his neighborhood, does not react to his surroundings with fearful disgust as Sara does. The heterogeneity of the city, rather, is a resource for him. His apartment building in London is "filled with Africans, Irish people, Pakistanis, and even a group of English students," and the very odors of "dope," "bargain aftershave, and boiled goat" that circulate the building are described as informational, rather than annoying, causing "the wallpaper to droop from the walls like ancient scrolls" (*TBA*, p. 9).

London is similarly depicted in *Sammy and Rosie Get Laid*. The film shows us a city that is complex, heterogeneous, and on the edge of chaos. Near the middle of the film, Rafi, a member of the Pakistani elite who is haunted by his past ties to political oppression and torture, urges his son Sammy to leave his neighborhood to go "home" to Pakistan, where he will be rich, famous, and respected. Rather than acquiesce to nostalgia for a homeland that was never his, Sammy refuses Rafi's conflation of home and nation, explaining that neither he nor his wife Rosie "are English; we're Londoners, you see."[33] Gayatri Spivak reads in Sammy's identification with London "all the overdetermination of the migrant diaspora

The promise and peril of metic intimacy

rather than the diasporic postcolonial."[34] For Spivak, the city is a staging ground for negotiation of "dominant-subordinate interraciality" that is "not a cultural exchange, but a moving target based on the city – *civitas* (for civil-ity rather than civilization), *polis* (for street politics rather than the political system)."[35] While Spivak describes Sammy, an Englishman of Pakistani heritage, as a "migrant" to distinguish his status from postcolonial subjects (both subaltern and elite), the term *metic* describes his situation more accurately, since Sammy does not move about, as we might expect a migrant to do, but remains located in and attached to his birthplace.[36] This does not mean that Sammy's identification as a Londoner translates into an unqualified identification with Britishness, but rather that the heterogeneity of the metropolis has an undermining effect on understandings of identities based on race, nation, and imperial domination.

Even so, the "street politics" of the city make clear that the politics of racism and imperial domination still operate in Britain. The opening scene of the film emphasizes the perils of living in the metropolitan contact zone, as we see an elderly black woman shot by white London policemen who invade her home in a botched raid. The shooting triggers a social upheaval – several nights of rioting in the neighborhood. Although the shooting is an "accident," like far too many "accidental" police shootings of black persons, it is an "accident" embedded in larger meaning-making systems – the conjunction of racial and class-based ideologies that construct the black British community as dangerous and in need of policing. While the "accident" triggers an upheaval that may create the potential for new communities to emerge, the film is ambivalent about whether that change will bring about a more survivable community or the same lethal policing and unrest.

The new social configurations that do emerge in the aftermath of the uprising are represented sexually (through different configurations of interracial and cross-class sex) and through the "queer domesticity" of two dinner parties.[37] Silver and Asha Sen both note the importance of the image of Woolf to Sammy's and Rosie's understanding of London.[38] Sen argues that "while Sammy's academic description of London shares similarities with Rosie's admiration of Virginia Woolf, it is displaced by the Woolf-inspired gender politics practiced by Rosie and her friends."[39] For Sen, "Woolf's politics contain no space for Rafi and drive him out into the public world of race riots where he is given a public identity based on Danny's perception of him as a great leader."[40] Silver, on the other hand, suggests that the image of Woolf in the film is polysemous: "what does the prominence of her image in this distinctly political film suggest? Does she preside over it as modernist, as feminist, as pacifist, as highbrow, as sapphist, as suicide, as failed liberal anti-imperialist?"[41] Silver answers her own questions with a careful "all of the above," but adds that in all cases, the image of Woolf framed by the flames of the urban riot is associated with feelings of terror.[42] I would suggest that this image also represents the interiorization of political violence, which is often peripheral to the domestic space figured in Woolf's novels.[43] In *Sammy and Rosie Get Laid*, latent haunting becomes manifest, as the ghost of a tortured Pakistani man follows Rafi through London, refusing to allow him to forget the violence that made possible his own position as part of the postcolonial elite. The latent becomes manifest in the social gatherings depicted in the film as well, as the people excluded from Mrs. Dalloway's party — the lesbian Miss Kilman, the immigrant Rezia, the colonial subjects of Peter Walsh's India — appear in the center of the action, rather than on the periphery of the story. In short, Sammy and Rosie's London becomes a gathering place for *metics* — those who nearly belong to the *polis*, but not quite. The status of the *metic* is different from that of the postcolonial elite (represented by Rafi) or the postcolonial subaltern (represented by the ghost). *Sammy and Rosie Get Laid* nevertheless makes clear that the *metic* status of someone like Sammy is predicated on the violence that precedes him — political violence in former imperial locations, and his father's exile and death in the putative "homeland."

Kureishi further explores the ambivalence of *metic* status in his first novel, *The Buddha of Suburbia*, which begins with the caveat:

My name is Karim Amir, and I am an Englishman born and bred, almost. I am often considered to be a funny kind of Englishman, a new breed as it were, having emerged from two old histories. But I don't care — Englishman I am (though not proud of it), from the South London suburbs and going somewhere. Perhaps it is the odd mixture of continents and blood, of here and there, of belonging and not, that makes me restless and easily bored. Or perhaps it was being brought up in the suburbs that did it. (*BS*, p. 3)

Rhetorically, this very declaration of Englishness mirrors the structural ambivalence that Karim lives in his everyday performance of English subjecthood. On the one hand, his Englishness is anchored by an assertive appeal to blood and birthright — "I am an Englishman born and bred." On the other hand, his subtle caveat — "almost" — calls attention to his status as the marked ethnic supplement to unmarked others' presumption of unproblematic national belonging. Wavering in his unproblematic assertion, he suggests that blood and birthright might be more of a marker of diasporic status than belonging – "perhaps it is the odd mixture of continents and blood, of here and there, of belonging and not, that makes me restless and easily bored." But he immediately undercuts the presumed influence of blood by appealing to the contingencies and banalities of birthplace "perhaps it was being brought up in the suburbs that did it" (*BS*, p. 3). Karim's rhetorical balancing act indicates his personal ambivalence about being English at a time when white supremacist groups such as the National Front were trumpeting their exclusionary, racist forms of hypernationalist rhetoric. Moreover, it demonstrates the "double writing" that Homi Bhabha associates with the nation's constitution of itself as a "People" – through the pedagogical appeal to archaic sameness projected onto the past (tradition), and the performative "temporality of the in-between" associated with contingency, particularity, and cultural difference within the heterogeneous space of the nation.[44]

For Bhabha, the "people" "represent the cutting edge between the totalizing powers of the 'social' as homogeneous, consensual community, and the forces that signify the more specific address to the contentious, unequal interests and identities within the population."[45] That "cutting edge" works more like a buzz saw upon the bodies of "others" who come to stand for difference in the nation's articulation of itself. Kureishi shows us what it might be like to flirt with this cutting edge, opening up new possibilities for constituting the people while also facing the risk of violence at the hands of purists who champion the archaic, pedagogical forms of the past. This sort of flirting produces dangerous intimacies, especially between men, that have the potential to be transformative when they are avowed, and lethal when they are not.

Through his depiction of a range of intimacies between South Asian and white men (from loving queer relationships to violent, phobic, and hate-filled encounters), Kureishi maps the currents of male–male desire that circulate in a nation where "Britishness" is at once considered an attribute of all subjects and synonymous with male whiteness. Thus when Karim opens his narrative by proclaiming "I am an Englishman," he is simultaneously laying claim to political subjecthood and calling into question the assumption that white, working-class, masculinity is the authentic marker of Englishness. In *My Beautiful Laundrette*, for example, the relationship between the Pakistani-British capitalist, Omar, and the working-class white hooligan, Johnny, eventually provides an alternative to the polarization of communities – the working-class (or working-poor) white community of squatters, who have turned to racism as one misguided expression of class warfare, and the materially privileged community of first- and second-generation South Asian immigrants, who find that their material privilege does not protect them from insidious racist violence.[46] Sex between the protagonists is sandwiched between moments of violence directed at Johnny and his compatriots or perpetrated by them against Omar's extended family. If, as Berlant and Warner argue, "sex opens a wedge to the transformation of those social norms that require only its static intelligibility or its deadness as a source of meaning,"[47] then the homoerotic ties between Johnny and Omar offer a potentially transformative alternative to the very public homosocial violence of the gang or the cartel.

Although Kureishi is a British writer, and thus his depictions must be contextualized within the particular race/class/gender formations of late twentieth-century England, the theoretical insights offered by Robyn Wiegman in her analysis of the homosocial underpinnings of racist violence in the USA nevertheless help illuminate the function of homosocial intimacy and violence in Kureishi's work. As Wiegman notes, racist violence against black men served (in racist hegemonic fantasy) to protect white supremacist men from the threat of sameness – the potential sameness of black and white men as equal political subjects.[48] For Wiegman, the unavowed logic of hate crimes directed at black males is therefore both gendered and erotically charged, a way of gendering African American men that hinders their symbolic access to the presumed universal (masculine) subjectivity. This threat of sameness provokes equally charged homosocial violences between black and white men in postcolonial Britain.[49]

Thus in *The Buddha of Suburbia*, Karim, "a funny kind of Englishman," is subject to the violence of racism (threats, racist epithets, beatings) as well as white men's fascination with his exoticized body. The theatre director Shadwell, for example, tells Karim that "Everyone looks at you, I'm sure, and thinks: an Indian boy, how exotic, how interesting, what stories of aunties and elephants we'll now hear from him," despite the fact that Karim has barely traveled farther from his suburban home than London (*BS*, p. 141). Shadwell's insistence that he play the part of Kipling's Mowgli in brownface foreshadows Karim's even more disturbing exploitation by Matthew Pyke, who uses his powerful position as a famous theatre director to elicit sexual favors from him (*BS*, p. 203). However, neither Karim, nor any of Kureishi's other protagonists (often biracial, bisexual, or marked as non-heteronormative) are portrayed as mere objects of white racial fear/desire. More often than not, his protagonists successfully negotiate the polarities of violent nationalisms and racisms in their efforts to forge intimacies across difference.

In his more recent work, Kureishi recognizes the importance of intraracial male bonding, especially among the South Asian Muslim community, as a response to the dehumanizing racist violence directed against them. In both *The Black Album* and "My Son the Fanatic," Kureishi shows why the *communitas* of Islamic fundamentalism might be appealing to a younger generation of men whose fathers sought to assimilate and yet were rewarded with racism and second-class citizenship.[50] Even so, he complicates the lure of this *communitas*. In his comments on his screenplays, Kureishi describes the racist nationalist and fundamentalist nationalist as kindred spirits, hampered by the same rigidity:

> Like the racist, the fundamentalist works only with fantasy. For instance, there are those who like to consider the West to be only materialistic and the East only religious. The fundamentalist's idea of the West, like the racist's idea of his victim, is immune to argument or contact with reality . . . this fantasy of the Other is always sexual, too. The West is re-created as a godless orgiastic stew of immoral copulation. If the black person has been demonised by the white, in turn the white is now being demonised by the militant Muslim. These fighting couples can't leave one another alone.[51]

As an alternative to these symbolic "fighting couples," Kureishi represents actual fighting couples, who must make the everyday effort to negotiate complicated hierarchies of race, class, status, and gender. In addition to the relationship between Omar and Johnny, which presents an alternative to the racial and economic polarizations depicted in *My Beautiful Laundrette*, the relationships between Shahid and Dee Dee in *The Black Album* and Karim and Charlie in *The Buddha of Suburbia* represent opportunities for moving beyond reified understandings of race and nation. And of course there are Sammy and Rosie, who represent the potential of a non-heteronormative future for the multiethnic metropolis – if we read the eclectic community that has gathered in their flat as emergent and sustainable.

CHAPTER 6

Orpheus, AIDS, and The Hours

> Landlocked in Montana here
> the end is limited by light, the final note
> will trail off at the farthest point we see,
> already faded, lover, where you bloat.
>
> All girls should be nicer. Arrows rain
> above us in the Indian wind. My future
> should be full of windy gems, my past
> will stop this roaring in my dreams.
> Sorry. Sorry. Sorry. But the arrows sing:
> no way to float her up. The dead sink
> from dead weight. The mission range
> turns this water black late afternoons.
> – Richard Hugo, "The Lady in Kicking Horse Reservoir"[1]

RESISTING THE "POLITICS OF ORPHEUS"

In his rather depressing homage to the body of a drowned woman, Richard Hugo constructs a chilling image of sedimentation – not of the lifeless woman who descends wordlessly to the bottom of the reservoir, but of the male poet, whose future should be "full of windy gems," but instead is sinking from "dead weight." The woman whose body provides the image is of little significance to the poet, who meditates instead on his foreclosed future, signified by the bloated female corpse. This substitutive logic is consistent with what Klaus Theweleit calls "the politics of Orpheus," where the "beauty of the bodies of dead women" is transformed into "the beauty of the poem."[2] Hugo's Orphic image resonates eerily with the details of Woolf's death. Her corpse remained tangled in debris at the bottom of the swollen river Ouse for three weeks before it was discovered. Although sanitized and made beautiful, this is the image that confronts viewers in the opening scene of Stephen Daldry's 2002 film, *The Hours*.[3] The film's representation of Woolf's suicide as a beautiful death reiterates the "politics of Orpheus," with a woman's death initiating the poetic beauty of the story. Narrating the story of Woolf's life through the lens of its ending – suggesting that her death was a sign of pathology and therefore that her life must have been a 59-year pathological prologue to that inevitable end – has the effect of caricaturing her as an invalidish mad genius, or, as Andrew O'Hehir describes her in his review of *The Hours*, a "self-absorbed bisexual nutcase genius."[4] Such a caricature diminishes Woolf's immense productivity and vitality, projecting an inevitable telos on a life that was varied and complex. The film also, in a perverse way, participates in what Lee Edelman calls "reproductive futurism," as the deaths of both writers in the film make space for others to live on: Richard's death enables the lesbian family of Clarissa, Sally, and Julia to move past Clarissa's infatuation with her past attachments to Richard, while "Mrs. Woolf's" death presumably allows Leonard to live on without the encumbrance of her madness.[5] Through visual repetition, "Mrs. Woolf's" death is also linked to the survival of the pregnant Laura Brown, who is inspired by her reading of *Mrs. Dalloway* to forgo her thoughts of suicide.

The timing of Woolf's own death, in March 1941, when the threat of German invasion was palpable – makes it tempting to read her suicide as a reaction to wartime despair. As Hermione Lee explains, a misstatement by the coroner at her inquest (he misquoted Woolf's suicide letter) led many of Woolf's contemporaries to interpret her suicide as the craven act of a frail aesthete who could not face the "terrible times" of war.[6] However, her suicide note indicates that Woolf thought she was going "mad" again, and as Susan Kenny argued over thirty years ago, it is likely that she killed herself in order to assert her autonomy, to avoid being subjected to a "rest cure."[7] Lee goes so far as to argue that "the letter, and the act it presaged, though an act *in extremis*, was rational, deliberate, and courageous."[8]

The interpretation of Woolf's suicide as an act of political despair, although challenged by scholars such as Lee or Sybil Oldfield, has persisted in the public imaginary.[9] In his introduction to *Postmodern Apocalypse*, for example, Richard Dellamora juxtaposes Woolf's suicide to that of Walter Benjamin. "Woolf's death," Dellamora argues, "seems to sound the knell . . . for the form of middle-class dissidence summed in the word 'Bloomsbury.' . . . Woolf's death demonstrated the vulnerability of Bloomsbury's attempts to reform politics by appeals to 'social conscience.'"[10] On the other hand, Dellamora reads Benjamin's suicide in 1940 as a "touchstone of postmodernity," the beginning of a postmodern era of possibility. "His act," argues Dellamora, "testifies to the end of the capability of Euro-American world historical movements – communism, fascism, and liberal or socialist democracy – to dominate human meaning."[11]

Why is it that the death of Woolf is invoked to symbolize the ending, even failure of the ideals espoused in her work, while Benjamin's death, according to Dellamora, is "a courageous protest against an order, triumphant at the time, that promised to extinguish both his liberty and his life"?[12] Fearing deportation to Nazi Germany, Benjamin fled occupied France only to kill himself when he learned that Spanish officials had closed the border on the very day he was to cross it. His suicide was precipitated, Hannah Arendt suggests, by "an uncommon stroke of bad luck."[13] Certainly, there were significant differences in the circumstances surrounding Woolf's death and Benjamin's; however, one would think that Benjamin's sudden action while in flight from the Nazis could just as easily be invoked to signify the tragic end of a political visionary, while Woolf's deliberate and planned action might be read as a conscientious protest.

Gender difference, rather than differences in political vision, accounts for the differing significations of these two suicides. The male death symbolizes a tragic, yet defiant agency, an engaged interaction with politics and culture, while the female death represents closure, individual pathology, singularity in retreat from politics and culture. This signification is consonant with prevailing discourses that link femaleness, the body, and death in the cultural imagination. Woolf's suicide evokes a sense of failure for critics like Dellamora because of what Julia Schiesari calls the "gendering of melancholia," and because women so often bear the burden of representing debased deaths against which heroic, transcendent, masculine death is defined.[14]

Schiesari argues that melancholia developed as a sign of social and moral distinction.[15] The grandeur of the male melancholic, whose intimate association with loss gives him presumably greater access to truth and creativity, is constructed at the expense of the abjected feminine. In this schema, women's sorrow is regarded as banal and devalued.[16] In short, the male melancholic (and Benjamin is on Schiesari's list of "great melancholics") has access to genius, while the depressed female is – well – just acting like a woman. Although the figure of Woolf challenges definitional boundaries of genius, interpretations of her suicide as biological failure or individual pathology reinscribe her in the feminized confines of the symptomatic body. She is mad Ophelia, whose death is private, natural, individual, emotional, while Benjamin is Hamlet, whose public death protests the rotten state of Denmark.

One need not have an investment in upholding the categories of "genius" or the transcendence of the mind over the drudgery of the body in order to understand that such categories are sustained by unequal gender dynamics. Transcendence, especially, is sustained through its opposite – the notion of inert biological limits. In his study on "Death, Women and Power," Maurice Bloch argues that in many cultures, two attitudes toward death exist simultaneously.[17] Bodily death, associated with the pollution of the decomposing corpse, individuates and evokes the biological limits of human sociality. A subsequent symbolic death, on the other hand, perpetuates the "eternal order of traditional authority."[18] "The devalued side," Bloch asserts, "is so often acted out by being associated with women while the other side . . . is associated either with men or with the group as an undifferentiated entity."[19] Value therefore is placed on transcendence and the continuity of the group at the expense of the biological individual.

Such a worldview permeated British nationalism during World War II, when Britishness was imagined as a cherished way of life under threat from fascists on the continent.[20] Within this ideological paradigm, individual, biological death would be perceived to be a menace to the coherence of the social order. As Marcuse argues, "The social order demands compliance with toil and resignation, heroism, and punishment for sin. The established civilization does not function without a considerable degree of unfreedom; and death, the ultimate cause of all anxiety, sustains unfreedom. Man is not free as long as death has not become really 'his own.'"[21] The person who makes death "her own," rather than the state's to dispense, undermines the ideology of nationalism. This connection was not unnoted by Woolf's contemporaries. Her suicide was considered unpatriotic by the Bishop of Lincoln's wife, who wrote a letter to *The Sunday Times* condemning Woolf for killing herself. The coroner, Mrs. Lincoln writes, "belittles those who are carrying on unselfishly for the sake of others . . . Many people possibly even more 'sensitive' have lost their all and yet they take their part nobly in this fight for God against the devil. Where would we all be if we listen to and sympathize with this sort of 'I cannot carry on'?"[22] While Mrs. Lincoln's letter was prompted by the coroner's misstatement, her ideological point is still made: life is not one's own to take; it is the state's right to place lives in jeopardy. It is the responsibility of proper subjects to endure life – even if they have "lost their all" – until the state or God requires them to lose their life, in which case they should dutifully give it up.

In other words, the flipside of being prepared to die for one's country is one's duty to live even a miserable life for it. As Georges Minois notes in his *History of Suicide*, "Weakness, cowardice, madness, perversion – suicide was everything except the manifestation of a human liberty, which was what the more audacious thinkers of the sixteenth through the eighteenth centuries had tried to suggest."[23] Recasting suicide as the exercise of human liberty directly challenges the state's right to appropriate the deaths of its citizens for the purposes of waging war. Woolf makes this connection clearly in *Mrs. Dalloway*, with the suicide of a male soldier, Septimus Smith. Woolf's depiction of Septimus' suicide challenges the conflation of proper male gender performance with English patriotism, soldiering, and dutifully "living on" for the sake of the nation. Drs. Holmes and Bradshaw serve as the mouthpieces for this normative conflation of "living on" and proper British masculinity. "He had actually talked of killing himself to his wife," Holmes says. "Quite a girl, a foreigner, wasn't she? Didn't that give her a very odd idea of English husbands? Didn't one own perhaps a duty to one's wife?" (*Mrs. D*, p. 139). For Holmes and his ilk, had Septimus been killed in the war like his compatriot Evans, his death would have been glorified, patriotic. Rezia would have had a "proper English husband," albeit a dead one.

Dr. Bradshaw reiterates this normative message even more explicitly, becoming a champion of biopower. For Foucault, biopower exerts normative control by "making live and letting die."[24] It is, according to Foucault, "continuous, scientific . . . the power to make live. Sovereignty took life and let live. And now we have the emergence of a power that I would call the power of regularization, and it, in contrast, consists in making live and letting die."[25] Hence, in response to rumors of Septimus' suicidal thoughts, Dr. Bradshaw invokes the police, who are metonymically linked in his speech to the "good of society":

In short, this living or not living is an affair of our own? But there they were mistaken. Sir William had a friend in Surrey where they taught, what Sir William frankly admitted was a difficult art – a sense of proportion. There were, moreover, family affection; honor; courage; and a brilliant career. All of these had in Sir William a resolute champion. If they failed him, he had to support police and the good of society, which, he remarked very quietly, would take care, down in Surrey, that these unsocial impulses, bred more than anything by the lack of good blood, were held in control. (*Mrs. D*, p. 153–54)

Despite, or perhaps because of this disciplining injunction, Septimus throws himself out his window, an action that inspires from Holmes not compassion, but a single utterance, "The coward!" (*Mrs. D*, p. 226). Only Rezia, a foreigner and a woman, is able to understand the explicit connection between soldiering (throwing one's self in front of a hand grenade, for example) and suicide (throwing one's self out a window). She inwardly salutes Septimus for his act of courage, even as she registers the shock of witnessing his death: "She had once seen a flag slowly rippling out from a mast when she stayed with her Aunt at Venice. Men killed in battle were thus saluted, and Septimus had been through the War" (*Mrs. D*, p. 228).

With this reading of Septimus' suicide in mind, one might be persuaded to see Woolf's suicide as neither craven nor heroic, but consistent with the pacifist political philosophy that she espoused for most of her life. Challenging the "ideology of death," Marcuse suggests, involves "construct[ing] some kind of 'normal' attitude toward death – normal in terms of the plain observable facts."[26] Woolf certainly developed this "normal" attitude towards death, writing in her diary: "this morning we discussed suicide if Hitler lands. Jews beaten up. What point in waiting? Better shut the garage doors. This is a sensible, rather matter of fact talk" (*D-V*, 15 May 1940). Marcuse argues that death considered in this commonsense manner as a biological limit, rather than the ultimate determinant of the meaning of one's life, "would partake of freedom, and individuals would be impowered to determine their own deaths."[27] Casting Woolf's suicide as the symbol of the failure of a political vision, as Dellamora does, is part of the meaning-making system that Marcuse finds so troubling. Moreover, Dellamora's act of interpretation misunderstands the nature of Woolf's political vision and the continuity of her last act with her career-long refusal to accept the ideology of death as inevitable.

OVERKILL IN *THE HOURS*

The made-for-Hollywood packaging of Woolf's death in *The Hours* creates a further temptation to read Woolf's death according to what David Román describes as the "Ouisa Syndrome" – recasting the experience of an Other into an encounter that is transformative for the straight, white, privileged, well-meaning, liberal onlooker.[28] Román names the "Ouisa Syndrome" after the female lead in John Guare's *Six Degrees of Separation*.[29] In that play, the white liberal character, Ouisa, appropriates the experience of a young, gay, African American man, making the experience into her own and using it to access her own humanity, even as she transforms the complexity of the black gay man's experience into "an anecdote 'to dine out on.'"[30] "Ouisa's journey," Román argues, "is universalized not only by the production, but by critics who see in Ouisa the spiritual awakening necessary to resolve the effects of a postmodern politics of doubt and despair."[31] Black gay male experience ironically becomes the vehicle for the uplift of the largely white, elite, liberal, audience. A similar experience evacuation is going on in the film version of *The Hours*. Through its narrative packaging as a story about dead authors who leave something significant in their writings for the survivors of their deaths, the film sends the clear message that the *important* experience is not the suffering of the protagonists, but the experience of watching their suffering and transforming it into "anecdotes to dine out on." Morbidly bookended by the spectacle of Woolf's drowned body, the film thus becomes a vehicle for the audience to remake itself into life-loving people who have learned the lesson that the "Mrs. Woolf" of the film teaches Leonard when he asks his "stupid question": "Why must someone die?" Sitting on a bench in a train station after being thwarted in her desire to go to London, "Mrs. Woolf" answers didactically: "That others may appreciate life."[32] This is the proper way to witness death, audience members. Be advised. The peroration has begun.

But what if "Mr. Woolf's" question were taken seriously, rather than generalized into a grand statement about aesthetic balance or the universal human condition? Why *does* Septimus have to die in *Mrs. Dalloway*? This is an aesthetic as well as political question that opens up other questions about how the postwar British society of the Dalloways treats its lower-class veterans – questions about the brutal effects of war and about the arrogance of experts and social elites. There is nothing inherently wrong with depicting such deaths – including Woolf's own suicide – in fictional works or popular film. However, one of the strengths of Woolf's *Mrs. Dalloway* is that it challenges us to situate particular deaths in their sociopolitical contexts, a task that can't be accomplished with platitudes about how edifying death is for the onlooker. Despite its remarkable, even brilliant use of intertextuality, *The Hours* does not share this strength. Why *does* the poet Richard have to die? For narrative symmetry, of course: he performs the Septimus role in the structure of *The Hours*. But how, in particular, does the depiction of the suicide of a gay man with AIDS engage with sociopolitical discourses that are specific to our own cultural location? How do we interpret the cultural work done through this depiction, without, Ouisa-like, simply making it into a humanistic anecdote to dine out on?

Orpheus, AIDS, and The Hours

One place to start is by tracing the intricate game of citation played by *The Hours*, which, as a film adaptation of a text that is already a spin-off of a modernist text, is already twice-removed from the concerns of Woolf's text.[33] Why such a spin-off on *Mrs. Dalloway* in the early twenty-first century? Silver, in her study of Woolf's iconicity, argues that "Virginia Woolf has become the site of conflict about cultural boundaries and legitimacy that continue to rage today."[34] In the wake of the AIDS crisis of the 1980s and 1990s, *Mrs. Dalloway*'s status as World War I novel is culturally resonant because, as I mentioned above, the text contains the seeds of a critique of biopower – a force that so cruelly discounted the lives of AIDS sufferers during the last two decades of the twentieth century. As a critique of the culture of death associated with World War I, the novel can be redeployed as a commentary on those death-filled years of the 1980s and 1990s. It is hard to know how to read that commentary in *The Hours*, because the film presents such a cultural hall of mirrors, and its distortions are just as significant as its reflections of Woolf's critique.

Since the film is obsessed with mirrors and mirroring, it should come as no surprise to say that *The Hours*, like *Mrs. Dalloway*, is haunted by doubles. To further complicate the mirror trope, Marleen Gorris uses the device of the shop window to indicate Clarissa's and Septimus' roles as doppelgängers in her own film production of *Mrs. Dalloway*.[35] When a car backfires, sounding like a gunshot, Clarissa stares out the florist's window straight into the face of a startled Septimus.

This facial mirroring doesn't take place in the novel, where Clarissa simply looks out the window and catches a glimpse of a car that might be the prime minister's (*Mrs. D*, p. 14). In the film version of *The Hours*, the scene in the flower shop becomes even more intricate. The florist, Barbara, for example, is played by the actress Eileen Atkins, who wrote the screenplay for Gorris' 1997 adaptation of *Mrs. Dalloway*. Atkins also played the role of Virginia Woolf in a 1990 made-for-TV adaptation of *A Room of One's Own*.[36] Barbara stalks Clarissa Vaughn in the shot/reverse-shot sequence while they are discussing Richard's novelistic "copy" of Clarissa's life story. Meryl Streep, who plays Clarissa in *The Hours*, stares out of the florist's shop window hoping to catch a glance of an actress – perhaps Vanessa Redgrave, who played Clarissa Dalloway in Gorris' *Mrs. Dalloway*. In Cunningham's novel, the actress that Clarissa hopes to glimpse is none other than . . . Meryl Streep, or perhaps Redgrave.[37]

This penchant for infinite mirroring seems fitting for texts that are so concerned with doppelgängers, which, as Andrew Webber explains, are often figured in narratives featuring "*mise-en-abyme*," whereby figures or structures are reflected within each other."[38] For Webber, the doppelgänger is a figure of simultaneous disavowal and recognition that, "may be seen to derive its power from the subliminal connivance of the apparently abused host subject or community . . . Even as it is disavowed it demands to be recognized as a projected symptom of profound anxiety in the host subject and the order of things."[39] A good example of the double as a figure of disavowal/recognition is the "exposure" scene in Kimberly Peirce's 1999 film, *Boys Don't Cry*.[40] In that scene, Brandon is dragged into the bathroom by his eventual rapists and murderers, who de-pants him in order to determine whether or not he has properly "male" genitalia. In the shot/reverse-shot sequence, Brandon envisions his double, who witnesses the spectacle of his violation. In this context, the doppelgänger represents something different from the gothic or paranormal, signaling instead the process of dissociation as a response to violence.

The double serves a psychological function in *Mrs. Dalloway* as well. Clarissa and Septimus are clearly doubles in the novel. Septimus is the shadow self of Clarissa – the repressed foil of her glossy, socialite existence. But even this pairing is haunted by a more sinister pairing, as Septimus is doubled by Evans, who appears as an apparition to him and draws him closer to death. (This is in accordance with the folk superstition that sighting one's doppelgänger is a premonition of one's own death.) Both Clarissa and Septimus sight doppelgängers as they contemplate suicide. Clarissa catches a glimpse of an old woman in the window across the street as she ponders the suicide of Septimus and then decides to live (*Mrs. D*, p. 186). Septimus, likewise, catches a glimpse of an old man across the street just before he jumps: "Life was good. The sun hot. Only human beings – what did *they* want? Coming down the staircase opposite an old man stopped and stared at him. Holmes was at the door. 'I'll give it you!' he cried, and flung himself vigorously, violently down on to Mrs. Filmer's area railings" (*Mrs. D*, p. 149). The paired pairing here suggests that perhaps a doppelgänger is not a presentiment of death. The resilience that Clarissa exemplifies is not psychological but rather social, dependent upon her relatively privileged status. In the novel, Clarissa and Sally are also paired in a couple that hints at the suppressed possibility for sexual pleasure between women – but this pairing is mirrored by the unpleasant possibility of a relationship between Elizabeth and Doris Kilman. In both cases, lesbian passion is shown as something of a dead end, a theme that uncannily resurfaces in *The Hours*, where Clarissa and Sally apparently suffer from what is colloquially known as "lesbian bed death." For a filmic text that ostensibly celebrates the possibility – repressed in the novel *Mrs. Dalloway* – of queer passion, *The Hours* is strangely ambivalent about the possibility of that passion's persistence.

SORROWFUL DUTY

In the novel *Mrs. Dalloway*, Clarissa does not see Septimus through the florist's window. What she does see in a shop window, just before going to the florist's, is a song from Shakespeare's *Cymbeline*, beginning with the lines, "Fear no more the heat of the sun" (*Mrs. Dalloway*, p. 9). These soothing words invoke a sense of reparation. Clarissa happens upon the verse as she is struggling to come to terms with the many losses precipitated by the Great War:

> What was she trying to recover? What image of white dawn in the country, as she read in the book spread open:
>
> > Fear no more the heat o' the sun
> > Nor the furious winter's rages
>
> This late age of the world's experience had bred in them all, all men and women, a well of tears. Tears and sorrows; courage and endurance; a perfectly upright and stoical bearing. Think, for example, of the woman she admired most, Lady Bexborough, opening the bazaar. (*Mrs. D*, p. 10)

If Clarissa's reading of the pastoral elegy is meant to invoke a sense of regeneration, to perform what Sacks would call the proper function of the elegy – a renunciation of attachment to the lost object – the source of Woolf's allusion, Shakespeare's *Cymbeline*, marks Clarissa's elegiac impulses as suspect, compelled by formal social imperatives. Within the context of Shakespeare's play, the elegiac performance does not *work* (if we think of commemoration as the work of the elegy) not because it is disingenuous, or ineffectual, but because there is no commemorative work to be done. Imogen, the lost object who is lamented, is not really dead, but simply drugged.[41] Nor is she a country boy from Wales, but the daughter of a king, a well-sheltered noblewoman who in the social arrangement of things is among the least likely to bear the ravages of the sun or the "furious winter's rages." Moreover, this elegant lament can't possibly be about the particularity of the lost loved one, whom the mourners have just met less than twenty-four hours previous to "his" death. The beautiful, extravagant mourning song thus says more about the disguised nobility of the lamenters than it does about the "dead" youth. In this sense, the song is a felicitous elegiac performance, but one that prompts us to recognize that the work of elegy is precisely *not* commemoration, but rather a testament to the dignity of the survivors. Moreover, the particular snippet Clarissa reads calls attention to the imperative function of elegy, as the grammatical form of the line is itself an imperative: "fear no more." As imperatives, elegies make demands on mourners to cease mourning, to "let go." Hence, after reading the lines, Clarissa immediately thinks of Lady Bexborough, a caricature of proper mourning who stoically opens a bazaar with the telegram announcing her son's death still in her hands (*Mrs. D*, p. 10). Life must go on, and dilatory veterans like Septimus who cannot "let go" of their losses must learn to do so. It is their duty.

While Woolf critiques this call to duty, *The Hours* reinvokes it. The film celebrates the smooth social surfaces that Woolf problematizes in the novel. Like the elegiac lament from *Cymbeline*, the film is an extravagantly beautiful cultural production that is less concerned with the particularity of the losses it depicts than its own surviving beauty. Here the symmetry between *Mrs. Dalloway* and *The Hours* does not so much break down as become obsessively formal, like an analogy machine that must, of necessity, ignore particularities and contingencies for the sake of producing likenesses. In the process, much of the political context of the subject matter of the film – the suicide of a gay man with AIDS – is evacuated.

It would be edifying to imagine that Richard makes death "his own" in defiance of biopower's compulsion to "make live and let die." Indeed, this seems to be an interpretation that the film urges, but it fails to account for the asymmetry between a returned heterosexual war veteran and a gay poet with AIDS whom dominant culture would prefer not to exist. It is hard to know whether Richard's death is a defiance of cultural wishes, or a dominant-cultural wish fulfillment. Tutored by the "Mrs. Woolf" of the film, we are supposed to know that we shouldn't ask why the poet dies, because he dies for us. His death makes for good art and for a pleasing, if painful, retrospective on the AIDS crisis. According to the logic of the film, we have to "let go" now and continue our lives after AIDS, as if the crisis were over.

With its insistent imperative to get on with mourning, the film invites the process that Berger condemns as "looking beyond" the massive suffering that is ongoing even as the film attempts closure by pairing the death of Richard with the beautiful death of "Mrs. Woolf."[42] This "closure" is more accurately a foreclosure of knowledge that the AIDS crisis is far from over. Despite tremendous advances in the treatment of HIV/AIDS since the advent of effective antiretroviral drug combinations in the mid 1990s, by the end of 2001 (the temporal setting of the Meryl Streep section of the film) an estimated 32,900,000 adults and 2,000,000 children in the world were living with HIV/AIDS.[43] The majority of these cases are in economically exploited regions of the world, another legacy of the colonial violence that haunts *Mrs. Dalloway*. If biopower endeavors to "make live" in the case of Septimus, it "lets die" in the case of Richard, and by extension the approximately 35,000,000 unmentioned persons with HIV/AIDS whose existence is displaced by the neat closure of the story. Woolf resists this imperative to "make live and let die" by portraying Septimus making death "his own," while *The Hours* makes an anecdote "'to dine out on'" in the beautiful deaths of its heroes.[44]

Epilogue:
Toward a survivable public mourning

> If we are interested in arresting cycles of violence to produce less violent outcomes, it is no doubt important to ask what, politically, might be made of grief besides a cry for war.
> – Judith Butler (*PL*, p. xii)

Because the incubation period for this book coincides with an extraordinary (and extraordinarily painful) time, it itself bears the traces of the long work of mourning many distinct but interconnected losses that have punctuated the past several years. I began piecing together the bare skeleton of my argument, a reading of Virginia Woolf's World War II writings, in late September 2001 for a November colloquium on women and war.[1] The world has changed quite dramatically since I first returned to Woolf's writing in search of non-apocalyptic, non-lethal frameworks for responding to the devastation of September 11. Like the vast majority of Americans, I remember exactly where I was when the twin towers collapsed, and, thinking about my own cherished experiences in New York City, I recalled Woolf's declaration of love for London, the city she navigated so deftly in her life and fiction:

> I forgot to make extracts from the papers, which boom, boom, echoing, emptily, the BBC. Hitler's speech – Churchill's – a ship sunk – no survivors – a raft capsized – men rowing for 10 or 12 or 30 hours. How little one can explode now, as perhaps one would have done, had it been a single death . . . Odd how often I think with what is love I suppose of the city: of the walk to the Tower: that is my England; I mean if a bomb destroyed one of those little alleys with the brass bound curtains & the river smell & the old woman reading I should feel – well, what the patriots feel –. (*D-V*, 2 February 1940)

These are strong words for Woolf, an ardent critic of militarism and patriotism, and in them we can trace some of the echoes of the ambivalence she struggled with as she responded to the effects of German air raids. These ambivalences raised troubling questions for Woolf, and

I found it reassuring to retrace her efforts to grapple with them in the shocked speechlessness of the fall of 2001. How does one maintain a commitment to peace when one's country is brutally attacked? How does one resist "that dreary false cheery hero-making strain" of nationalism without discounting the truly heroic efforts of, for example, the many rescue workers who perished on September 11 (*D-V*, 30 June 1940)? Is it possible to critique the abuses of power at home when the "homeland" also stands in opposition to abuses of power abroad? Three years and two wars later, these questions – submerged or politely muted in the immediate aftermath of September 11 – bubbled to the surface in a bitter and divisive 2004 US presidential election. The stakes of public mourning were very high, as one side attempted to mobilize images of the catastrophe to legitimate its own military invasions, and the other struggled to separate the grief, anger, and fear precipitated by the terrorist attacks from the uses made of them to justify the invasion and occupation of Iraq. In the early days of November 2004, many found themselves rocked by another kind of grief, as those who chose to use the catastrophe of September 11 to legitimate invasion won the day. The left lost not only an election, but a battle of commemoration.

One of tactics in this battle of commemoration was the manipulation of forms of mourning that are made public, and those relegated to the out-of-sight realm of the private. For example, on 11 June 2004, the US news media broadcast continuous live coverage of the "National Day of Mourning" declared by US President George W. Bush in order to mark the passing of former president Ronald Reagan.[2] The pageantry of President Reagan's funeral procession drew largely reverential commentaries, although its lavish stagecraft did not escape the notice of media critics such as Caryn James and Alessandra Stanley, who covered the arts and television for the *New York Times*. Stanley credits Nancy Reagan for her production of a "pageant over two decades in the making," as if it were an elaborate Broadway performance "green-lighted by the most powerful production company in the world, the United States Government."[3] "[A]s television lovingly records every detail of Mr. Reagan's majestic state funeral this week," writes Stanley, "it has become clear that his widow had one last big production in her: the Reagans began planning the funeral when he took office in 1981, and Mrs. Reagan has fine-tuned the details every year since he fell ill. Mrs. Reagan . . . has written, directed and produced the final, definitive film of the couple's career."[4] James notes that the Reagan funeral cited the funeral procession of John F. Kennedy, but in a manner choreographed to supersede it: "History may offer a simple reason for the elaborate Reagan ceremonies: each funeral must distinguish itself from the last or risk losing its impact . . . History is a hard act to follow, but the funeral preparations show that the Reagan camp is still unmatched at turning imagery to its advantage."[5]

The sheer saturation of this imagery (with photos of the former president's flag-draped casket adorning the front pages of the major US newspapers for several days running) provided an uncanny reminder of images that had been conspicuously absent from public view since March 2003 – those of the flag-draped coffins of more than 800 US soldiers (not to mention the approximately 10,000 Iraqi civilians) who were killed in the Iraq war as of 1 June 2004.[6] Juxtaposing the spectacle of national mourning decreed for President Reagan with the officially decreed "private" status of ceremonies for fallen US soldiers, and the unrecognized status of Iraqi civilian losses, illustrates the differentiating function of public mourning.[7] A three-tiered system of recognizing loss implicitly emerges from this juxtaposition – publicly mourned loss, publicly recognized but privately mourned loss, and disavowed loss. In the first two instances, public recognition of death not only acknowledges the loss of the person but also affirms the previous presence of the person as a subject who was valued and will be missed. The third category – incorporating, for example, those who perished during the first decade of the AIDS pandemic, those "disappeared" by death squad governments, or those who through force of military circumstance are categorized under the desubjectivizing sign of "collateral damage" – remains virtually invisible in mainstream public discourse.

To refuse to recognize the loss of a person is, as Butler notes, to refuse to recognize the very personhood of the deceased:

certain forms of grief become nationally recognized and amplified, whereas other losses become unthinkable and ungrievable . . . the differential allocation of grievability that decides what kind of subject is and must be grieved, and which kind of subject must not, operates to produce and maintain certain exclusionary conceptions of who is normatively human: what counts as a livable life and a grievable death? (*PL*, p. xiv)

Butler's question, posed in *Precarious Life*, echoes the questions she raised earlier in *Antigone's Claim*. Antigone's "predicament," argues Butler,

does offer an allegory for the crisis of kinship: which social arrangements can be recognized as legitimate love, and which human losses can be explicitly grieved as real and consequential loss? Antigone refuses to obey any law that refuses public recognition of her loss, and in this way prefigures the situation that those with publicly ungrievable losses – from AIDS, for instance – know too well.[8]

Analyzing Antigone's "predicament," therefore, has the potential to make conscious, if not unravel, the ideologies of domination embedded in Creon-like imperatives to mourn properly.

Writing on the eve of World War II, with keen awareness of the growing menace of fascism in Europe, Woolf, too, invoked the figure of Antigone in her antifascist triptych, *Three Guineas*. As a bereaved sister who bravely questions Creon's autocratic attempts to legitimate his power by managing public grief, Antigone performs an act of commemoration that is socially engaged and stubbornly resistant to hegemonic cooptation. Her actions (deemed traitorous by Creon) also call to mind contemporary Antigone figures such as Kristen Breitweiser, Jeremy M. Glick, or members of "September Eleventh Families For Peaceful Tomorrows" – mourners who challenge the state's attempt to usurp the meaning of their loved ones' deaths.[9] Such resistant mourning is a continuation of resilient, *metic*, modernist cultural work that imagines a post-Antigonean politics of mourning – where public mourning does not serve the vengeful imperatives of the Creon-like state, and where dissent is not (as it were) buried alive.

CREONIC IMPERATIVES AND LETHAL MOURNING

Paying heed to the words of Antigone, Woolf argues, opens up a space for analyzing the "unwritten laws" that prop up ideologies of domination and conquest (*TG*, p. 184 fn. 42). In addition to "finding" and exposing such laws, Antigone mourns in a way that, as Butler notes, confounds any clear separation between forms of kinship and the state, or, as Woolf put it, the public sphere and the private house (*TG*, p. 142).[10] This confounding entails something more than suggesting that the private is to the public, or the psychic is to the social, as the micro is to the macro, but rather that the relationship between the two is made up of complex networks of feeling, thinking, remembering, and reacting.

With respect to loss, for example, Butler suggests that, "many people think that grief is privatizing, that it returns us to a solitary situation and is, in that sense, depoliticizing. But I think that it furnishes a sense of political community of a complex order, and it does this first of all by bringing to the fore the relational ties that have implications for theorizing fundamental dependency and ethical responsibility" (*PL*, p. 22). For Butler, this reminder of connectedness and dependence (strikingly different from the Bush administration's rhetoric of autonomous retribution as a response to nationalist grief) opens up the possibility for empathy, rather than vengeance, to be cultivated in response to trauma.[11] This gesture of opening up, rather than closing in, might be seen as the beginning of a postnationalist response to threat, something similar to the border-indifferent humanity that Woolf invokes when she suggests that even love of country, "some love of England dropped into a child's ears" might spark, rather than vengeance, the desire to "give to England first what she desires of peace and freedom for the whole world" (*TG*, p. 109).

How, as I asked in my introduction, might a particular act of remembrance shape the meanings we give to the past, and how does that construction of the past shape our possible futures? Woolf was certainly aware of the potential for loss to be invoked as the justification for military aggression. As I noted in Chapter 1, Woolf reacted to BBC broadcasts of battle news by commenting, "It is the myth making stage of war we are in" (*D-V*, 3 June 1940). In the myth-making stage of war, calls to remember are the common staples of wartime propaganda. Mobilizing memory of loss is the rhetorical strategy, for example, of the World War I recruitment poster by Fred Spear, which pictures a drowning woman and baby, captioned by the single word, "Enlist" (fig. 1).[12] As appraiser Rudy Franchi explains, "Visually, the poster plays on America's shock at the sinking of the steamship Lusitania by a German U-boat in May of [. . . 1915], which claimed over a thousand lives. The United States was not yet involved in the war, and the uproar incited by the poster was a factor in America's decision to enter it."[13]

Such an undeniably compelling mobilization of the spectacle of loss is "myth making" not because the image is somehow "untrue," but rather because, as Sontag notes, such images are so inescapably rhetorical, and dependent upon a pedagogy that will enable the viewer to read the image as corroboration of a particular belief.[14] Each side in a conflict will have its own traumas to tally and avenge, and for the spectacle of loss to be mobilized in an effective way, its viewers will have to be instructed how to remember – how to selectively remember – or rather how to forget the traumas of the other side. As part of the rhetoric of retribution, even the same images of atrocity – as in the case of the photographs of slaughtered children that, according to Sontag, were re-captioned and "passed around at both Serbian and Croat propaganda meetings" – might be invoked by both sides as justification for their actions.[15] While it would be a mistake to cite the reciprocal practice of mobilizing images of atrocity for military purposes as evidence of the moral equivalence of parties in a conflict, a healthy suspicion of the rhetoric of retribution might help to

Fig. 1 Fred Spear, "Enlist," 1915, Smithsonian Institution.

circumvent the vicious cycle of perpetrating new atrocities as a means of avenging old.[16]

In *Antigone*, Creon, mobilizing the rhetoric of retribution, arranges the spectacle of remembrance to reinforce his regime-consolidating pedagogy. In response to his edict, the Thebans must commit to memory the lesson communicated through his differentially allocated rights of commemoration – retrospectively marking one brother as a friend to the people of Thebes, and the other as a threat. Creon forbids the burial of Polyneices because he believes that honoring him in death would cast dishonor upon the Theban soldiers who fought on behalf of the city, and thus undo one of the outcomes of the battle – the determination of who counts as "wicked" and who "just":

> Such is my mind in the matter; never by me
> shall the wicked man have precedence in honor
> over the just. But he that is loyal to the state
> in death, in life alike, shall have my honor.[17]

Thus the unburied body of Polyneices serves as a redundant reminder of what his death has already substantiated. (Creon's insistence on redundancy – literally his penchant for overkill – is his undoing.) For Antigone (and her successors), to publicly mourn is to publicly dissent, not because she takes up (a somehow neutrally coded) mourning and politicizes it, but because the process of commemoration has already been politicized through Creon's prohibition against forms of mourning that undermine his credibility as a legitimate ruler.[18] In order to consolidate his authority, Creon must not only manage public memory, but also public forgetting – especially of Polyneices' claim, as the eldest son of Oedipus, to the Theban throne. Creon's edict – to remember one brother and forget the other – is also an injunction to forget the violent genealogy that led to the consolidation of Creon's power. Thus the threat that Antigone poses to the state is her refusal to forget as she is instructed.

What is perhaps most troubling in the play is that neither Creon nor Antigone questions the right of the sovereign to punish dissent with death. We might say of Antigone what Marcuse says of Socrates: "In accepting his death, Socrates puts his judges in the wrong, but his philosophy of death acknowledges their right – the right of the polis over the individual."[19] Despite this, *Antigone* itself seems to prompt us to question whether or not absolute sovereignty is a wise policy. Creon, after all, calls himself a "vain silly man"[20] in his last speech, and the Chorus concludes by valuing wisdom above obedience: "Wisdom is far the chief element in happiness / and, secondly, no irreverence towards the gods."[21] The Chorus' diplomatic rebuke opens up a small fissure in the seemingly inexorable structure of the tragedy. Are the allegiances (to the particularity of the body or the universality of the state) that are presented by the play as irreconcilable *necessarily* so? Or is their construction as irreconcilable part of the lethal machinery of the problem? Within the tragedy, Antigone's demise may have been fated all along – either because she is "cursed" by "the doomed self-destruction of [her] mother's bed," or because of the purportedly inevitable tension between one's allegiance to family and allegiance to the *polis*.[22] But this sense of inevitability may be more a function of the tragic emplotment of events rather than attributable to something intrinsically irremediable in the events themselves.[23] After all, classicists suggest that there were variant versions of the Antigone story, depicting the survival of many of the characters (Oedipus, Jocasta, Polyneices, and Haemon) who are killed off in Sophocles' tragedies.[24] Perhaps resistant mourning is survivable after all?

The desire to see justice "in time" to make a difference motivates Woolf's return to *Antigone* as she seeks alternatives to both fascism and war in *Three Guineas*. "Is dominance craving submission?" she asks. "And, most pertinent and difficult of all the questions that our silence covers, what possible satisfaction can dominance give to the dominator?" (*TG*, p. 129). In answer she suggests, "Let us then grope our way amateurishly enough among these very ancient and obscure emotions which we have known ever since the time of Antigone, and Ismene and Creon at least" (*TG*, p. 130). As Diana Swanson notes, Woolf uses the figure of Antigone to indicate the "longevity" of daughters' rebellions against tyrannical father figures.[25] The rebellious daughter, in Swanson's reading, "begins to place herself in a horizontal rather than a vertical relationship to men."[26] This is certainly the case insofar as Woolf explores the power dynamics of relations between sisters and brothers in both *The Years* and *Three Guineas*. But she is also revaluing the child's perspective in her engagement with Freud's "Oedipus Complex."[27] Although Freud is interested in locating and describing the workings of infantile drives, he formulates the Oedipus complex from the narcissistic viewpoint of the parent, who imagines him/herself as the object of both the loving and murderous desires of the child. Oedipus is figured as the child who kills his father and marries his mother in this drama, rather than as the child whose parents attempted, unsuccessfully, to kill him in order to save themselves. To look at the Oedipus complex from the point of view of Antigone is to reimagine Oedipal drives as originating in parents' desires for, or designs upon, their children. From Woolf's perspective "infantile fixations" more accurately describe fathers' obsessions with their children. And their desire (although Woolf is certainly not naïve about incest) is to possess and control their children, especially if they happen to be daughters. Antigone's plaint – "what parents I was born of, God help me!"[28] – has some resonance here, for when Oedipus blinds himself, he dooms (not because of his sin, but because of his expectations of his daughter) Antigone to a wandering life of subservience to his blindness.[29] Thus the child suffers from the father's self-destruction, and in his blindness he can't see the effects of his actions on his children. In the same way, Creon fails to see that his edict will cause Haemon to suffer, until it is too late. Woolf's refiguring of the Oedipus complex, therefore, suggests an ethics that begins with recognizing the desires of authority figures to exact obedience from those whose very vulnerability makes resistance a risky, perhaps life-effacing, gambit.

FEELING WHAT PATRIOTS FEEL

In her World War II writing, Woolf finds in her own vulnerability the inspiration to imagine an alternative to the domination drive that she identifies as the source of both fascism and war. She was residing in the countryside of Sussex during the ferocious Nazi bombings of 1940, although, at the time, she and her husband also held the lease on a London flat that was damaged by a Nazi bomb (on 18 September 1940). In the southeast corner of England, Sussex was in the direct flight line of Nazi bombers heading toward London, thus throughout the air raids of 1940, bombs dropped regularly on the towns and fields near the Woolfs' home. In her diary entry of 29 September 1940, Woolf records the bombs dropping "so close I cursed L[eonard] for slamming the window." In a previous entry, she describes being caught outside in an air raid:

They came very close. We lay down under the tree. The sound was like someone sawing in the air just above us. We lay flat on our faces. Hands behind head. Don't close yr teeth said L. They seemed to be sawing at something stationary. Bombs shook the window of my lodge. Will it drop I asked? If so, we shall be broken together. I thought, I think, of nothingness – flatness, my mood being flat. Some fear I suppose. (*D-V*, 16 August 1940)

This passage, in its breathtaking shorthand, communicates a sense of the fragility of the mere human body, huddling under a tree for protection from an air raid: "hands behind head" – as if leaves, branches, and bone could really save one from a bomb.

Despite, or perhaps because of her experiences during the Nazi bombardment, Woolf remained fiercely critical of militarism and the ideologies that foster it. In "Thoughts on Peace in an Air Raid," she describes an air raid to an American audience that is far removed from the impact of the bombs and exhorts her readership to work for peace. Women, Woolf argues, cannot sit silently and passively in their more or less secure air raid shelters just because (in 1940) "all the idea-makers who are in a position to make ideas effective are men" (*DM*, p. 244). Challenging her female readers, Woolf asks, "Are we not stressing our disability [our lack of voice] because our ability exposes us perhaps to abuse, perhaps to contempt?" (*DM*, p. 244). For Woolf, to remain silent is tantamount to desertion, for, she contends, "there is another way of fighting for freedom without arms; we can fight with the mind. We can make ideas that will help the young Englishman who is fighting up in the sky to defeat the enemy" (*DM*, p. 244). That fight, the fight for real and not rhetorical freedom, means, for Woolf, "thinking against the current, not with it" (*DM*, p. 244). And this type of thinking entails a commitment to end the ideologies of domination, wherever they manifest themselves:

> Down here, with a roof to cover us and a gas mask handy, it is our business to puncture gas bags and discover the seeds of truth. It is not true that we are free ... If we were free we should be out in the open, dancing, at the play, or sitting at the window talking together. What is it that prevents us? "Hitler!" the loudspeakers cry with one voice. Who is Hitler? What is he? Aggressiveness, tyranny, the insane love of power made manifest, they reply. Destroy that, and you will be free. (*DM*, p. 245)

"But how?" we might answer her back, sixty-eight years later. For Woolf, the key is in her imagination of a future generation of men and women who do not believe that war is inevitable or honorable. Her concern is for, as she stated above, "not this one body in this one bed, but millions of bodies yet to be born" (*DM*, p. 243). As Woolf argues in *Three Guineas*, "memory and tradition" (we might call it ideology and education) form subjects for whom aggressiveness, love of power, and domination are admired, rather than deplored traits (*TG*, p. 18). For Woolf, as I mentioned in Chapter 1, the creative thinkers of the world must find ways to refashion memory and tradition so that a new breed of freedom-loving subjects can be formed: "We must create more honourable activities for those who try to conquer in themselves their fighting instinct, their subconscious Hitlerism. We must compensate the man for the loss of his gun" (*DM*, p. 247).

As an antidote to the fear that possesses one during an air raid, "the mind reaches out and instinctively revives itself by trying to create" (*DM*, p. 247). To "compensate the man for the loss of his gun," Woolf argues, "we must give him access to his creative feelings. We must make happiness" (*DM*, p. 248). The verb in Woolf's assertion is crucial. We must "make" happiness as an honorable activity, rather than expect it as a reward for other, more lethal forms of "honorable" activity. Happiness is therefore not a payment within an ethical economy – something that one receives as compensation at the end of a life conceived of as a long term of duty – but a practice that must be continuously cultivated during life. Woolf's imperative to "make happiness" therefore articulates an alternative to the ideology of death.

Consider the stark economy of the "Ideology of death," for example, in the rhetoric of reward that was outlined in a handwritten letter carried by the perpetrators of the terrorist attacks of September 11. According to the

CNN description of these letters, the terrorists were instructed to bring "knives, your will, your ID's onto the planes for battle" and the letter explains that the terrorists are about to "begin to live the happy life, the infinite paradise."[30] In other words, the perpetrators were instructed to *make terror* in order to win happiness. Just to be clear – Islamic extremists do not hold a monopoly on the ideology of death; indeed Marcuse's analysis, enfolded as it was in his attempts to analyze the ideological workings of the brutal fascist regimes of the 1930s and 1940s, suggests that Christian doctrines of suffering, sacrifice, and rebirth contributed to a philosophy transvaluing biological life, making it a prelude to a better life to be gained through an honorable death.[31]

As an alternative to the logic of heroic sacrifice, Woolf imagines the possibility of a "good life" that is not determined retrospectively by a "good" death. "Making happiness" therefore entails the conscious cultivation of creativity, or, as Scarry would put it, of the imagination, of "making," rather than "unmaking" the world.[32] Woolf thus articulates an ethical dimension to the Paterian sensibility she explores in her earlier fiction and criticism. For Pater, "we are all under sentence of death, but with a sort of indefinite reprieve . . . we have an interval, and then our place knows us no more . . . our one chance lies in expanding that interval, in getting as many pulsations as possible into the given time."[33] Woolf's imperative to "make happiness" expands Pater's emphasis on living consciously during the interval between life and death, suggesting that there might be a political dimension to the project of valuing that "interval" rather than fixating on the end.

In Sophocles' story, Antigone is exiled and entombed outside the boundaries of the city, sentenced to non-human status because Creon cannot sanction challenges to his control over the meaning of commemoration.[34] She is buried alive, but reading her story through the "modernist patch" opens up the possibility of a different ending.[35] What coalitions would have been necessary – among the sisters and enslaved persons of Thebes, and of course the Chorus which stands and rebukes Creon even as it does nothing to intervene – to have similarly rescued Antigone from her tomb? This is not merely an academic question, but a necessarily practical one for our own historical moment.

Notes

INTRODUCTION: "THE CAPTIVATING SPELL OF THE PAST"

1. Theodor Adorno, "The Meaning of Working Through the Past," trans. Henry W. Pickford, *Can One Live after Auschwitz? A Philosophical Reader*, ed. Rolf Tiedemann (Stanford: Stanford University Press, 2003), pp. 3–18, p. 18.
2. Raymond Williams, "Afterword," *Modern Tragedy* (Stanford: Stanford University Press, 1967), p. 98.
3. Joseph Roach, *Cities of the Dead* (New York: Columbia University Press, 1996), p. 5. Roach describes the process of surrogation – the uneasy replacement of someone who is gone with a surrogate who takes on that person's function. My thanks to Katie N. Johnson for introducing me to Roach's work.
4. Edward Said, *Culture and Imperialism* (New York: Vintage Books, 1994), p. 4.
5. Adorno, "Working Through the Past," p. 17.
6. Ibid., p. 12.
7. Paul Gilroy, *Postcolonial Melancholia* (New York: Columbia University Press, 2005), p. 2.
8. Said, *Culture and Imperialism*, p. 8.
9. Jed Esty, *A Shrinking Island: Modernism and National Culture in England* (Princeton: Princeton University Press, 2004), p. 2.
10. Brenda Silver, *Virginia Woolf Icon* (Chicago: University of Chicago Press, 1999), pp. 154–55.
11. Raymond Williams, *The Politics of Modernism: Against the New Conformists* (London and New York: Verso, 1989), p. 38.
12. Bonnie Kime Scott, *Refiguring Modernism: The Women of 1928* (Bloomington: Indiana University Press, 1995), p. 183.
13. Williams, *Politics*, p. 40.
14. Esty, *Shrinking*, p. 197.
15. Jessica Berman, *Modernist Fiction, Cosmopolitanism and the Politics of Community* (New York: Cambridge University Press, 2001), p. 117.

16. Christine Froula, *Virginia Woolf and the Bloomsbury Avant-Garde: War, Civilization, Modernity* (New York: Columbia University Press, 2005), p. 16.
17. Martha C. Nussbaum, *For Love of Country* (Boston: Beacon Press, 2002), p. 7.
18. In the notes to his English translation of *Antigone*, Charles Segal explains, "The word used by Antigone for having no home (literally, 'changing her home') here, as in 911–12/852 and used later by Kreon in 950/890, is *metoikos*, whose primary meaning for most Athenians would be '*metic*,' that is, a resident alien." *Antigone*, trans. Reginald Gibbons and Charles Segal (New York: Oxford University Press, 2003), p. 150, www.questia.com/PM.qst?a=o&d=103543279 (accessed 20 February 2006). My thanks to my colleague Denise McCoskey for explaining the resonances of the ancient Greek use of the term, and for pointing out the significance of its occurrence in Sophocles' *Antigone*.
19. Berman, while focusing on Woolf's cosmopolitanism, also notes that, "When Woolf famously contends that as a woman she has no country, she is not simply proclaiming her cosmopolitan sympathies but also clearly remarking on her exclusion from the very idea of the citizen" (*Modernist Fiction*, p. 22).
20. Williams, *Politics*, p. 40.
21. Esty, *Shrinking*, p. 197.
22. Ibid., p. 197.
23. Alex Zwerdling, *Virginia Woolf and the Real World* (Berkeley: University of California Press, 1986); Froula, *Woolf and Bloomsbury*; Anna Snaith, *Virginia Woolf: Public and Private Negotiations* (New York: Palgrave Macmillan, 2003); Williams, *Politics*.
24. Esty, *Shrinking*, p. 97.
25. *BA*, p. 8; Esty, *Shrinking*, p. 88.
26. Chalmers Johnson uses the term "empire of bases" to describe the imperial formation of the USA and its militarized satellites in *The Sorrows of Empire: Militarism, Secrecy, and the End of the Republic* (New York: Henry Holt and Co., 2004), p. 23.
27. Theodor Adorno, "Cultural Criticism and Society," *Can One Live after Auschwitz? A Philosophical Reader*, ed. Rolf Tiedemann (Stanford: Stanford University Press, 2003), pp. 146–62, p. 162.
28. Ibid., p. 146.
29. Rita Felski, "Modernist Studies and Cultural Studies: Reflections on Method," *Modernism/Modernity* 10.3 (September 2003), 501–17, pp. 510–11.
30. Chalmers Johnson uses the term "blowback" to describe the resentment and violence directed at imperial and neoimperial powers by the less powerful (*Sorrows*, p. 8).
31. Raymond Williams, *Marxism and Literature* (Oxford: Oxford University Press, 1977), p. 132.
32. Sigmund Freud, "Mourning and Melancholia," *Collected Papers*, vol. 4, ed. Ernest Jones, trans. Joan Riviere (London: Hogarth Press, 1953), p. 155.

33. Ibid., p. 155.
34. Williams, *Politics*, p. 97.
35. Gilroy, *Postcolonial Melancholia*, p. 90.
36. Freud, "Mourning," p. 155.
37. Elaine Scarry, *The Body in Pain: The Making and Unmaking of the World* (New York: Oxford University Press, 1985), pp. 124–25.
38. Michael André Bernstein, *Foregone Conclusions: Against Apocalyptic History* (Berkeley: University of California Press, 1994), p. 9.
39. The last words of *To the Lighthouse* are Lily Briscoe's: "I have had my vision" (p. 209).
40. Susan Sontag, *Regarding the Pain of Others* (New York: Farrar, Straus, and Giroux, 2003), p. 6.
41. Pat Barker, *Double Vision* (New York: Farrar, Straus, and Giroux, 2003), p. 113.
42. Ruth Leys, *Trauma: A Genealogy* (Chicago: University of Chicago Press, 2000).
43. Herbert Marcuse, "The Ideology of Death," *The Meaning of Death*, ed. Herman Feifel (New York: McGraw-Hill, 1959), p. 64.
44. Ibid., p. 64.
45. Eve Kosofsky Sedgwick, *Touching Feeling: Affect, Pedagogy, Performativity* (Durham, NC: Duke University Press, 2003), p. 37.
46. Johnson, *Sorrows*, pp. 283–312.
47. Brenda Silver discusses the phenomenon of "versioning" in *Virginia Woolf Icon* (Chicago: University of Chicago Press, 1999), p. 13.
48. Michel Foucault, *The History of Sexuality: An Introduction*, trans. Robert Hurley, vol. 1 (New York: Random House, 1990), p. 147.
49. Ibid., p. 137.
50. Hanif Kureishi, "Sex and Secularity," Introduction to *Collected Screenplays 1* (London: Faber and Faber, 2002), p. xi.

1 WOOLF'S RESILIENCE

1. Avery F. Gordon, *Ghostly Matters: Haunting and the Sociological Imagination* (Minneapolis: University of Minnesota Press, 1996), p. 8
2. Ibid., p. 42.
3. Erica L. Johnson draws on Gordon's theories to push the haunting metaphor even further, suggesting that Woolf proposes a "shift from ontological to *hauntological* subject construction" in *Orlando*, in "Giving up the Ghost: National and Literary Haunting in *Orlando*," *Modern Fiction Studies* 50.1 (2004), 110–28, pp. 114–15.
4. A rich theoretical literature on the substitutive logic of consolation and its effects has been central to my thinking here, especially Peter Sacks, *The English Elegy: Studies in the Genre from Spenser to Yeats* (Baltimore: Johns Hopkins University Press, 1985) and [Aranye] Louise O. Fradenburg, "'Voice Memorial': Loss and Reparation in Chaucer's Poetry," *Exemplaria* 2.1 (1990),

169–202. Alex Zwerdling and Tammy Clewell both address Woolf's refusal to make easy translations from loss to consolation. Alex Zwerdling, *Virginia Woolf and the Real World* (Berkeley: University of California Press, 1986); Tammy Clewell, "Consolation Refused: Virginia Woolf, the Great War, and Modernist Mourning," *Modern Fiction Studies* 50.1 (2004), 197–223.
5. Sigmund Freud, *The Ego and the Id*, trans. Joan Riviere, ed. James Strachey (New York: W. W. Norton, 1960), pp. 23–24.
6. Wendy Brown, *States of Injury: Power and Freedom in Late Modernity*, (Princeton: Princeton University Press, 1995), p. 74.
7. See, for example, Louise DeSalvo, *Virginia Woolf: The Impact of Childhood Sexual Abuse on Her Life and Work* (New York: Ballantine, 1989); David Eberly, "Semicolons and Safety Pins," *Virginia Woolf: Turning the Centuries*, ed. Ann L. Ardis and Bonnie Kime Scott (New York: Pace University Press, 2000), pp. 134–40; Suzette Henke, "Virginia Woolf and Post-Traumatic Subjectivity," *Virginia Woolf: Turning the Centuries*, ed. Ann L. Ardis and Bonnie Kime Scott (New York: Pace University Press, 2000), pp. 147–52; Roger Poole, *The Unknown Virginia Woolf*, 4th edition (Cambridge: Cambridge University Press, 1995); Mark Spilka, *Virginia Woolf's Quarrel with Grieving* (Lincoln: University of Nebraska Press, 1980); and Diana L. Swanson, "My Boldness Terrifies Me: Sexual Abuse and Female Subjectivity in *The Voyage Out*," *Twentieth Century Literature* 41.4 (1995), 284–309.
8. *M*, p. 11; Elaine Scarry, *The Body in Pain: The Making and Unmaking of the World* (New York: Oxford University Press), p. 4.
9. Ibid., p. 3.
10. By "radial," I am referring to Woolf's description of her prose in her correspondence with painter Jacques Raverat. In a different context, Maggie Humm, following John Berger, uses the term "radial" to describe the visual descriptions in Woolf's *Three Guineas* in "Memory, Photography, and Modernism: The 'dead bodies and ruined houses' of Virginia Woolf's *Three Guineas*," *Signs* 28.2 (2002), p. 646.
11. Thomas Caramagno, *The Flight of the Mind: Virginia Woolf's Art and Manic-Depressive Illness* (Berkeley: University of California Press, 1992), p. 2.
12. Susan Sontag, "Illness as Metaphor," *Illness as Metaphor and AIDS and Its Metaphors* (New York: Picador, 2001), p. 58.
13. Both Jane Marcus and Brenda Silver address the tendency to metaphorize Woolf herself. Jane Marcus, "The Asylums of Antaeus: Women, War, and Madness – Is There a Feminist Fetishism?" *The New Historicism*, ed. H. Aram Veeser (New York: Routledge, 1989), p. 806; Brenda Silver, *Virginia Woolf Icon* (Chicago: University of Chicago Press, 1999.)
14. Scarry, *Body*, pp. 66–67, 325–26.
15. Both DeSalvo and Eberly suggest that Woolf's prose is a symptom of dissociation.
16. Linguistic dexterity is enhanced in hypomanic states, as Kay Redfield Jamison explains in *Touched with Fire: Manic Depressive Illness and the Artistic Temperament* (New York: Free Press, 1993), p. 108.

17. For a discussion of Woolf's rendering of absence, see Clewell's reading of *Jacob's Room* and *To the Lighthouse* in "Consolation Refused."
18. Scarry, *Body*, p. 3.
19. Peter Whybrow, *A Mood Apart: The Thinker's Guide to Emotion and Its Disorders* (New York: Harper Perennial, 1998), pp. 4–5.
20. Ibid., p. 4.
21. Ibid., p. 5.
22. For a discussion of collective tendencies to misperceive (or not perceive at all) the communications of trauma survivors, see Judith Lewis Herman, *Trauma and Recovery* (New York: Basic Books, 1992), pp. 7–9.
23. Scarry, *Body*, pp. 164–65.
24. Ibid., p. 171.
25. Ibid., p. 171.
26. Ibid., p. 171.
27. Judith Butler, *The Psychic Life of Power* (Stanford: Stanford University Press, 1997), pp. 192–93.
28. Ibid., p. 193. Clewell suggests that Woolf is doing just this in "venting bereaved hostility onto Jacob rather than allowing this anger to foment within the self" ("Consolation Refused," p. 205).
29. Butler, *Psychic Life*, pp. 191–92; Freud "Mourning and Melancholia," pp. 164–65.
30. Jamison, *Touched with Fire*, p. 105.
31. Quotation from the "megaphonic" voice in Woolf's *BA*, p. 187 (italics in original).
32. Christine Froula, *Virginia Woolf and the Bloomsbury Avant-Garde* (New York: Columbia University Press, 2005), p. xii.
33. Penny Farfan reads this section of "A Sketch of the Past" as an affirmation of Woolf's belief in the social importance of the artist in "Writing/Performing: Virginia Woolf *Between the Acts*," *Text and Performance Quarterly* 16 (1996), 205–15, p. 211.
34. Michael André Bernstein, *Foregone Conclusions: Against Apocalyptic History* (Berkeley: University of California Press, 1994), p. 9.
35. Zwerdling, *Virginia Woolf and the Real World*, p. 289.
36. Poole, *The Unknown Virginia Woolf*, p. 245.
37. Nancy Topping Bazin and Jane Hamovit Lauter, "Virginia Woolf's Keen Sensitivity to War," *Virginia Woolf and War*, ed. Mark Hussey (Syracuse, NY: Syracuse University Press, 1991), pp. 14–39. Several other scholars have read *Between the Acts* as a representation of Woolf's despair. See Sallie Sears, "Theater of War: Virginia Woolf's *Between the Acts*," *Virginia Woolf: A Feminist Slant*, ed. Jane Marcus (Lincoln: University of Nebraska Press, 1983), p. 215; Patricia Laurence, "The Facts and Fugue of War: From *Three Guineas* to *Between the Acts*," *Virginia Woolf and War*, ed. Mark Hussey (Syracuse, NY: Syracuse University Press, 1991), p. 244; and Karen Schneider, "Of Two Minds: Woolf, the War and *Between the Acts*," *Journal of Modern Literature* 16 (1989), 93–112, p. 95.

38. See, for example, diary entries for 23 September 1939; 7 October 1939; 2 February 1940; and 14 June 1940.
39. James F. English, *Comic Transactions: Literature, Humor, and the Politics of Community in Twentiety-Century Britain* (Ithaca, NY: Cornell University Press, 1994), p. 102.
40. Farfan, "Writing/Performing," p. 214.
41. Stephen Barber, "Lip-Reading: Woolf's Secret Encounters," *Novel Gazing: Queer Readings in Fiction*, ed. Eve Kosofsky Sedgwick (Durham, NC: Duke University Press, 1997), pp. 401–41, p. 432.
42. Bernstein, *Conclusions*, p. 1. Patricia Klindienst Joplin and Lucio Ruotolo have both commented on the significance of setting *Between the Acts* in the summer of 1939. Patricia Klindienst Joplin, "The Authority of Illusion: Feminism and Fascism in Virginia Woolf's *Between the Acts*," *Virginia Woolf: A Collection of Critical Essays*, ed. Margaret Homans (Englewood Cliffs, NJ: Prentice Hall, 1993), pp. 210–26, p. 214; Lucio P. Ruotolo, *The Interrupted Moment: A View of Virginia Woolf's Novels* (Stanford: Stanford University Press, 1986), p. 206.
43. Bernstein, *Conclusions*, p. 3.
44. Melba Cuddy-Keane describes Woolf's open historiographic methods in "Virginia Woolf and the Varieties of Historicist Experience," *Virginia Woolf and the Essay*, ed. Beth Carole Rosenberg and Jeanne Dubino (New York: St. Martin's Press, 1997), pp. 57–77, p. 66.
45. English notes the connection between homophobia and the consolidation of nationalist sentiments, suggesting that Woolf achieves a critique of nationalism through "joke-work." English, *Comic Transactions*, p. 127.
46. In Chapter 4, I discuss Sontag's critique of Woolf's depiction of imaginary consensus at greater length.
47. John Berger, "Hiroshima," *The Sense of Sight* (New York: Pantheon Books, 1985), p. 295.
48. Ibid. (Berger's emphasis)
49. Scarry, *Body*, p. 62.
50. Ibid., p. 109.
51. Sears, "Theater of War," pp. 212–13, 217.
52. Quentin Bell, *Virginia Woolf: A Biography*, vol. 2 (New York: Harcourt Brace Jovanovich, 1972), p. 107.
53. Ibid., p. 106.
54. *D-V*, 3 October 1924; partially cited in Bell, *Virginia Woolf*, vol. 2, p. 106.
55. Melba Cuddy-Keane, "The Politics of Comic Modes in Virginia Woolf's *Between the Acts*," *PMLA* 105 (1990), 273–85, p. 282.
56. English, *Comic Transactions*, p. 106. Discussing Woolf's "meditation on the artist and community," English suggests that *Between the Acts* is a failed satire (pp. 105–6), perhaps because La Trobe's parodic pageant does not fully "neutralize the nationalist effect" (p. 124).
57. Cuddy-Keane, "Politics," p. 282.

58. Several scholars have analyzed the generic features of *Between the Acts*. Among them, Melba Cuddy-Keane reads the novel as a comedy. David McWhirter reads the novel as a modernist form of tragicomedy, while Catherine Wiley and Karin E. Westman analyze the pageant and the novel, respectively, as examples of Brechtian "epic theatre." Cuddy-Keane, "Politics"; David McWhirter, "The Novel, the Play, and the Book: *Between the Acts* and the Tragicomedy of History," *English Literary History* 60 (1993), 787–812; Catherine Wiley, "Making History Unrepeatable in *Between the Acts*," *Clio* 25 (1995), 3–20; Karin E. Westman, "History as Drama: Towards a Feminist Materialist Historiography," *Virginia Woolf and the Arts: Selected Papers from the Sixth Annual Conference on Virginia Woolf*, ed. Dianne F. Gillespie and Leslie K. Hankins (New York: Pace University Press, 1997), pp. 335–43.
59. Scarry, *Body*, p. 137 (Scarry's emphasis).
60. Jo-Ann Wallace, "Woolf's 'Spinsters': The Body and the Blank Page of History," *English Studies in Canada* 16 (1990), 201–14, p. 202.
61. The former position is taken by Bazin and Lauter in "Virginia Woolf's Keen Sensitivity to War," while the latter is taken by Wallace, "Woolf's 'Spinsters,'" and Patricia Cramer, "Virginia Woolf's Matriarchal Family of Origins in *Between the Acts*," *Twentieth Century Literature* 39 (1993), pp. 166–84.
62. Scarry, *Body*, pp. 254–55.
63. *D-V*, 17 October 1940; also noted in Ruotolo, *Interrupted Moment*, p. 205.
64. Judith Butler, *Bodies that Matter: On the Discursive Limits of "Sex"* (New York: Routledge, 1993), p. 12.
65. Homi K. Bhabha, "DissemiNation: Time, Narrative, and the Margins of the Modern Nation," *Nation and Narration*, ed. Homi K. Bhabha (New York: Routledge, 1990), pp. 219–322, p. 297.
66. Ibid., p. 299.
67. Butler, *Bodies*, p. 3.
68. Ibid., p. 223.
69. Butler most explicitly links the politics of citation with authority in *Excitable Speech: A Politics of the Performative* (New York: Routledge, 1997), p. 51.
70. Bhabha, "DissemiNation," p. 297.
71. Ibid., p. 300.
72. Judith Butler, *Gender Trouble* (New York: Routledge, 1991), p. 63.
73. Eileen Barrett suggests that Woolf would have been aware of this sexological terminology through her connection with Radclyffe Hall and her discussion of sexology with friends such as E. M. Forster and Lytton Strachey in "Unmasking Lesbian Passion: The Inverted World of Mrs. Dalloway," *Virginia Woolf: Lesbian Readings*, ed. Eileen Barrett and Patricia Cramer (New York: New York University Press, 1997), pp. 146–64, p. 149.
74. English connects La Trobe's lesbianism to her position as a member of the community of outsiders of *Three Guineas* (English, *Politics*, p. 106). Julie Abraham, too, reads La Trobe as an outcast figure but interprets her

historical pageant as a critique of the "heterosexual plot," suggesting that history "ends and begins with the heterosexual couple," in *Are Girls Necessary? Lesbian Writing and Modern Histories* (New York: Routledge, 1996), p. 166.
75. Joplin, "Authority of Illusion," p. 212.
76. Farfan, "Writing/Performing," p. 209.
77. Butler, *Bodies*, p. 225.
78. Butler, *Gender Trouble*, p. 146.
79. Georgia Johnston also investigates the connections between performativity and class identification in "Class Performance in *Between the Acts*: Audiences for Miss La Trobe and Mrs. Manresa," *Woolf Studies Annual* 3 (1997), 61–75.
80. Joplin, "Authority of Illusion," pp. 210–11.
81. Jacques Lacan, "The Mirror State as Formative of the Function of the I as Revealed in Psychoanalytic Experience," *Ecrits: A Selection*, trans. Alan Sheridan (New York: Norton, 1977), pp. 1–7, p. 2.
82. Scarry, *Body*, pp. 62, 121.
83. Butler, *Gender Trouble*, p. 145 (Butler's emphasis). Farfan makes use of this Butlerian concept in her argument as well. Whereas Farfan focuses more specifically on the "master plot of heterosexual romance," my aim has been to extend Butler's insights more generally to the construction of national subjects. Farfan, "Writing/Performing," p. 210.
84. Focusing on the imbrication of history with the repetition of regulatory norms, Della Pollock, among others, reads Butler pessimistically in "Introduction: Making History Go," *Exceptional Spaces: Essays in Performance and History*, ed. Della Pollock (Chapel Hill: University of North Carolina Press, 1998), pp. 1–45, p. 2. Butler, on the other hand, suggests that we cannot choose to disregard the formative effect of discursive norms, but we can attempt to employ these norms not-according-to-their-directions, in order to expose, and potentially change, their normative force (*Gender Trouble*, p. 145).

2 STEIN'S SHAME

1. Brenda Silver, *Virginia Woolf Icon* (Chicago: University of Chicago Press, 1999), p. 3.
2. Catharine R. Stimpson, and Brenda Wineapple, "An Icon Is an Icon Is a Challenge to Teach," *The Chronicle of Higher Education*, 22 January 1999, p. B6.
3. Catharine R. Stimpson, "The Somagrams of Gertrude Stein," *Poetics Today* 6.1–2 (1985), 67–80, p. 70.
4. Eve Kosofsky Sedgwick, *Touching Feeling: Affect, Pedagogy, Performativity* (Durham, NC: Duke University Press, 2003), p. 37.
5. Ibid., p. 37.
6. Marianne Hirsch, *Family Frames: Photography, Narrative, and Postmemory* (Cambridge, MA: Harvard University Press, 1997), p. 22.

7. James E. Young, *At Memory's Edge: After-Images of the Holocaust in Contemporary Art and Architecture* (New Haven, NJ: Yale University Press, 2000), p. 2.
8. For a critique of the Military Commissions Act of 2006, which regulates the detention of "alien unlawful enemy combatants," "secret detentions," and "'alternative' interrogation techniques," see Amnesty International's report on the "Military Commissions Act of 2006."
9. Robert Casillo, *The Genealogy of Demons: Anti-Semitism, Fascism, and the Myths of Ezra Pound* (Evanston, IL: Northwestern University Press, 1988), p. 3.
10. Adolf Hitler, *Mein Kampf* (selections), *Sources of the Western Tradition*, ed. Marvin Perry, Joseph R. Peden, and Theodore H. Von Laue (Boston: Houghton Mifflin Co., 1987), p. 299.
11. The Southern Poverty Law Center, for example, has produced an "Intelligence Report" since 1981 tracking and documenting the activities of hate groups such as the Ku Klux Klan, Aryan Nations, and the National Socialist Movement (www.splcenter.org/intel/law.jsp). National Public Radio ran a weeklong series charting "Europe's Right Turn" in Denmark, Belgium, and France on 20–22 November 2006. Sylvia Poggioli, "Europe Looks Inward, Tilts to the Right," *NPR.org*, www.npr.org/templates/story/story.php?storyId=6522463.
12. In *Identification Papers*, Diana Fuss argues that metaphors associated with identification fall into three main categories: identification as falling, identification as incorporation, and identification as contagion. While all three of these identificatory tropes operate in H.D.'s late writing, the trope of contagion is especially significant in her writing on Pound. Diana Fuss, *Identification Papers* (New York: Routledge, 1995), p. 13.
13. During World War II, Pound broadcast pro-fascist and anti-Semitic diatribes on Rome Radio. (These broadcasts led to his arrest in 1945 for treason, but he was eventually declared unfit to stand trial and committed to St. Elizabeth's hospital.)
14. H.D., *End to Torment: A Memoir of Ezra Pound* (New York: New Directions, 1979), pp. 4–5.
15. Ibid., p. 11.
16. Ibid., p. 20.
17. Ibid., p. 5.
18. Ibid., p. 27.
19. Donna Krolik Hollenberg, *Between History and Poetry: The Letters of H.D. and Norman Holmes Pearson* (Iowa City: University of Iowa Press, 1997), p. 203.
20. For an analysis of the trial, see Conrad L. Rushing, "Mere Words: The Trial of Ezra Pound," *Critical Inquiry* 14.1 (1987), 111–33.
21. Norman Holmes Pearson, letter to H.D., 8 April 1958, Hollenberg, *Letters*, p. 219.
22. Sedgwick, *Touching Feeling*, p. 37; Hollenberg, *Letters*, p. 219.

23. Edward Said, *Culture and Imperialism* (New York: Vintage Books, 1994), p. 4; Avery F. Gordon, *Ghostly Matters: Haunting and the Sociological Imagination* (Minneapolis: University of Minnesota Press, 1996), p. 42; Theodor Adorno, "Cultural Criticism and Society," *Can One Live after Auschwitz? A Philosophical Reader*, ed. Rolf Tiedemann (Stanford: Stanford University Press, 2003), pp. 146–62, p. 146.
24. Gordon, *Ghostly Matters*, p. 4. Stimpson and Wineapple address scholarly reactions to Stein's "complicated" politics in "An Icon Is an Icon Is a Challenge to Teach."
25. Arthur Lachman, "Gertrude Stein as I Knew Her," *Gertrude Stein Remembered*, ed. Linda Simon (Lincoln: University of Nebraska Press, 1994), pp. 3–9, p. 3.
26. Linda Simon (ed.), *Gertrude Stein Remembered* (Lincoln: University of Nebraska Press, 1994), p. 1.
27. Diana Souhami, *Gertrude and Alice* (San Francisco: Pandora, 1991), p. 124.
28. Stimpson, "Somagrams" ("Somagrams," 67–71).
29. Blanche Wiesen Cook, "'Women Alone Stir My Imagination': Lesbianism and the Cultural Tradition," *Signs* 4.4 (1979), 718–39, p. 730.
30. Ibid., p. 730. Cook's charge of anti-Semitism requires further assessment, especially given Stein's own understanding of anti-Semitic attacks on Jews such as pogroms in Russia and the Dreyfus affair. In an 1896 college composition, Stein demonstrated a keen awareness of how anti-Semitism targeted even assimilated Jews: "A Jew admitted into the society of Gentiles is admitted on sufferance only. As long as they like him personally all is well, but the instant he does aught that is blameworthy, swiftly comes opprobation, not only to the man but his race." Gertrude Stein, "The Modern Jew Who Has Given up the Faith of His Fathers Can Reasonably and Consistently Believe in Isolation," ed. Amy Feinstein, *PMLA* 116.2 (2001), 416–28, pp. 427.
31. Jean E. Mills, "Gertrude Stein Took the War Like a Man," *The Gay and Lesbian Review*, March–April (2003), 16–18, p. 16.
32. Ibid., p. 17.
33. Ibid., p. 17.
34. Ibid., p. 17.
35. Butler argues that politics cannot be presumed to follow from identity: "This antifoundationalist approach to coalitional politics assumes neither that 'identity' is a premise nor that the shape or meaning of a coalitional assemblage can be known prior to its achievement" (*Gender Trouble*, p. 21).
36. Leigh Gilmore, "A Signature of Lesbian Autobiography: Gertrice/Altrude," *Autobiography and Questions of Gender*, ed. Shirely Neuman (London: Frank Cass & Co. Ltd., 1992), pp. 63–64.
37. Ibid., p. 64.
38. For a historical discussion of butch/femme culture, see Elizabeth Lapovsky Kennedy and Madeline D. Davis, *Boots of Leather, Slippers of Gold: The History of a Lesbian Community* (New York: Routledge, 1993).
39. Stimpson, "Somagrams," p. 69.

40. For examples of modes of female masculinity available to Stein, see Judith Halberstam, *Female Masculinity* (Durham, NC: Duke University Press, 1998).
41. By "legitimate" I mean intelligible and acceptable to many contemporary lesbians. I don't mean to suggest that butch/femme relationships are acceptable to homophobic culture at large. Butler discusses the "norms of cultural intelligibility" in *Gender Trouble*, arguing that "'intelligible' genders are those which in some sense institute and maintain relations of coherence and continuity among sex, gender, sexual practice, and desire" (p. 23).
42. Gilmore, "Gertrice/Altrude," p. 57.
43. Ibid., p. 61.
44. Sidonie Smith, *Subjectivity, Identity, and the Body: Women's Autobiographical Practices in the Twentieth Century* (Bloomington: Indiana University Press, 1993), p. 66.
45. Ibid., p. 66.
46. Ibid., p. 68.
47. Ibid., p. 71.
48. Ibid., p. 72.
49. Ibid., pp. 79–80.
50. Ibid., p. 80.
51. Ibid., pp. 75, 78.
52. Ibid., p. 82.
53. Gertrude Stein, "Melanctha," *Three Lives and Q.E.D.*, ed. Marianne DeKoven, Norton Critical Edition (New York: W. W. Norton & Co., 2006), pp. 53–147, p. 147.
54. Marianne DeKoven, "Race, Sexuality, and Form in 'Melanctha,'" *Three Lives and Q.E.D.*, ed. DeKoven, pp. 402–7, p. 403; Sonia Saldívar-Hull, "Racism in 'Melanctha,'" *Three Lives and Q.E.D.*, ed. DeKoven, pp. 358–67, p. 367.
55. Ibid., p. 361.
56. Jamie Hovey, "Sapphic Primitivism in Gertrude Stein's *Q.E.D.*," *Modern Fiction Studies* 42.3 (1996), 547–68, p. 547.
57. Sontag, *Illness as Metaphor*, p. 45.
58. According to the *Oxford English Dictionary*, "melancholy" comes from the root Melano- (black) plus choler (bile). The etymology for melancholy is listed as follows: "<Anglo-Norman *malencolie, malancolie, melancolie, melencolie* and Middle French *melancolie* (c 1180 in Old French; French *mélancolie*) < post-classical Latin *melancholia* (5th cent.; already in classical Latin as a Greek loanword) < ancient Greek μελανχολια–condition of having black bile < μελαν - (see MELANO-) + χολη βιλε (cf. CHOLER *n.*¹) + ια-IA¹. Cf. Old Occitan *melancolia, melanconia* (13th cent.), Spanish *melancolia* (1490; 1251 as *malenconia*), Italian *malinconia* (late 13th cent.; c1243 as *mellenconia*), Middle High German *melancolia, melancoli, melancolei* (14th cent.; German *Melancholie*), Middle Dutch *melancolie, merancolie, mirancolie* (Dutch *melancholie*), Swedish *melankoli* (1557). Cf. MELANCHOLIA *n*"

(*OED*). Melanctha comes from the same root, "Melano-" (black) combined with the root Chthonic" (earth). Thus Melanctha would mean "black earth," although name books list the meaning as "black flower" (http://baby-names.adoption.com/search/Melanctha.html).
59. Stein, "Melanctha," p. 54.
60. Ibid., p. 147.
61. The epigraph to "Melanctha" is "Each one as she may," which DeKoven reads as a "pun on the name May Bookstaver, Stein's lover from 1900–1902, on whom the characters Melanctha, and Helen in *Q.E.D.* are based" (*Three Lives and Q.E.D.*, p. 53 fn.1).
62. Stein, "Melanctha," p. 61.
63. Janet Malcolm reports Fäy's role in the persecution of Freemasons in "Gertrude Stein's War: The Years in Occupied France," *The New Yorker*, 2 June 2003, www.newyorker.com/fact/content/articles/030603fa_fact2. (accessed 24 November 2006). Barbara Will remarks on the possibility that Stein joked about nominating Hitler for the peace prize in 1934 in "Gertrude Stein and Zionism," *Modern Fiction Studies* 51.2 (2005), 437–55, p. 451. Priscilla Wald, Jayne L. Walker, and Leon Katz, among others, discuss Stein's admiration for Weininger. Priscilla Wald, *Constituting Americans: Cultural Anxiety and Narrative Form* (Durham, NC: Duke University Press, 1995); Jayne L. Walker, *The Making of a Modernist: Gertrude Stein from Three Lives to Tender Buttons* (Amherst: University of Massachusetts Press, 1984); Leon Katz, "The First Making of *The Making of Americans*," PhD diss. Columbia University, 1963.
64. See Gertrude Stein, *Wars I Have Seen* (New York: Random House, 1945), p. 11; Stein, "Introduction to the Speeches of Maréchal Pétain," *Modernism/Modernity* 3.3 (1996), 93–96; Wanda Van Dusen, "Portrait of a National Fetish: Gertrude Stein's "Introduction to the Speeches of Maréchal Pétain," *Modernism/Modernity* 3.3 (1996), 69–92; Linda Wagner Martin, *"Favored Strangers": Gertrude Stein and Her Family* (New Brunswick: Rutgers University Press, 1995), pp. 246–47; Richard Bridgman, *Gertrude Stein in Pieces* (New York: Oxford University Press, 1970), pp. 316–18; Phoebe Stein Davis, "'Even Cake Gets to Have Another Meaning': History, Narrative, and 'Daily Living' in Gertrude Stein's World War II Writings," *Modern Fiction Studies* 44.3 (1998), 568–607, p. 568; and Barbara Will, "Lost in Translation: Stein's Vichy Collaboration," *Modernism/Modernity* 11.4 (2004), 651–68, p. 651.
65. Van Dusen, "Portrait," p. 70.
66. Ibid., p. 71.
67. Stein Davis, "'Even Cake,'" p. 600.
68. Will, "Lost in Translation," p. 665.
69. Will, "Gertrude Stein and Zionism," p. 451.
70. Malcolm, "Gertrude Stein's War."
71. Ibid.

72. Janet Malcolm, "Strangers in Paradise: How Gertrude Stein and Alice B. Toklas got to Heaven," *The New Yorker*, 13 November 2006, www.newyorker.com/fact/content/articles/061113fa_fact1 (accessed 24 November 2006).
73. Craig Seligman, in a biography for *Salon* magazine, notes that "Malcolm was born in prewar Prague, one of two daughters (the other is the writer Marie Winn) of secular Jews; the family got out of Europe just in time, in 1939." Craig Seligman, "Janet Malcolm," *Brilliant Careers. Salon.com*, 29 February 2000, http://archive.salon.com/people/bc/2000/02/29/malcolm/index.html (accessed 29 November 2006).
74. Gertrude Stein, *The Making of Americans* (Norman, IL: Dalkey Archive Press, 1995), p. 180.
75. Wald, *Constituting Americans*, p. 252.
76. Ibid., p. 257.
77. Ibid., p. 251.
78. Butler, *Psychic Life of Power*, p. 191.
79. Ibid., p. 193. Wald notes that Stein wrote to Mabel Weeks about both texts (*Three Lives* and *The Making of Americans*), specifically linking the former texts to writing on the "margins" and the latter text to her attempt to write the "Great American Novel" (Wald, *Constituting Americans*, pp. 239–40).
80. Butler, *Psychic Life of Power*, p. 94.
81. Fuss, *Identification Papers*, p. 2.
82. Ibid., pp. 5–6 (Fuss' emphasis).
83. Thorton Wilder, "Introduction to *Four in America*," *Gertrude Stein Remembered*, ed. Linda Simon (Lincoln: University of Nebraska Press, 1994), p. 132.
84. Stein, "Hersland (old man) died," unpublished notebook to *The Making of Americans*, Gertrude Stein and Alice B. Toklas Papers. Yale Collection of American Literature. Beinecke Rare Book and Manuscript Library.
85. Stein, *The Making of Americans*, p. 498.
86. Ibid., p. 498.
87. Ibid., p. 498.
88. Herbert Marcuse, "The Ideology of Death," *The Meaning of Death*, ed. Herman Feifel (New York: McGraw-Hill, 1959), p. 64.
89. Ibid., pp. 64–5.
90. Ibid., p. 65.
91. Elaine Scarry, *The Body in Pain: The Making and Unmaking of the World* (New York: Oxford University Press, 1985), pp. 12–13, 66.
92. Sigmund Freud, "Thoughts for the Times on War and Death (1915)," *Freud: On War, Sex and Neurosis*, ed. Sander Katz, trans. Joan Riviere *et al.* (New York: Arts & Science Press, 1947), pp. 294–95.
93. Ibid., p. 295.
94. Ibid., p. 264.
95. Marcuse, "Ideology," p. 64; Freud, "Thoughts," 295.
96. See for example Lisa Ruddick, *Reading Gertrude Stein: Body, Text, Gnosis* (Ithaca, NY: Cornell University Press, 1990), pp. 4–6; Bridgman, *Gertrude*

Stein in Pieces, p. 133; Walker, *Making of a Modernist*, pp. 1–18; and Stephanie L. Hawkins, "The Science of Superstition: Gertrude Stein, William James, and the Formation of Belief," *Modern Fiction Studies* 51.1 (2005), 60–87, p. 61.
97. LeRoy Panek, *Probable Cause: Crime Fiction in America* (Bowling Green: Bowling Green State University Popular Press, 1990), p. 40.
98. Gertrude Stein, *Everybody's Autobiography* (Cambridge, MA: Exact Change, 1993), p. 2.
99. Ibid., p. 127.
100. Maureen T. Reddy, *Sisters in Crime: Feminism and the Crime Novel* (New York: Continuum, 1988), p. 6.
101. Gertrude Stein, *Blood on the Dining-Room Floor*, ed. John Herbert Gill (Berkeley: Black Lizard, 1982). Gill points out the autobiographical details and historical references of the story in his "Afterword," pp. 83–100.
102. Stein, *Blood*, p. 50.
103. Ibid., p. 51.
104. Gertrude Stein, "Why I Like Detective Stories," *How Writing Is Written*, ed. Robert Bartlett Haas (New York: Black Sparrow Press, 1974), pp. 146–50, p. 149.
105. Gertrude Stein, "American Crimes and How They Matter," *How Writing Is Written*, ed. Robert Bartlett Haas (New York: Black Sparrow Press, 1974), pp. 100–5, p. 101.
106. Ibid., p. 101.
107. Ibid., pp. 103–4.
108. Gertrude Stein, *The Geographical History of America*, ed. William H. Gass (Baltimore, MD: Johns Hopkins University Press, 1995), p. 45.
109. Ibid., p. 45.
110. Marcuse, "Ideology of Death," p. 74.
111. Stein, *Geographical History*, p. 46.
112. Ibid., p. 46.
113. Ibid., p. 62.
114. Gill, "Afterword," pp. 94.
115. Stein, *Geographical History*, p. 63.
116. Ibid., p. 64.
117. Julie Abraham reads this passage differently, suggesting that it represents a longing for consolation, in *Are Girls Necessary? Lesbian Writing and Modern Histories* (New York: Routledge, 1996), p. 94. The negatives in the sentence, "I wish I knew a history as a history which is not which is not there are no fears," however suggest that Stein does *not* wish for history to pretend "there are no fears."
118. Stein, *Geographical History*, pp. 78–79.
119. Ibid., p. 112.
120. Abraham discusses Stein's preference for a history of "daily living" over a history of "events" in *Are Girls Necessary?*, pp. 89–91.
121. Gertrude Stein, "American Biography and Why Waste It," *Useful Knowledge* (Barryhill, NY: Station Hill Press, 1988), pp. 162–69, p. 162.

122. Ibid., p. 163.
123. Ibid., p. 169.
124. Gertrude Stein, "Transatlantic Interview," *How Writing Is Written*, ed. Robert Bartlett Haas (New York: Black Sparrow Press, 1974), p. 16.
125. Ibid., p. 16.
126. Ibid., pp. 16–17.
127. Van Dusen, "Portrait of a National Fetish," p. 74; Stein, "Transatlantic Interview," p. 17.
128. Stein, *Wars*, p. 111.
129. Ibid., pp. 111–21.
130. Gertrude Stein, *Reflection on the Atomic Bomb*, ed. Robert Bartlett Haas (Los Angeles: Black Sparrow Press, 1973), p. 161.
131. Ibid., p. 161 (Robert Haas' editorial insertion).
132. Scarry, *Body*, p. 66.
133. Ibid.

3 H.D.'S WARS

1. Susan Stanford Friedman, *Penelope's Web: Gender Modernity, and H.D.'s Fiction* (Cambridge: Cambridge University Press, 1990), pp. 152–53.
2. Sections of "The Walls Do Not Fall" circulated on many lists, including the HDSOC-L (H.D. Society) list, the WOMPO (women's poetry discussion) list, the New-Poetry list, and the UB Poetics discussion group.
3. On the pressure to mourn after September 11, see David Eng, "The Value of Silence," *Theater Journal* 54 (2002), 85–94. David Simpson analyzes the political (mis)uses of post-9/11 commemorative culture in *9/11: The Culture of Commemoration* (Chicago: University of Chicago Press: 2006).
4. Michael S. Roth, *The Ironists Cage: Memory, Trauma, and the Construction of History* (New York: Columbia University Press, 1995), pp. 11–12.
5. Ibid., p. 8.
6. Cathy Caruth, *Unclaimed Experience: Trauma, Narrative, and History* (Baltimore, MD: Johns Hopkins University Press, 1996), pp. 91–92.
7. Susan Stanford Friedman, whose work on H.D. has been indispensable to scholars, uses the term "Madrigal cycle" to describe *Paint it Today*, *Asphodel*, and *Bid Me to Live (A Madrigal)*. For a complete discussion of her characterization of the novels as a cycle, see *Penelope's Web*, p. 285 fn. 2. According to Friedman, *Pilate's Wife* was written between 1924 and 1934. During her lifetime, H.D. submitted the manuscript for publication, but it was rejected. Susan Stanford Friedman, "Dating H.D.'s Writing," *Signets: Reading H.D.*, ed. Susan Stanford Friedman and Rachel Blau DuPlessis (Madison, WI: University of Wisconsin Press, 1990), p. 48.
8. Michael André Bernstein, *Foregone History: Against Apocalyptic History* (Berkeley: University of California Press, 1994) p. 9.
9. Bernstein argues that "It is essential to recognize here that whenever our sense of what the Shoah destroyed includes, along with their actual deaths,

Notes to pages 82–83

the potential achievements and never realized futures of the children who were murdered, we are already engaged in sideshadowing. The logic of historical inevitability, on the other hand, explicitly suggests that the murdered children were already doomed to perish in the Shoah the instant they were born, hence it would be inconsistent to mourn the adult lives they never experienced or the accomplishments they never attained" (ibid., p. 15).

10. For accounts of H.D.'s difference from male modernists, see Susan Stanford Friedman's "Creating a Women's Mythology" in *Signets: Reading H.D.*, ed. Susan Stanford Friedman and Rachel Blau DuPlessis (Madison, WI: University of Wisconsin Press, 1990), pp. 373–405, and Melody Zajdel, "'I See Her Differently': H.D.'s *Trilogy* as Feminist Response to Masculine Modernism," *Sagetrieb* 5 (1986), 7–16.
11. William Butler Yeats, "Easter 1916," *Selected Poems and Four Plays*, ed. M. L. Rosenthal (New York: Scribner, 1996), p. 83.
12. William Butler Yeats, "Second Coming," *Selected Poems and Four Plays*, ed. M. L. Rosenthal (New York: Scribner, 1996), p. 89.
13. Cyrena N. Pondrom examines the intertextuality of *Trilogy* and *Four Quartets*, but she does not comment on the ideological significance of the two poems' rhetorical similarities, in "*Trilogy* and *Four Quartets*: Contrapuntal Visions of Spiritual Quest," *Agenda* 25.3–4 (1987–88), 155–65.
14. As Fradenburg and Carla Freccero note, "salvific" histories can serve to persuade a culture that certain sacrifices are necessary, even good: "One important aspect of the salvific virtue of history in Caxton's account is its incitement to glory, to sacrifice ... Through the knowledge history makes about life and death, young men will be more likely to risk their lives for the common good. Caxton thus registers the lethal productivity of history but also legitimizes it: jeopardy redemptively produces the defense of countries and the 'public weal'; and records of 'other strange men's hurts' teach us how to live – that is, if 'we' are good fighting men." [Aranye] Louise O. Fradenburg and Carla Freccero, "The Pleasures of History," *GLQ* 1.4 (1995), p. 372. Such histories record, legitimize, and therefore perpetuate jeopardy. Suggesting that certain kinds of deaths are glorious, salvific histories reproduce "good fighting men" willing to kill and die for their country. Literature, as well as history, participates in this formation of "good fighting men."
15. [Aranye] Louise O. Fradenburg discusses the implications of women's association with the particular in "Voice Memorial: Loss and Reparation in Chaucer's Poetry," *Exemplaria* 2.1 (1990), p. 185.
16. For a discussion of H.D.'s response to the ideology of patriotic motherhood, see Friedman, *Penelope's Web*, pp. 189–90.
17. Ibid., p. 216.
18. Bernstein, *Foregone History*, p. 1.
19. Herbert Marcuse, "The Ideology of Death," *The Meaning of Death*, ed. Herbert Feifel (New York: McGraw Hill, 1959), p. 64.

20. Although "Burnt Norton" was written before the outbreak of war, Eliot and his Bloomsbury contemporaries would have been aware of the political menace Nazi Germany presented in 1935, the year Hitler denounced the Versailles Treaty.
21. The first five lines of "Burnt Norton" are:

> Time present and time past
> Are both perhaps present in time future,
> And time future contained in time past.
> If all time is eternally present
> All time is unredeemable.   ("BN" lines 1–5)

22. "Little Gidding," the last quartet, was composed in 1942, the same year that mainstream newspapers in Britain began to issue reports on the extermination of Jews in Nazi death camps. Victoria Harrison, "When a Gift is Poison: H.D., The Moravian, The Jew, and World War II," *Sagetrieb* 15 (1993), p. 74.
23. For Scarry, the structure of war is a contest whereby the materiality of the wounded or killed body is used to substantiate abstract concepts and values. The values of the side which succeeds in "out-injuring" the other prevail. Elaine Scarry, *The Body in Pain: The Making and Unmaking of the World* (New York: Oxford University Press, 1985), p. 64.
24. Walter Benjamin, "Theses on the Philosophy of History," *Illuminations*, ed. Hannah Arendt, trans. H. Zolin (New York: Schocken Books, 1969) p. 256.
25. Lee Quimby, *Anti-Apocalypse: Exercises in Genealogical Criticism* (Minneapolis: University of Minnesota Press, 1994), p. xvii.
26. Bernstein, *Foregone History*, p. 2.
27. Elinor Shaffer, "Secular Apocalypse: Prophets and Apocalyptics at the End of the Eighteenth Century," *Apocalypse Theory and the Ends of the World*, ed. Malcolm Bull (Cambridge, MA: Blackwell Publishing, 2003), p. 137.
28. The italicized portions of the verse are direct references to the Book of Revelation 21: 10–11, 14, 22.
29. H.D.'s accounts of Nazi anti-Semitism in Vienna and her correspondence with Freud in London are published in H.D., *Tribute to Freud* (New York: New Directions, 1974), pp. 58–63.
30. Harrison, "When a Gift," p. 73.
31. The Book of Revelation 21: 4–5.
32. Peter Sacks, *The English Elegy: Studies in the Genre from Spenser to Yeats* (Baltimore, MD: Johns Hopkins University Press, 1985), p. 2.
33. Ibid., p. 4.
34. Ibid.
35. Ibid., p. 5.
36. Ibid., p. 8.
37. Fradenburg argues that "It is not possible to speak of the 'acceptance' of loss without simultaneously denying loss. That renunciation, acceptance, and

closure are so commonly insisted upon both by the elegy and by theoretical and critical treatments of the genre must, then, give us pause" ("Voice Memorial," p. 184).
38. Ibid., p. 183.
39. Sigmund Freud, "Thoughts for the Times on War and Death (1915)," *Freud: On War, Sex, and Neurosis*, ed. Sander Katz, trans. Joan Riviere *et al.* (New York: Arts & Science Press, 1947), pp. 294–95.
40. Ibid., 295.
41. Sigmund Freud, *The Interpretation of Dreams. The Standard Edition of the Complete Psychological Works*, vol. 5, trans. James Strachey (London: Hogarth Press, 1953) p. 509. Cited in Caruth, *Unclaimed Experience*, p. 93 (Freud's emphasis).
42. Caruth, *Unclaimed Experience*, p. 105 (Caruth's emphasis).
43. Ibid., p. 92 (Caruth's emphasis).
44. Ibid., p. 104.
45. Freud's and Lacan's accounts clearly foreclose this possibility by beginning with a child who is already dead.
46. Judith Butler, *The Psychic Life of Power* (Stanford: Stanford University Press, 1997), p. 7.
47. Ibid., pp. 7–8.
48. I am thinking here of the explosion of "talk show" discourse on incest that is described in Louise Armstrong, *Rocking the Cradle of Sexual Politics* (Reading, MA: Addison-Wesley Publishing, 1994).
49. Butler, *Psychic Life*, p. 7. Elizabeth Wilson suggests that in middle-class white families, there is a general unwillingness to see incest as part of a continuum of abuse and neglect that children face in "Not in this House: Incest, Denial, and Doubt in the White Middle Class Family," *The Yale Journal of Criticism* 8.1 (1995), 35–58.
50. Caruth, *Unclaimed Experience*, p. 105.
51. John Berger, "Hiroshima," *The Sense of Sight: Writings by John Berger* (New York: Pantheon Books, 1985), p. 295.
52. Ibid., p. 295.
53. Both Friedman and Dianne Chisholm note the intertextuality of Freud's and H.D.'s writing. Friedman reads *The Gift* as "a continuation of the specific analysis she began with Freud" (*Penelope's Web*, p. 286). Dianne Chisholm reads *The Gift* as a revision of Freud's theory of implicitly melancholic femininity in *H.D.'s Freudian Poetics: Psychoanalysis in Translation* (Ithaca, NY: Cornell University Press, 1992), p. 134.
54. Susan Edmunds describes H.D.'s use of montage techniques in *Out of Line: History, Psychoanalysis, and Montage* (Stanford: Stanford University Press, 1994). Friedman describes H.D.'s "dark room" metaphors in *Penelope's Web*.
55. Friedman reads this passage as H.D.'s working through her "war phobia" through recourse to the "safe" space of childhood memory (*Penelope's Web*, p. 335).

56. It is not a coincidence that *Uncle Tom's Cabin* would have been young Hilda's first play, given the extraordinary popularity of "Tom plays" during the late nineteenth century. Judith Williams discusses the history of the play's reception in "Uncle Tom's Women," *African American Performance and Theater History: A Critical Reader*, ed. Harry J. Elam Jr. and David Krasner (New York: Oxford University Press, 2001), p. 19.
57. H.D.'s tendency to see race as symbolic, and therefore to be blind to the racist implications of her own representations, is persistent throughout her career. As Susan Edmunds notes regarding H.D.'s last poem, *Hermetic Definition*, H.D. registers her ambivalent, appropriative/appreciative attitude toward two postcolonial men (Lionel Durand and St.-John Perse) and an African American man (Rafer Johnson) (*Out of Line*, p. 152); H.D., *Hermetic Definition* (New York: New Directions, 1972).
58. See Williams, "Uncle Tom's Women," for an analysis of the tradition of minstrelsy in "Tom shows."
59. Hilda's penchant for projecting representational reality on the body of the black man prefigures her assertion that the character Pete, in *Borderline*, represents a naturalness that neurotic, over-civilized whites fail to possess. See Jean Walton, "White Neurotics, Black Primitives, and the Queer Matrix of *Borderline*," *Out Takes: Essays on Queer Theory and Film*, ed. Ellis Hanson (Durham, NC: Duke University Press, 1999), pp. 243–70.
60. H.D., *Palimpsest* (Carbondale, IL: Southern Illinois University Press, 1968), p. 6.
61. Edmunds, *Out of Line*, pp. 113–14; H.D., *Helen in Egypt* (New York: New Directions, 1961), pp. 17–21.
62. Friedman, *Penelope's Web*, p. 338.
63. Sigmund Freud, "From the History of an Infantile Neurosis," *The Standard Edition of the Complete Psychological Works*, vol. 17, trans. James Strachey (London: Hogarth Press, 1955), p. 16.
64. Ibid., p. 40.
65. Ibid., p. 35.
66. Ibid., p. 95.
67. Ibid., p. 20.
68. Ibid., p. 21.
69. Susan Stanford Friedman's *Psyche Reborn: The Emergence of H.D.* (Bloomington: Indiana University Press, 1990) and Friedman, *Penelope's Web* are exemplary in demonstrating H.D.'s concern with rebirth in *Trilogy*.
70. Nicholas Abraham and Maria Torok, "A Poetics of Psychoanalysis: 'The Lost Object – Me,'" *SubStance* 43 (1984), p. 5.
71. Ibid., p. 4.
72. Ibid., p. 4.
73. Ibid., p. 4 (Abraham and Torok's italics).
74. Friedman, *Psyche Reborn*, pp. 9–13.
75. Friedman also reads *The Gift* and *Trilogy* as paired texts, suggesting that "*The Gift* is personal, clearing up the tangles of brushweed in the forests of

memory so that she could step into the clearing as the clairvoyant poet of *Trilogy* who mediates between the sacred and the profane" (*Penelope's Web*, p. 350).
76. Lewis Spence, *Ancient Egyptian Myths and Legends* [reprint] (New York: Dover, 1990), p. 63. Originally published as *Myths & Legends of Ancient Egypt* (London: G. Harrap, 1915).
77. Ibid., p. 106.
78. Ibid., p. 67.
79. Ibid., pp. 68–69.
80. Isis figures most prominently in "The Walls Do Not Fall"; Mary in "Tribute to the Angels"; and Mary Magdalene in "The Flowering of the Rod."
81. Spence, *Ancient Egyptian*, pp. 68–69.
82. When Isis cut open the tree, she "mourned so loudly over it that one of the young princes dies of terror" (ibid., p. 69).
83. Ibid., p. 71.
84. H.D., *Tribute to Freud*, p. 37.
85. Ibid., p. 37.
86. Sigmund Freud, *Moses and Monotheism*, trans. Katherine Jones (New York: Random House, 1939), p. 140.
87. Ibid., p. 168.
88. Ibid., p. 5.
89. H.D., *Tribute to Freud*, p. 37.
90. H.D., *Asphodel*, ed. Robert Spoo (Durham, NC: Duke University Press, 1992), p. 103.
91. H.D., *Paint It Today*, ed. Cassandra Laity (New York: New York University Press, 1992), p. 3.
92. Ibid., p. 5.
93. Ibid., p. 6.
94. For a discussion of the patriotic mother in wartime propaganda, see Jane Marcus, "The Asylums of Antaeus: Women, War, and Madness – Is There a Feminist Fetishism?" *The New Historicism*, ed. H. Aram Veeser (New York: Routledge, 1989), p. 141.
95. H.D., *Asphodel*, p. 129.
96. H.D., *Bid Me to Live* (Reading Ridge, CT: Black Swan, 1983), p. 50.
97. Ibid., p. 86.
98. Lee Quimby, *Anti-Apocalypse: Exercises in Genealogical Criticism* (Minneapolis: University of Minnesota Press, 1994), p. xxii.
99. Jennifer Terry, "Theorizing Deviant Historiography," *differences* 3.2 (1991), p. 56 (emphasis in the original).
100. Burke, "Introduction," *PW*, p. x; Friedman, *Psyche Reborn*, p. 6.
101. Burke, "Introduction," *PW*, p. xi.
102. Ibid., pp. xi–xiii.
103. Marcuse, "Ideology of Death," p. 68.
104. Plato, *Phaedo*, trans. David Gallop (New York: Oxford University Press, 1998), lines 67a5, 84a5–84b.

105. Marcuse, "Ideology," p. 71.
106. D. H. Lawrence, *St Mawr* and *The Man Who Died* (New York: Vintage, 1953), p. 205.
107. Ibid., p. 207.
108. Michel Foucault, *History of Sexuality: An Introduction*, vol. 1, trans. Robert Hurley (New York: Random House, 1990), p. 157.
109. Burke carefully outlines the etymology of Mnevis' name in her introduction to *Pilate's Wife*, p. ix.
110. Nicole Loraux, *Mothers in Mourning*, trans. Corinne Pache (Ithaca, NY: Cornell University Press, 1998), p. 68.
111. Ibid., p. 71.
112. Ibid., p. 77.
113. *Fahrenheit 9/11*, dir. Michael Moore (Lions Gate Films, 2004).
114. Loraux, *Mothers*, p. 78.
115. H.D., *Asphodel*, p. 122.
116. Ibid., p. 122.
117. Friedman, *Penelope's Web*, pp. 189–90.
118. Ibid., p. 186.
119. H.D., *Bid Me to Live*, pp. 24–25.
120. Judith Butler, *Antigone's Claim: Kinship Between Life and Death* (New York: Columbia University Press, 2000), p. 37.
121. Louis Silverstein, "Louis Silverstein's H.D. Chronology," *Imagists.org*, www.imagists.org/hd/hdchron.html, pp. 36–37.
122. H.D., *Asphodel*, p. 123.

4 PICTURES, ARGUMENTS, AND EMPATHY

1. Susan Sontag, *On Photography* (New York: Picador 1977), p. 175.
2. Raymond Williams, *The Politics of Modernism: Against the New Conformists* (New York: Verso, 1989), p. 38.
3. Susan Sontag, "Why Are We in Kosovo?" *The New York Times*, 2 May 1999, *The New York Times Online*, http://query.nytimes.com/gst/fullpage.html?res=9C07E1DA163DF931A35756C0A96F958260&sec=&spon=&partner= permalink&exprod=permalink.
4. "Compassion," *Oxford English Dictionary Online*, 2nd edition, 2002 Draft Additions "compassion fatigue," dictionary.oed.com. Marjorie Garber, "Compassion," *Compassion: The Culture and Politics of an Emotion*, ed. Lauren Berlant (New York: Routledge, 2004), p. 19.
5. Lauren Berlant, "The Subject of True Feeling: Pain, Privacy, and Politics," *Cultural Studies and Political Theory*, ed. Jodi Dean (Ithaca, NY: Cornell University Press, 2000), p. 62.
6. Friedrich Schiller, *On the Aesthetic Education of Man in a Series of Letters*, ed. and trans. Elizabeth M. Wilkinson and L. A. Willoughby (Oxford: Oxford University Press, 1967), p. 53.

7. Theodor Adorno, "Education after Auschwitz," trans. Henry W. Pickford, *Can One Live after Auschwitz? A Philosophical Reader*, ed. Rolf Tiedemann (Stanford: Stanford University Press, 2003), pp. 19–33, pp. 30–31.
8. John Berger, "Hiroshima," *The Sense of Sight* (New York: Pantheon Books, 1985), p. 295.
9. Martha C. Nussbaum, *Cultivating Humanity: A Classical Defense of Reform in Liberal Education* (Cambridge, MA: Harvard University Press, 1998), p. 93.
10. Ibid., p. 90.
11. Berlant, "Subject of True Feeling," p. 44.
12. Ibid., p. 62.
13. Joseph Conrad, *Heart of Darkness*, ed. Paul B. Armstrong, 4th edition (New York: W. W. Norton & Co., 2005).
14. "Heart of Darkness," *Online News Hour*, 11 May 2004, www.pbs.org/newshour/bb/middle_east/jan-june04/prisoners_5-11.html.
15. Berlant, "Subject of True Feeling," p. 46.
16. Joan Walsh, "The Abu Ghraib Files," *Salon.com*, 14 March 2006, www.salon.com/news/abu_ghraib/2006/03/14/introduction (accessed 2 October 2006).
17. Federation News Agency, Sarajevo, "Bosnians Honour Susan Sontag by Renaming Sarajevo Square After Her," *BBC Worldwide Monitoring*, 27 January 2005.
18. Primo Levi, *The Drowned and the Saved*, trans. Raymond Rosenthal (New York: Vintage Books, 1989), p. 17. In *Survival in Auschwitz*, trans. Stuart Woolf (New York: Simon & Schuster, 1996), p. 88, Levi notes that at Auschwitz, the term for prisoners who had been starved, abused, and humiliated so severely that they were unable to communicate, was "*Muselmänner*" – translated literally as "Muslims." Giorgio Agamben discusses the etymology of the term *Muselmann* in *Remnants of Auschwitz* (New York: Zone Books, 2002), pp. 41–48, but I shall refrain from using the term because of its problematic association with stereotypes about alleged Islamic fatalism.
19. The distinction that Dominick LaCapra makes between "primary memory" and "secondary memory" is similar to the distinction that I'm making here between witnessing and recognition, insofar as "secondary memory," for LaCapra, involves distance and the ability to contextualize. Dominick LaCapra, *History and Memory after Auschwitz* (Ithaca, NY: Cornell University Press, 1998), pp. 20–21. For LaCapra, however, "secondary memory" is something of the historian's craft, involving the ability to communicate the import of an event to others, and to fact check the reports of those who have "primary memory" of events (*History*, p. 21).
20. Paul Ricoeur, *The Course of Recognition*, trans. David Pellauer (Cambridge, MA: Harvard University Press, 2005), pp. 19, 23.
21. If we follow the Hegelian trajectory of the theory of subject-making put forth by Butler, for example, the desire "to be" is a "pervasively exploitable desire" that requires (but exceeds in the drama of foreclosed dependency on one's

Notes to pages 123–27

"passionate attachments") "the recognition of the other." Judith Butler, *The Psychic Life of Power* (Stanford: Stanford University Press, 1997), pp. 7, 9.
22. Ricoeur, *Recognition*, p. 24.
23. Hence the process of memorializing the *Shoah* seems more urgent now, as living witnesses become fewer with the passing of time. See Michael Roth, *The Ironist's Cage: Memory, Trauma, and the Construction of History* (New York: Columbia University Press, 1995); Levi, *The Drowned and the Saved*; and Tony Judt, "From the House of the Dead: On Modern European Memory," *New York Review of Books* 52.15, 6 October 2005.
24. Tony Judt, *Postwar: A History of Europe since 1945* (New York: Penguin, 2005), p. 804.
25. Susan Sontag, "Waiting for Godot in Sarajevo," *Where the Stress Falls* (New York: Picador, 2001), p. 321. Bruce Robbins criticizes Sontag for expecting too much of the American intelligentsia in his book, *Feeling Global: Internationalism in Distress* (New York: New York University Press, 1999), p. 13. While it is the case that not all American leftists are privileged enough to travel, as Sontag did to Sarajevo during the Bosnian war, Robbins misses Sontag's main point in her "A Lament for Bosnia" (*The Nation*, 25 December 1995) – that relatively few American "intellectuals who consider themselves people of conscience" spoke out about the "ethnic cleansing" committed in Bosnia until it was too late for the over 8,000 Bosniaks who were slaughtered in the Srebrenica massacre of 1995.
26. Sontag, "Waiting," p. 321.
27. Ibid., p. 320.
28. Ibid., p. 321.
29. Susan Sontag, *On Photography* (New York: Farrar, Straus, and Giroux, 1977), p. 17.
30. Susan Sontag, *Regarding the Pain of Others* (New York: Farrar, Straus, and Giroux, 2003), p. 84.
31. Ibid. pp. 110–11.
32. Ibid. p. 111.
33. Judith Butler, "Photography, War, Outrage," *PMLA* 120.3 (2005), 822–27, p. 823.
34. Ibid., p. 823.
35. Ibid., p. 826.
36. Ibid., p. 826.
37. Nancy K. Miller, "Regarding Susan Sontag," *PMLA* 120.3 (2005), 828–33, p. 831; Sontag, *Regarding the Pain of Others*, p. 110.
38. Sontag, *On Photography*, p. 3.
39. Sontag, *Regarding the Pain of Others*, p. 6.
40. *TG*, p. 11; Sontag, *Regarding the Pain of Others*, p. 46.
41. Ibid., p. 13.
42. Sontag, *On Photography*, p. 19.
43. Susan Sontag, "Regarding the Torture of Others," *New York Times Magazine*, 23 May 2004, p. 27.

44. Sontag, *Regarding the Pain of Others*, p 3.
45. Ibid., p. 8.
46. Ibid., p. 5.
47. Ibid., p. 126.
48. Diane Gillespie, "'Her Kodak Pointed at His Head': Virginia Woolf and Photography," *Virginia Woolf: Themes and Variations: Selected Papers from the Second Annual Conference on Virginia Woolf*, ed. Vara Neverow-Turk and Mark Hussey (New York: Pace University Press, 1993), pp. 113–47; Maggie Humm, "Memory, Photography, and Modernism: The 'dead bodies and ruined houses' of Virginia Woolf's *Three Guineas*," *Signs* 28.2 (2002), pp. 645–63.
49. Natasha Aleksiuk even suggests that Cameron, like her grand-niece, constructed deliberately performative biographical renderings in "'A Thousand Angles': Photographic Irony in the Work of Julia Margaret Cameron and Virginia Woolf," *Mosaic: A Journal for the Interdisciplinary Study of Literature* 33.2 (2000), 125–43, p. 125.
50. Gillespie, "Her Kodak," p. 132.
51. Humm, "Memory, Photography," pp. 646–47.
52. Ibid., p. 646.
53. Jeanette Winterson, *Art Objects: Essays on Ecstasy and Effrontery* (New York: Vintage International, 1997), pp. 27, 15.
54. Ibid., p. 113–14.
55. Ibid., p. 10.
56. Ibid., p. 13.
57. David Román, *Acts of Intervention: Performance, Gay Culture, and AIDS* (Bloomington: Indiana University Press, 1998), p. 169.
58. Pat Barker, *Double Vision* (New York: Farrar, Straus, and Giroux, 2003), p. 113.
59. Ibid., p. 45.
60. Ibid., p. 47.
61. Ibid., p. 45.
62. Ibid., p. 84.
63. Ibid., p. 100.
64. Ami Klin and Fred R. Volkmar, "Asperger's Syndrome: Guidelines for Assessment and Diagnosis," *Yale Child Study Center* (New Haven: Learning Disabilities Association of America, 1995), info.med.yale.edu/chldstdy/autism/asdiagnosis.html.
65. A caveat on the use of developmental disabilities and mental illnesses as symbolic elements in narratives: this is a form of what Sontag called using "illness as metaphor," where disability or illness stands for larger social phenomena. Given the concerns of the novel with our affective responses to suffering, it is clear that Barker is using illness as a metaphor for our emotional engagement with others. Barker's description is not about actual persons with Asperger's syndrome or borderline personality disorder in quite the same way that her *Regeneration Trilogy* can be said to be about persons

suffering from post-traumatic stress disorder. Thus my analysis is not about the facts of Asperger's or borderline personality disorder, but their mobilization as metaphors within Barker's narrative.
66. Barker, *Double Vision*, p. 71.
67. Nussbaum, *Cultivating Humanity*, p. 93.
68. Barker, *Double Vision*, p. 160.
69. Ibid., p. 27.
70. Ibid., p. 56.
71. Ibid., p. 227.
72. Ibid., pp. 227–28.
73. Ibid., pp. 152, 237–38 (emphasis in original).
74. Ibid., pp. 151–52.
75. Paul Farmer, "An Anthropology of Structural Violence," *Current Anthropology* 45.3 (2004), 305–32, p. 307.

5 THE PROMISE AND PERIL OF *METIC* INTIMACY

1. Colin McCabe, "Interview: Hanif Kureishi on London," *Critical Quarterly* 41.3 (1999), 37–56, p. 37.
2. Pat Barker, *Double Vision* (New York: Farrar, Straus, and Giroux, 2003)
3. Judith Butler, *Undoing Gender* (New York: Routledge, 2004), p. 20.
4. Lauren Berlant and Michael Warner, "Sex in Public," *Critical Inquiry* 24 (Winter 1998), p. 553.
5. On *Männerbünde*, see Jay Geller, "Freud, Blüher, and the Secessio Inversa: Männerbünde, Homosexuality, and Freud's Theory of Cultural Formation," *Queer Theory and the Jewish Question*, ed. Daniel Boyarin, Daniel Itzkovitz, and Ann Pellegrini (New York: Columbia University Press, 2003), pp. 90–120.
6. Berlant and Warner, "Sex in Public," p. 565.
7. Paul Gilroy, *Postcolonial Melancholia* (New York: Columbia University Press, 2005), p. xv.
8. As Patricia Laurence points out, cross-class or interracial sexual intimacy may also simply reproduce relations of domination, as they apparently did in E. M. Forster's orientalizing treatment of south Asian and Asian men. Patricia Laurence, *Lily Briscoe's Chinese Eyes* (Columbia, SC: University of South Carolina Press, 2003), pp. 184–98.
9. For anthropological explanations of the "translocal" see Arjun Appadurai, *Modernity at Large: Cultural Dimensions of Globalization* (Minneapolis: University of Minnesota Press, 1996), p. 192; and Tom Boellstorff, "The Perfect Path: Gay Men, Marriage, Indonesia," *GLQ* 5.4 (1999), 475–510.
10. Martha Nussbaum, "Introduction," *For Love of Country?*, ed. Joshua Cohen for *Boston Review* (Boston, MA: Beacon Press, 2002), p. xiii.
11. Martha Nussbaum, "Patriotism and Cosmopolitanism," *For Love of Country?*, ed. Joshua Cohen for *Boston Review* (Boston, MA: Beacon Press, 2002),

p. 5; Rabindranath Tagore, *The Home and the World*, trans. Surendranath Tagore (New York: Penguin Books, 1985).
12. Nussbaum explains the etymology of the word "cosmopolitan" in "Patriotism and Cosmopolitanism," p. 7.
13. My thanks to Brooke Rollins, whose talk at Miami University on January 19, 2007, alerted me to Lycias' *metic* status.
14. At the party are Nicholas, a gay Polish expatriate; René, a Frenchman living in London; Maggie, who, as his wife, holds French citizenship as well; Sarah, who is described as slightly deformed and a bit queer; and Eleanor, who as a spinster occupies a position outside heteronormative economies of desire. Moreover, as Maren Linett notes, Woolf had originally described Nicholas as a Jewish man in her earlier drafts of *The Years*. Maren Linett, "The Jew in the Bath: Imperiled Imagination in Woolf's *The Years*," *Modern Fiction Studies* 48.2 (2002), 341–61, p. 355.
15. See Introduction, note 18 above.
16. Abel Pargiter, the paterfamilias of the Pargiter family, comments on Sara's "deformity" when Sara's character is first introduced in the novel: "She [Sara's mother] held out her hand partly to coax the little girl, partly, Abel guessed, in order to conceal the very slight deformity that always made him uncomfortable. She had been dropped when she was a baby; one shoulder was slightly higher than the other; it made him feel squeamish; he could not bear the least deformity in a child" (*TY*, p. 122).
17. Stephen Barber, "Lip-Reading: Woolf's Secret Encounters," *Novel Gazing: Queer Readings in Fiction*, ed. Eve Kosofsky Sedgwick (Durham, NC: Duke University Press, 1997), p. 401.
18. Berlant and Warner, "Sex in Public," p. 558.
19. Linett examines the significance of this scene in relation to Woolf's simultaneously held antifascist and anti-Semitic views in her reexamination of Woolf's complicated attitudes towards Jewishness, fascism, intellectual liberty, and marriage to Leonard Woolf ("The Jew in the Bath").
20. Ibid., p. 357.
21. In my preliminary research I could find, with the exception of the discussion of Woolf by Ocampo's biographers, only four essays on Woolf and Ocampo: Fiona G. Parrott, "Friendship, Letters and Butterflies: Victoria Ocampo and Virginia Woolf," *STAR* (*Scotland's Transatlantic Relations*) *Project Archive*, April 2004, www.star.ac.uk; Nicola Luckhurst, "Photoportraits: Gisele Freund and Virginia Woolf," *Virginia Woolf Out of Bounds: Selected Papers from the 10th Annual Conference on Virginia Woolf*, ed. Jessica Schiff Berman and Jane Goldman (New York: Pace University Press, 2002), pp. 197–205; Elena Aguirre, "Virginia Woolf, Victoria Ocampo, Alfonsina Storni: tres mujeres mentales," ed. Teresita Frugoni de Fritzsche, *Primeras Jornadas Internacionales de Literatura Argentina/Comparística: Actas* (Buenos Aires, Argentina: Facultad de Filosofía y Letras, Universidad de Buenos Aires, 1996), pp. 337–44; and (thank you to Nancy Paxton who alerted me to the fourth essay) Laura Maria Lojo Rodriguez, "'A gaping mouth but no

words': Virginia Woolf Enters the Land of Butterflies," *The Reception of Virginia Woolf in Europe*, ed. Mary Ann Caws and Nicola Luckhurst (London: Continuum, 2002), pp. 218–46.
22. We may fault Ocampo for invading Woolf's privacy (as Woolf claims in her diary), but (judging from how often Freund's photographs are reproduced in works on Woolf) one would be hard pressed to find Woolf scholars who aren't secretly grateful to Ocampo for making the 1939 photo session possible. On the stunning nature of Freund's color photos of Woolf and the issues surrounding Freund's portraits of modernist authors, see Luckhurst, "Photoportraits."
23. Doris Meyer, *Victoria Ocampo: Against the Wind and Tide* (New York: Braziller, 1979); Patricia Owen Steiner, *Victoria Ocampo: Writer, Feminist, Woman of the World* (Albuquerque: University of New Mexico Press, 1999).
24. Victoria Ocampo, 1935 letter to Virginia Woolf, quoted in Meyer, *Victoria Ocampo*, pp. 125–26 (emphasis in original).
25. Victoria Ocampo, undated letter to Virginia Woolf, quoted in Meyer, *Victoria Ocampo*, p. 126 (emphasis in original).
26. Jane Marcus, *Hearts of Darkness: White Women Write Race* (New Brunswick, NJ: Rutgers University Press, 2004), p. 56.
27. Virginia Woolf, *The Waves* (New York: Harcourt, 1959), p. 47.
28. Robin Hackett, *Sapphic Primitivism: Productions of Race, Class, and Sexuality in Key Works of Modern Fiction* (New Brunswick, NJ: Rutgers University Press, 2004), p. 61.
29. Ibid., pp. 61–62.
30. Adam Phillips, *On Kissing, Tickling, and Being Bored: Psychoanalytic Essays on the Unexamined Life* (Cambridge, MA: Harvard University Press, 1993). My thanks to Robyn Wiegman for introducing me to Phillips' work.
31. Ibid., p. 11.
32. Ibid.
33. *Sammy and Rosie Get Laid*, dir. Stephen Frears, screenplay by Hanif Kureishi (Chanel Four Films, 1987).
34. Gayatri Chakravorty Spivak, *Outside in the Teaching Machine* (New York: Routledge, 1993), p. 250.
35. Ibid., p. 250–51.
36. Ibid., p. 249–50.
37. Nayan Shah uses the term "queer domesticity" to describe heterogeneous communal living and intimate proximity in "Perversity, Contamination and the Dangers of Queer Domesticity," *Queer Studies: An Interdisciplinary Reader*, ed. Robert J. Corber and Stephen Valocchi (Oxford: Blackwell, 2003), pp. 121–41.
38. Silver, *Icon*, pp. 163–71.
39. Asha Sen, "Re-Writing History: Hanif Kureishi and the Politics of Black Britain," *Passages: A Journal of Transnational & Transcultural Studies* 2.1 (2000), 61–80, p. 72.
40. Ibid., p. 73.

41. Silver, *Icon*, p. 164.
42. Ibid.
43. Both the Armenian genocide and the Amritsar massacre haunt the story of dinner parties and doctor's visits in *Mrs. Dalloway*, as Kathy J. Phillips points out in *Virginia Woolf against Empire* (Knoxville: University of Tennessee Press, 1994), pp. 7, 10.
44. Homi K. Bhabha, "DissemiNation: Time, Narrative and the Margins of the Modern Nation," *Nation and Narration*, ed. Homi K. Bhabha (New York: Routledge, 1990), p. 299.
45. Ibid., p. 297.
46. *My Beautiful Laundrette*, dir. Stephen Frears, screenplay by Hanif Kureishi (Channel Four Films, 1985).
47. Berlant and Warner, "Sex in Public," p. 565.
48. Robyn Wiegman, *American Anatomies: Theorizing Race and Gender* (Durham, NC: Duke University Press, 1995).
49. Ibid., p. 90.
50. Hanif Kureishi, "My Son the Fanatic," *Critical Quarterly* 37.1 (1995), pp. 57–65.
51. Hanif Kureishi, "Sex and Secularity," Introduction to *Collected Screenplays*, vol. 1 (London: Faber and Faber, 2002), p. x.

6 ORPHEUS, AIDS, AND *THE HOURS*

1. Richard Hugo, "The Lady in Kicking Horse Reservoir," *The Lady in Kicking Horse Reservoir* (New York: W. W. Norton, 1973).
2. Klaus Theweleit, "The Politics of Orpheus between Women, Hades, Political Power and the Media: Some thoughts on the Configuration of the European Artist, Starting with the Figure of Gottfried Benn or: What Happens to Eurydice?" *New German Critique* 36 (1985), 133–56, p. 156.
3. *The Hours*, dir. Stephen Daldry, screenplay by David Hare (Miramax, 2002).
4. Andrew O'Hehir, "Who's Afraid of Virginia Woolf?" *Salon.com*, 27 December 2002, http://dir.salon.com/story/ent/movies/review/2002/12/27/hours/index.html?pn=2.
5. Lee Edelman, *No Future: Queer Theory and the Death Drive* (Durham, NC: Duke University Press, 2004), p. 2.
6. Hermione Lee, *Virginia Woolf* (New York: Knopf, 1997), p. 753.
7. Susan M. Kenny, "Two Endings: Virginia Woolf's Suicide and *Between the Acts*," *Women Reading Women's Writing*, ed. Sue Roe (New York: St. Martin's Press, 1987), p. 284.
8. Lee, *Virginia Woolf*, p. 744.
9. Sybil Oldfield is the editor of a collection of condolence letters sent to Leonard Woolf after Virginia's death, *Afterwords: Letters on the Death of Virginia Woolf* (New Brunswick, NJ: Rutgers University Press, 2005).
10. Richard Dellamora, *Postmodern Apocalypse: Theory and Cultural Practice at the End* (Philadelphia: University of Pennsylvania Press, 1995), p. 1.
11. Ibid.

12. Ibid., p. 3.
13. Hannah Arendt, "Introduction" to Walter Benjamin, *Illuminations*, ed. Hannah Arendt, trans. Harry Zohn (New York: Schocken Books, 1969), p. 17.
14. Juliana Schiesari, *The Gendering of Melancholia: Feminism, Psychoanalysis, and the Symbolics of Loss in Renaissance Literature* (Ithaca, NY: Cornell University Press, 1992).
15. Ibid., p. 8.
16. Ibid., p. 11.
17. Maurice Bloch, "Death, Women, and Power," *Death and the Regeneration of Life*, ed. Maurice Bloch and Jonathan Parry (Cambridge: Cambridge University Press, 1982), pp. 214–22. My thanks to Aranye Louise O. Fradenburg for introducing me to Bloch's text and ways to read the gendered representations of death, as well as Patricia C. Ingham, whose lectures as we team taught helped to bring the import of this reading home.
18. Ibid., p. 225.
19. Ibid., pp. 225–26.
20. Paul Gilroy analyzes the nostalgic resurgence of embattled nationalist sentiment in *Postcolonial Melancholia* (New York: Columbia University Press), p. xii.
21. Herbert Marcuse, "The Ideology of Death," *The Meaning of Death*, ed. Herman Feifel (New York: McGraw-Hill, 1959), p. 74.
22. Quoted in Lee, *Virginia Woolf*, pp. 753–54.
23. Georges Minois, *History of Suicide: Voluntary Death in Western Culture*, trans. Lydia G. Cochrane (Baltimore: Johns Hopkins University Press, 1999), p. 321.
24. Michel Foucault, *Society Must Be Defended*, ed. Mauro Bertani and Alessandro Fontana, trans. David Macey (New York: Picador, 2003), p. 247.
25. Ibid.
26. Marcuse, "Ideology of Death," p. 69.
27. Ibid.
28. David Román, *Acts of Intervention: Performance, Gay Culture, and AIDS* (Bloomington: Indiana University Press, 1998).
29. John Guare, *Six Degrees of Separation* (New York: Random House, 1990).
30. Román, *Acts of Intervention*, p. 172.
31. Ibid., p. 159.
32. *The Hours*, dir. Stephen Daldry.
33. Michael Cunningham, *The Hours* (New York: Farrar, Straus, and Giroux, 1998).
34. Brenda Silver, *Virginia Woolf Icon* (Chicago: University of Chicago Press, 1999) p. 3.
35. *Mrs. Dalloway*, dir. Marleen Gorris, screenplay by Eileen Atkins (First Look Pictures, 1997).
36. *A Room of One's Own*, Television Broadcast, dir. Patrick Garland (Public Broadcasting Service, 1990).

37. Cunningham, *The Hours*, p. 27.
38. Andrew Webber, *The Doppelganger: Double Visions in German Literature* (Oxford: Clarendon Press, 1996), p. 6.
39. Ibid., p. 9.
40. *Boys Don't Cry*, dir. Kimberly Peirce (Hart-Sharp Entertainment, 1999).
41. William Shakespeare, *Cymbeline*, Penguin Shakespeare Series (New York: Penguin, 2005), Act IV, Scene 2.
42. John Berger, "Hiroshima," *The Sense of Sight* (New York: Pantheon Books, 1995), p. 295.
43. *World Heath Organization 2004 Report on the Global AIDS Epidemic* (2004), http://data.unaids.org/Global-Reports/Bangkok-2004/UNAIDS_Bangkok_press/GAR2004_html/GAR2004_15_en.htm.
44. Román, *Acts of Intervention*, p. 172.

EPILOGUE: TOWARD A SURVIVABLE PUBLIC MOURNING

1. Madelyn Detloff, "'Feeling What Patriots Feel': Woolf's 'Thoughts on Peace' in the Shadow of War", paper presented at the Not for Men Only: Women Respond to War – Huntington Library Women's Studies Seminar, San Marino, CA, 10 November 2001.
2. President George W. Bush, "Providing for the Closing of Government Departments and Agencies on June 11, 2004," Executive Order 13343, 6 June 2004.
3. Alessandra Stanley, "A Pageant over 2 Decades in the Making," *The New York Times*, 10 June 2004, national edition, sec. A.
4. Ibid.
5. Caryn James, "Good Grief: The Appeal of Public Sorrow", *The New York Times*, 10 June 2004, national edition, sec. B1 and B5.
6. Figures for US deaths are from CNN.com special coverage of the War on Iraq. Figures for Iraqi deaths are from Iraq Body Count, Hamit Dardagan and John Sloboda, Iraq Body Count.Net. Current figures are much higher.
7. In response to public outcry over the policy of not showing coffins returning to Dover Air Force Base, Pentagon officials have argued that "only individual graveside services, open to cameras at the discretion of relatives, give 'the full context' of a soldier's sacrifice." Dana Milbank, "Curtains Ordered for Media Coverage of Returning Coffins," *The Washington Post*, 21 October 2003, p. 23.
8. Judith Butler, *Antigone's Claim: Kinship between Life and Death* (New York: Columbia University Press, 2000) p. 24.
9. September Eleventh Families For Peaceful Tomorrows describes itself as an "advocacy organization founded by family members of September 11th victims who have united to turn our grief into action for peace," *Our Mission*, 20 June 2004, www.peacefultomorrows.org/mission.html. Jeremy M. Glick is the son of a victim of the September 11 attacks. He signed and

publicly defended the "NOT IN OUR NAME Statement of Conscience," and was subsequently harassed by television news host Bill O'Reilly for signing the statement "Fox News' Bill O'Reilly Threatens Physical Assault on and Ejects a 9/11 Family Member from His Show," *Not in Our Name*, 4 February 2003, www.notinourname.net/media/fox_news_oreilly2_feb03.html (accessed 20 June 2004).

Kleinberg, Kristen Breitweiser, Patty Casazza, and Lori Van Auken (the "Jersey Girls") are widows whose husbands were killed in the September 11 attacks. Their mourning process led them to call for an independent commission to investigate the September 11 bombings. This became the National Commission on Terrorist Attacks Upon the United States. David Crary (Associated Press), "Relatives of 9–11 Victims Distraught over Report Bush Received Advance Warnings," *Common Dreams News Center*, 2002, www.commondreams.org/cgi-bin/print.cgi?file=/headlines02/0516-09.htm (accessed 20 June 2004).

10. Butler, *Antigone's Claim*, pp. 2–3.
11. R. Clifton Spargo suggests that the "ethics of mourning" involves recognizing the forms of connectedness that Butler describes somewhat differently as a sense of shared vulnerability. Spargo argues that ethical mourning evokes a Levinasian sense of "responsibility" for the other, and that this relationship of responsibility cannot be assuaged through the conventional tropes of elegiac substitution. Resistant mourning, such as Antigone's, is therefore highly ethical for Spargo, because it calls to mind "the injustice that may be done to the living other at any given moment." R. Clifton Spargo, *The Ethics of Mourning: Grief and Responsibility in Elegiac Literature* (Baltimore, MD: Johns Hopkins University Press, 2004), p. 4.
12. Jane Marcus analyzes the iconography of the British World War I posters, arguing that they are in part a patriarchal resignification of the powerful iconography of women's suffrage posters, in "The Asylums of Antaeus: Women, War, and Madness – Is there a Feminist Fetishism?" *The New Historicism*, ed. H. Aram Veeser (New York: Routledge, 1989).
13. Rudi Franchi *Antiques Roadshow. Broadcast Highlights Indianapolis Hour 2*, WGBH 2002, www.pbs.org/wgbh/pages/roadshow/series/highlights/2002/indianapolis/indianapolis2.htm (accessed 20 June 2004).
14. Susan Sontag, *Regarding the Pain of Others* (New York: Farrar, Straus, and Giroux, 2003), p. 13.
15. Ibid., p. 11.
16. Unfortunately, as images from Abu Ghraib make painfully clear, this vicious cycle is still churning. See, for example, Seymour M. Hersh, "Torture at Abu Ghraib," *The New Yorker*, 5 May 2004.
17. Sophocles, *Antigone*, trans. David Grene in *Sophocles I* (Chicago: University of Chicago Press, 1992), lines 226–29.
18. As Butler points out, along with the nation-building function of commemoration, "we have to consider how the norm governing who will be a grievable human is circumscribed and produced in these acts of permissible and

celebrated public grieving, how they sometimes operate in tandem with a prohibition on the public grieving of others' lives, and how this differential allocation of grief serves the derealizing aims of military violence" (*PL*, p. 37).

19. Herbert Marcuse, "The Ideology of Death," *The Meaning of Death*, ed. Herman Feifel (New York: McGraw-Hill, 1959), p. 67.
20. Sophocles, *Antigone*, line 1414.
21. Ibid., lines 1420–21.
22. Ibid., line 915. Hegelian readings especially seem to suggest that Antigone represents a conflict between kinship and the state. Butler deconstructs this dialectic, arguing that Antigone's place within kinship structures is far from uncomplicated. See Butler, *Antigone's Claim*, pp. 3–5.
23. For a critique of the logic of inevitability in tragic emplotments, see Michael André Bernstein, *Foregone Conclusions: Against Apocalyptic History* (Berkeley: University of California Press, 1994).
24. George Steiner, *Antigones* (New York: Oxford University Press, 1984), pp. 111–12.
25. Diana Swanson, "An Antigone Complex? Psychology and Politics in *The Years* and *Three Guineas*," *Virginia Woolf: Texts and Contexts*, ed. Beth Rigel Daugherty and Eileen Barrett (New York: Pace University Press, 1996), p. 37.
26. Ibid., p. 36.
27. Diana Swanson, Christine Froula, and Elizabeth Abel each examine Woolf's response to and revision of Freud's "Oedipus Complex." It is not my intention to retrace the ground of these important analyses, but my reading is indebted to, and enriched by, theirs. Swanson, "An Antigone Complex?"; Christine Froula, "St. Virginia's Epistle to an English Gentleman; or Sex, Violence, and the Public Sphere in Woolf's *Three Guineas*," *Tulsa Studies in Women's Literature* 13.1 (1994), 27–56; Elizabeth Abel, *Virginia Woolf and the Fictions of Psychoanalysis* (Chicago: University of Chicago Press, 1989).
28. Sophocles, *Antigone*, line 919.
29. This is Antigone's position in *Oedipus at Colonus*, where she is praised for submitting to "the drudgery / of playing nursemaid to an old man, roaming / barefoot and hungry through the woodland wild." Sophocles, *Oedipus at Colonus* (Northbrook, IL: AHM Publishing Corporation, 1975), lines 347–49.
30. "Written Instructions Link Hijackers on 3 Flights," *CNN.com/US*, 28 September 2001, www.cnn.com/2001/US/09/28/inv.document.terrorism/index.html (accessed 19 June 2004).
31. Marcuse, "Ideology of Death," p. 65.
32. Elaine Scarry, *The Body in Pain: The Making and Unmaking of the World* (New York: Oxford University Press, 1985), p. 325. Judith Lee discusses Woolf's ethics of "making" in relation to Scarry's analysis of the making/unmaking of the world in "This Hideous Shaping and Moulding: War and the Waves," *Virginia Woolf and War: Fiction, Reality, and Myth*, ed. Mark Hussey (Syracuse, NY: Syracuse University Press, 1991), pp. 180–202.
33. Walter Pater, *The Renaissance: Studies in Art and Poetry. The 1893 Text*, ed. Donald L. Hill (Berkeley: University of California Press, 1980), p. 190.

34. This is a clever attempt at management of spectacle on the part of Creon, for in relegating Antigone to the status of the not-human, her death can be made to appear not directly attributable to Creon in the same way that it would have if she had been publicly stoned, as Creon's original edict declared.
35. This process calls to mind the narrative strategy that Rachel Blau DuPlessis calls "writing beyond the ending" in *Writing Beyond the Ending: Narrative Strategies of Twentieth-Century Women Writers* (Bloomington: Indiana University Press, 1985).

Index

Abraham, Nicolas, and Torok, Maria 101
Abu Ghraib photos 121, 130
abuse 90, 100
Adorno, Theodor 1, 2, 8, 9, 59, 120
AIDS 17, 160, 161, 164, 168
Antigone 7, 18, 114, 140, 168, 169, 171, 173, 176
antimetaphor 69, 70, 75, 78, 79
anti-Semitism 56, 68, 87, 136, 141, 142
apocalyptic rhetoric 4, 12, 16, 79, 81, 82, 83, 86, 88, 90, 106, 108, 109, 166
Atkins, Eileen 161

backshadowing *see* Bernstein, Michael André
Barber, Stephen 34, 141
Barker, Pat 12, 13, 17, 130, 135, 136
Bazin, Nancy Topping 34
Bell, Quentin 39
Benjamin, Walter 85, 155, 156
Benstock, Shari 60
Berger, John 37, 90, 120, 125, 128
Berlant, Lauren 120, 121, 136, 152
Berman, Jessica 6
Bernstein, Michael André 12, 33, 35, 56, 81, 83, 86
Bhabha, Homi K. 43, 46, 48, 151
biopower *see* Foucault
Bloch, Maurice 157
Bloomsbury 5, 6, 9, 31
"Bluebeard" story 97
Borden, Lizzie *see* Stein, Gertrude, "Lizzie Borden stories"
Borges, Jorge Luis 140, 143
Boys Don't Cry (film) 162
Brown, Wendy 24, 26
Burke, Joan 109
Butler, Judith 18, 30, 43, 44, 46, 52, 54, 68, 80, 89, 114, 125, 136, 137, 139, 166, 168, 169

Caramagno, Thomas 25
Caruth, Cathy 81, 89, 90, 91

child abuse, child sexual endangerment *see* abuse
commemoration 11, 23, 124, 163, 164, 167, 168, 169, 170, 171, 172, 176
Conrad, Joseph 121
contagion metaphors 56
Cook, Blanche Wiesen 60, 62
cosmopolitanism 4, 6, 7, 10, 17, 120, 122, 125, 137, 138
Cuddy-Keane, Melba 39, 40
cultural studies 5, 10
Cymbeline 163

Davis, Phoebe Stein 66
Dellamora, Richard 155, 156, 159
DeSalvo, Louise 24, 26

Eberly, David 24
Edmunds, Susan 91, 98
effective history *see* genealogy
elegy 81, 82, 83, 87, 89, 163
Eliot, T. S. 14, 81, 82, 83
empathy 120, 121, 124, 127, 129, 132, 133, 169
English, James 34
Esty, Jed 5, 7, 8, 10

Farfan, Penny 34, 49
Felski, Rita 10
forensics 56, 76, 79
Foucault, Michel 17, 18, 108, 158, 161, 164, 165
Fradenburg, Aranye Louise O. 88
Freud, Sigmund 10, 11, 13, 24, 30, 69, 71, 88, 89, 91, 99, 101, 105, 173
Freund, Gisèle 142, 143, 148
Friedman, Susan Stanford 91, 99, 102, 109, 113
Froula, Christina 6, 7, 31
Fuss, Diana 69

genealogy, genealogical history 108, 109
Gilbert, Sandra 26
Gillespie, Diane 128

Index

Gilmore, Leigh 61, 62
Gilroy, Paul 3, 10, 137
Gordon, Avery 23, 55, 59
Gorris, Marlene 161
Gregg, Frances 106
Gubar, Susan 26

H.D. (Hilda Doolittle Aldington)
  works
    Asphodel see "Madrigal" trilogy
    Bid Me to Live see "Madrigal" trilogy
    End to Torment 57
    "The Flowering of the Rod" see *Trilogy*
    The Gift 16, 81, 82, 91, 106, 109
    Helen in Egypt 98
    "Madrigal" trilogy 16, 81, 83, 106, 114
    Paint it Today see "Madrigal" trilogy
    Palimpsest 98
    Pilate's Wife 16, 80, 81, 83, 109, 112, 114
    "Tribute to the Angels" see *Trilogy*
    Tribute to Freud 105
    Trilogy 16, 80, 81, 82, 83, 86, 95, 101, 102, 106, 112
    "The Walls Do Not Fall" see *Trilogy*
Hackett, Robin 146
Hapgood, Hutchins 72
Harrison, Victoria 87
Henke, Suzette 24
Herman, Judith 13
Hirsch, Marianne 54
The Hours (film) 17, 154, 159, 160, 161, 162, 164
The Hours (novel) 161
Hugo, Richard 154
Humm, Maggie 128

ideology of death *see* Marcuse, Herbert
imperative to mourn "properly" 169, 170, 172
"imperial loss" 10, 11, 17
intimacy 121, 136, 137, 138, 139, 141, 142, 148, 151, 152
Isis and Osiris myth 102, 104, 106, 109, 112

James, Caryn 167
Jamison, Kay Redfield 30
Johnson, Chalmers 17
Joplin, Patricia Klindienst 48
Judt, Tony 124

Kenny, Susan 155
Kureishi, Hanif
  on London 136, 148
  works
    The Black Album 148, 153
    The Buddha of Suburbia 150, 151, 152, 153

My Beautiful Laundrette 151, 153
"My Son the Fanatic" 153
Sammy and Rosie Get Laid 148, 153
"Sex and Secularity" 19, 153

Lacan, Jacques 89
Lauter, Jane Hamovit 34
Lawrence, D. H. 80, 108, 109, 111
Lee, Hermione 155
Levi, Primo 123
Leys, Ruth 13
Linett, Maren 141
Loraux, Nicole 112, 114

Malcolm, Janet 15, 67
Marcus, Jane 145
Marcuse, Herbert 14, 16, 24, 70, 71, 74, 75, 77, 83, 110, 157, 159, 172
Mary Magdalene story 104
metic 4, 7, 17, 137, 138, 139, 140, 141, 142, 148, 149, 150, 169
Meyer, Doris 140, 143
Miller, Nancy 126
Mills, Jean E. 60
Minois, Georges 158
Mnevis, Menis 112, 114
modernism 3, 4, 5, 6, 8, 9, 10, 11, 14, 23, 80, 119, 169
Mrs. Dalloway (film) 161
Münsterberg, Hugo 71

Nussbaum, Martha 7, 120, 129, 132, 138

Ocampo, Victoria 138, 142
Oldfield, Sybil 155
Orpheus (politics of Orpheus) 154, 155
Osiris *see* Isis and Osiris myth
outrage fatigue 119

"patching" 2, 4, 11, 15, 16, 23, 80, 119, 176
Pater, Walter 176
patriotic motherhood 107, 113
Pearson, Norman Holmes 58
Pétain, Henri Phillppe (Maréchal Pétain) 59, 66
Phillips, Adam 147
Plato 110, 120
Poole, Roger 24, 34
postmemory 54, 56, 68
Pound, Ezra 9, 56, 57
public mourning
  see commemoration

queer *metics* 137, 138, 139, 141, 142
Quinby, Lee 108

racism, racial stereotypes 64, 93, 94, 149, 151, 152, 153
Raverat, Jacques 25, 39
Reagan, President Ronald (funeral) 167
recognition 123, 124, 168, 173
Reddy, Maureen T. 72
resilience 3, 14, 23, 26, 78, 169
resistant mourning 172
Ricouer, Paul 123
Roach, Joseph 2
Román, David 129, 154
Roth, Michael S. 81

Sacks, Peter 88, 89, 163
Sackville-West, Vita 143, 147
Said, Edward 2, 3, 5, 8, 59
Scarry, Elaine 11, 15, 24, 26, 28, 29, 37, 38, 39, 40, 42, 71, 78, 79
Schiesari, Julia 156
Scott, Bonnie Kime 6
Sears, Sally 39
Sedgwick, Eve Kosofsky 15, 53
Sen, Asha 149
sentimental nationalism 120, 122
Shaffer, Elinor 86
shame 15, 53, 55
sideshadowing
  see Bernstein, Michael André
Silver, Brenda 5, 53, 149, 161
Simon, Linda 59
Skinner, B. F. 71
Smith, Sidonie 62
Snaith, Anna 7
Sontag, Susan
  on "ethnic cleansing" 124
  on Sarajevo 16, 119, 122, 124, 125
  Waiting for Godot (production) 122
  works
    Illness as Metaphor 65
    On Photography 119, 124, 127
    Regarding the Pain of Others 12, 13, 25, 36, 122, 125, 126, 127, 128, 130, 133, 135, 170
    "Regarding the Torture of Others" 12, 127, 133
Spilka, Mark 24
Spivak, Gayatri 148
Stanley, Alessandra 167
Stein, Gertrude
  detective stories 72, 76
  Jewish identity 56, 59, 66, 67, 70
  lesbianism 56, 59
  Lizzie Borden stories 73
  masculinity 59
  works
    "American Biography and Why Waste It" 76
    "American Crimes and How They Matter" 73
    The Autobiography of Alice B. Toklas 62
    Blood on the Dining-Room Floor 16, 72, 75
    Everybody's Autobiography 16, 72
    Four in America 69
    The Geographical History of America 16, 74, 75
    The Making of Americans 15, 56, 68, 69, 70, 71, 72, 74, 77
    "Melanctha" 64–66
    Narration 75
    "Notebooks" to *The Making of Americans* 70
    Reflection on the Atomic Bomb 16, 78–79
    "Sacred Emily" 69
    "Tender Buttons" 71
    Three Lives 77
    "Transatlantic Interview" 77, 78
    Wars I Have Seen 78
Steiner, Patricia Owen 140, 143
Stimpson, Catharine 53, 61
structural violence 134
surrogation 1
Swanson, Diana 24, 173

Terry, Jennifer 108
Theweleit, Klaus 17, 154
translocal 137
trauma 4, 12, 13, 14, 16, 23, 25, 26, 81, 89, 91, 92, 94, 99, 101, 102, 123, 170

Uncle Tom's Cabin 93

Van Dusen, Wanda 66, 78
vicarious compunction 15, 54, 59, 68

Wald, Patricia 68
Warner, Michael 136, 152
Webber, Andrew 161
Whybrow, Peter 28
Wiegman, Robyn 152
Wilder, Thornton 69
Will, Barbara 66
Williams, Raymond 1, 5, 6, 7, 8, 10, 11, 119
Wineapple, Brenda 53
Winterson, Jeanette 129
witnessing *see* recognition
Woolf, Virginia
  making "happiness" 175, 176
  mental illness 24, 25
  suicide 17, 154, 155, 156, 157, 159, 164
  works
    Between the Acts 8, 15, 24, 31, 32, 33, 39
    Diary 23, 31, 32, 33, 38, 40, 42, 78, 139, 142, 166, 170, 174
    "The Leaning Tower" 5
    Letters 25, 142, 143, 144, 145, 147

"The Memoirs of Sarah Bernhardt" 51
Moments of Being 32
Mrs. Dalloway 17, 38, 150, 155, 158, 160, 161, 162, 163, 165
"Old Bloomsbury" 138, 139, 140
"On Being Ill" 24, 26, 29
"Reminiscences" 26, 27
A Room of One's Own 27, 42, 45
"A Sketch of the Past" 146
"Thoughts on Peace in an Air Raid" 18, 30, 31, 33, 38, 44, 174, 175
Three Guineas 7, 9, 13, 15, 16, 18, 24, 33, 34, 36, 40, 44, 57, 120, 122, 126, 127, 128, 135, 140, 143, 169, 170, 173, 175

"22 Hyde Park Gate" 139
The Voyage Out 146–47
The Waves 145
The Years 138, 140, 148, 173
World War I 2, 11, 80, 83, 107, 114, 120, 140, 141, 161, 163
World War II 2, 3, 8, 12, 16, 31, 33, 34, 59, 67, 77, 78, 80, 84, 92, 104, 122, 157, 166, 169, 174

Yeats, William Butler 14, 82, 83
Young, James 54, 56

Zwerdling, Alex 7, 34

Printed in Great Britain
by Amazon.co.uk, Ltd.,
Marston Gate.

Printed in Great Britain
by Amazon.co.uk, Ltd.,
Marston Gate.